meaning
& memory

Gary Pacernick

meaning

& memory

interviews

with fourteen

jewish poets

THE OHIO STATE UNIVERSITY PRESS

Columbus

Library of Congress Cataloging-in-Publication Data

Pacernick, Gary.
   Meaning and memory : interviews with fourteen Jewish poets / Gary
Pacernick.
      p.   cm.
   ISBN 0-8142-0879-7 (alk. paper) — ISBN 0-8142-5079-3 (pbk. : alk. paper)
   1. American poetry—Jewish authors—History and criticism—Theory, etc. 2.
English poetry—Jewish authors—History and criticism—Theory, etc. 3. Poets,
American—20th century—Interviews. 4. Jewish authors—United States—
Interviews. 5. Jewish authors—Great Britain—Interviews. 6. Poets, English—20th
century—Interviews. 7. Jewish poetry—Authorship. 8. Poetry—Authorship. I.
Title.
   PS591.J4 P34 2001
   811′.54098924—dc21

                                                                    2001001106

Text and jacket design by Diane Gleba Hall.
Type set in Minion by Sans Serif, Inc.
Printed by Thomson-Shore, Inc.

The paper used in this publication meets the minimum requirements of the
American National Standard for Information Sciences—Permanence of Paper
for Printed Library Materials. ANSI Z39.48-1992.

9   8   7   6   5   4   3   2   1

IN MEMORY OF My Mother and Father: Sally and Edward Pacernick
And to All the Poets

Seek good and not evil,
 that you may live . . .
Hate evil and love good;
 enthrone justice in the courts . . .
 —AMOS: 5–6

By the rivers of Babylon we sat
 down and wept
 when we remembered Zion.
 —PSALM 137

Man cannot approach the divine by reaching beyond the
human; he can approach Him through becoming human.
 —MARTIN BÜBER

Fearful, I see my hand is on the latch
I am the woman, and about to enter
 —ALICIA OSTRIKER

CONTENTS

ACKNOWLEDGMENTS

I AM INDEBTED to the poets for making the interviews possible. Their answers to my questions are the core of the book. I would not have begun this project if my wife, Dorothea, hadn't suggested that I interview Jewish poets. In addition, she helped and encouraged me throughout the long process leading to this book. I also owe a debt of thanks to my transcribers: Jeanne Brent Buckley and Eileen Ribbler. Wright State University's College of Liberal Arts and the Graduate Research Council awarded me several grants that helped to pay my travel expenses.

Acknowledgment is gratefully made to the following publications, which first printed these interviews, sometimes in slightly different form:

"Allen Ginsberg: An Interview by Gary Pacernick." *American Poetry Review* 26, no. 4 (July–Aug. 1997): 23–27.

"Carl Rakosi: An Interview by Gary Pacernick." *American Poetry Review* 26, no. 1 (Jan.–Feb. 1997): 13–19.

"A Conversation with David Ignatow." *Another Chicago Magazine,* 1997.

"Gerald Stern: An Interview by Gary Pacernick." *American Poetry Review* 27, no. 4 (July–Aug. 1998): 41–47.

"Interview: Alicia Ostriker." *The American Voice* 45 (1998): 61–76.

"Interviews with Ruth Fainlight and Elaine Feinstein." *The Centennial Review* 43, no. 3 (Fall 1999): 467–500.

"An Interview with Dannie Abse." *Chiron Review* 61 (Spring 2000): 16–17.

"Interview with Harvey Shapiro." *The Missouri Review* 21, no. 2 (1998): 91–109.

"Interview with Marge Piercy." Reprinted from *Prairie Schooner* 71, no. 4 (Winter 1997), by permission of the University of Nebraska Press. Copyright 1997 by the University of Nebraska Press.

"An Interview with Stanley Kunitz." *Michigan Quarterly Review* 36, no. 4 (Fall 1997): 646–54.

"Staying Power: A Lifetime of Poetry, an Interview with Philip Levine." *Kenyon Review,* n.s., 21, no. 2 (Spring 1999).

INTRODUCTION

As I begin my sixtieth year during this May of 2000, I see myself as a thirteen-year-old boy sitting alone in the damp basement of my grandfather's Hasidic synagogue, waiting for the other bar mitzvah boy to finish his mafter and haftarah portions of the Torah plus the blessings. I don't like being isolated from my family and friends, but I know why I must endure this solitary exile.

The other boy's uncle is the synagogue's biggest benefactor and money speaks, even in this Hasidic synagogue. My pious grandfather's religious zeal can't compete with the power of money. When it is finally my turn, I climb up the stairs to the main floor where my grandfather and father and the other male congregants—the only ones who count toward the minyan—wait for me to take my place on the bema next to the rabbi.

While women and girls throw candy down at me from behind the curtain on the balcony where they are required to sit, I sing in a rich voice that reverberates in the rafters. My voice is high and sonorous. I'm supposed to be a man, but I'm still a boy—a boy enraptured with baseball, who would love to trade his suit, tie, and yarmulke for blue jeans and T-shirt and race out of the synagogue and down the alley to the baseball diamonds at Central High School. Many of my friends will be there, and I could join them in the American pastime.

But I can't. I'm afraid even to think such a thought. Something about these men in long black coats and beaverskin hats, and the others, like my grandfather, draped in prayer shawls, rocking back and forth, reciting, singing, crying out the liturgy they know by heart, strikes fear and awe in me.

There's something haunting in the light that shines through the tiny windows near the ceiling of the synagogue. Is this the Lord's light illuminating the dark world, a world where Jews have lived in fear for their rights and even their lives for centuries? And who can forget the fiery hell of Europe during World War II? Some of the congregants, even some of my relatives, are survivors. Their aura of suffering and the savage murder of millions of martyrs are always with me in ways I may never fully understand, making me fearful and ashamed, as well as angry, defiant, and, yes, guilty.

Guilty that I am here, alive and breathing, celebrating my coming into manhood, while so many boys and girls disappeared from the earth, their voices silenced yet their spirits still alive. I look down from the bema at my father and grandfather, two quiet, reserved men with tears in their eyes, moved by the ancient Hebrew words that I have chanted before the entire congregation.

As I write these words, I immediately think of a related event. No bar mitzvah would be complete without the evening banquet. This is supposed to be a time of joy and celebration. Who can resist the pleasures of music and dance, food and drink galore? But everyone in my family is nervous as we prepare to leave the house. Why is this?

The explanation is that my bar mitzvah falls on an obscure Jewish fast day when all food, drink, and entertainment are strictly prohibited. No one dares tell my grandfather about the conflict. The desperate strategy is to keep our indiscretion a secret until the very last minute and then pray that he will agree to attend the party.

As soon as my grandfather finds out, disaster strikes. He is enraged and devastated: King Lear struck dumb with grief and rage by Cordelia's shocking answers to his questions. I am his favorite; we walk together to his synagogue, and I sit next to him while he recites and chants prayers. But the law comes before my bar mitzvah party.

He refuses to leave the house and join us at the banquet hall. A dark cloud hovers over the celebration. Finally, after the dinner, my grandfather arrives. He sits silently, sadly, for the rest of the evening—my grandfather, who lives for his religion and compromises with the 613 commandments barely enough to survive in the world. Yet I can't forget my stern, orthodox, otherworldly grandfather who was silent in America, his silence resonant with an ancient tradition. If he and his family, including my father, hadn't left Europe when they did, my world would not exist.

These scenes that I can't forget come from a place that now barely exists outside of my memory. For many years I journeyed farther and farther from that mythic place. This was my time in the wilderness, a dark wilderness where I was almost destroyed by a foe that I could neither comprehend nor withstand. It was a form of suffering that I had to survive to create a new life.

As a freshman at the University of Michigan, I identified with these words from the preface to Hawthorne's *The Snow Image and other Twice-told Tales:* "I sat down by the wayside of life, like a man under enchantment, and a shrubbery sprung up around me, and the bushes grew to be saplings, and the saplings became trees, until no exit appeared possible, through the entangling depths of my obscurity." I was overwhelmed by feelings of isolation, fear, and foreboding. Hawthorne must have experienced the pain of depression or imagined how it felt, in language and cadence recalling Psalm 137: "By the rivers of Babylon we sat down and wept."

Then I read Whitman's *Leaves of Grass* and couldn't put down the book, for it offered hope, optimism, energy. "I celebrate myself and sing myself, / and what I assume you shall assume, / for every atom belonging to me as good belongs to you." I was captivated by these two antithetical fathers of American literature, who for me represented the frightening world in which I was locked within myself versus the larger world of freedom and promise.

At the university I immersed myself in texts written by English and American writers. Images of the Hasidic synagogue and my grandfather and grandmother and other images of my youth receded into the far reaches of my memory. I decided to major in English and enrolled in the English honors program. To my surprise there were no American writers on the very ambitious reading list. Well, T. S. Eliot slipped in but there was no Whitman, Dickinson, or Stevens.

Evidently the professors wanted us to read the real English writers: Chaucer, Shakespeare, Spenser, Donne, Milton, and on and on to the twentieth century. I studied hard; I did well as far as grades; but inside I still felt empty, alone, scared—lost in a place of dark obscurity where "no exit appeared possible." This had to do at least in part with my loss of Jewish identity and the void that opened around me as I tried to find my place as an American poet and scholar.

Yet I had to go on, to survive. I chose graduate school over law school and traveled to the University of Minnesota. Because Allen Tate, the poet and critic, taught there, I felt that he might help me to realize my new dream of being a writer of poems. Then I could emulate my poetic heroes: Whitman, Yeats, Dylan Thomas, Hart Crane, not to mention Shakespeare, etc. After I showed Mr. Tate my first two poems, he signed me into his graduate seminar in creative writing.

I tried my best to write the sonnets, sestinas, and villanelles that my teacher assigned for the class, though the poems I wrote on my own pleased me more. And I decided to do my dissertation on Hart Crane. I was probably drawn to his tormented life as much as to his verbal pyrotechnics, but at that time it was his language that stood out. I too wanted to create a modern American poetry that emulated the greatness of Shakespeare and Marlowe as well as Whitman.

During this time, I wrote a short story about a father who takes his son for a ride in his horse and buggy to the outskirts of their city, where the son discovers that he is about to become his father's sacrificial offering to the Lord. To my surprise Mr. Tate loved the story, because it reminded him of old men in the South who fought duels to preserve their honor.

The novelist Ian MacMillan reminded me in a recent note that during the summer of 1965, while attending the University of Iowa, I read my poems to him and his wife. He remembered that one of the poems was about a pogrom—"something like grapes from the young vine, etc." Looking through my old folders, I found that poem, perhaps my first Jewish poem, in which I imaginatively returned to my father's Ukraine. It was a trip that I would imagine many times.

Seeking a cure for my depression, I left Allen Tate and Minnesota and drove from my dark winter wilderness to the sunny desert and Tempe, Arizona, where I finished my doctoral dissertation on Hart Crane at Arizona State University and met regularly with my friend the blind therapist, who had helped me in the past. By word and deed he assured me that hope was still possible. When I met the woman who was to become my wife, I felt as if I were beginning a new life. And then I turned back toward the East and my past.

After driving east for days, my pregnant wife, Dotti, and I arrived in Dayton, Ohio, where our daughter Jennifer was born, and I began to teach as an assistant professor of English at Wright State University. Almost five years later, my father, Edward, died after a long illness and my younger daughter, Eden, was born. I was thirty-three years old. Returning to Detroit for the funeral, I was transported back to my youth. Even the rabbi, my father's friend, who conducted the funeral and led the Shiva services, looked like my father— "short, stocky, pale-skinned, bald—with small, sad, blue eyes." Listening to him speak and tell stories, I imagined that he had memorized the Talmud.

Poems began to pour out of me. Many were monologues in which my relatives spoke and revealed their secrets to me. Some resembled stories, parables, and dreams. They were all centered in the Jewish world in which I had been born and raised. Could I, as an American poet, write these poems? I began to wonder about my predecessors. Who were they? I knew about Karl Shapiro and Delmore Schwartz and, of course, Allen Ginsberg, but I thought of them as American poets. I did not think of them as poets of the Jewish experience.

Having read some of my recent poems, the poet Milton Kessler told me that I was a Jewish poet, and he suggested that I read the Jewish Objectivists: Oppen, Rakosi, Zukofsky, and especially Reznikoff. Just knowing that American Jewish poets existed who wrote about their Jewishness was a revelation to me. I began to feel that my inner life as a Jew and as a poet could be unified.

By now I had a large group of poems about my youth and the people with whom I grew up. These people spoke to me of key moments in their lives. After meeting Robert Britton, head of studio acting at Wright State, I gave him copies of my poems. Before I knew it, Bob had created a multimedia play with music and dance based on my poems, and I titled the play *I Want to Write a Jewish Poem*. It was performed onstage and later produced for public television. In addition, many of these poems appeared in magazines and journals, and a book of the poems, *The Jewish Poems,* was published. I had begun my life as an American Jewish poet.

HAVING DISCOVERED that there were a number of important Jewish poets in America whose work reflected their Jewishness, I decided to edit an anthology of their work. When a publisher was not forthcoming but the director of a press suggested that I was well qualified to write a critical and scholarly study of American Jewish poetry, I had a decision to make, and I decided to undertake the project.

After years of work, the book that I produced was brought out under the title *Memory and Fire: Ten American Jewish Poets*. It was based on my reading of Allen Ginsberg, David Ignatow, Philip Levine, Howard Nemerov, Muriel Rukeyser, Charles Reznikoff, Jerome Rothenberg, Karl Shapiro, Louis Simpson, and Louis Zukofsky. I also studied criticism and scholarship about Jewish literature and Judaism past and present to gain a perspective on my subject.

Each of the ten poets I chose for my book is unique, and it was challenging, to say the least, to assess and explain the Jewish element of their work. Several of them resisted my claim that they should even be considered Jewish poets as opposed to American poets or just poets. But I proposed a thesis based on memory and fire, history and prophecy.

I defined memory as "imaginative remembrance (history) of a tradition beginning with the Covenant between God and Israel and extending through the long Diaspora of the Jewish people to the present day." Fire "suggests the prophetic viewpoint that concentrates on harsh criticism of existing social, political, and economic conditions, strong advocacy of freedom and justice, and application to a secular context of the divine voice and will." I wrote that the poets of memory try to imagine the past in order to celebrate tradition while the poets of fire attempt to transform the present by means of a messianic vision.

My thesis was based on my reading of all the poems written by each of the poets; however, during this process I began to focus on what I considered their "Jewish poems," which referred to or suggested their Jewishness. My study indicated to me that memory and fire were the keys to understanding these poems. "In their deeply human stories, myths, visions, and prophecies these poets reveal the suffering, exile, and alienation of past and present Jewish life; however, through their art of memory and fire they also remember Zion and chant their versions of the Lord's song in a strange new land."

Two years later the American Jewish Archives published my second study of the subject, *Sing a New Song: American Jewish Poetry since the Holocaust*. Here I surveyed the work of twenty-seven poets from Stephen Berg and Michael Blumenthal through Theodore Weiss and C. K. Williams. This time I advocated "an inductive as opposed to a deductive, an open as opposed to a fixed, approach to American Jewish poets and poetry."

The title of my previous book had been suggested by my reading of Muriel Rukeyser's prose. I had also been struck by her sonnet "To Be a Jew in the Twentieth Century," in which she asserts that it is a "gift" to live out one's Jewishness, because it keeps the spirit open. While I wrote about each poet separately, my overall premise was that they "affirm Jewishness by imagining it anew as part of their affirmation of humanness, of man's spiritual promise and the holiness of the earth. The poetry is part of an ongoing quest. It marks not the end of the canon but its continuation and change."

AS IN ANY discussion of a controversial subject among Jews, the issue of Jewish poets in America has elicited fierce debate. Two formidable Jewish critics, Robert Alter and Harold Bloom, question the very authenticity of poems written by American Jews. For one thing, these critics suggest, the poets are not steeped in traditional Jewish texts—the Bible, Talmud, Midrash, etc.

Harold Bloom gloomily argues that these poets are not American enough to bathe themselves in the great Protestant sublime tradition. Since they are not prepared to accede to a Gentile master, such as Emerson or Whitman, they can never go through what Bloom considers the essential process of breaking free of the father-poet and writing their own "strong" poems.

Other critics accept the reality that there are Jewish writers and poets and that their work has value and is worth studying. Perhaps they recognize in the writing of American Jewish poets something essential that has been articulated by Elie Wiesel: "Jew by conviction or Jew in spite of himself, the Jewish writer *cannot be* anything else. What is most ironic is that even his rejection of his Jewishness identifies him."

One of the challenges of breaking free of orthodoxy in literature, as in life, is the loss of absolutes. Even the word *Jew* becomes difficult to define. In the introduction to his anthology *Jewish-American Literature,* Abraham Chapman states, "Jew is a three-letter word and beyond this there is no common agreement on any definition of precisely who or what is Jewish." In his study of the subject, reprinted in Chapman's anthology, the distinguished anthropologist Melville J. Herskovits concludes, "A Jew is a person who calls himself a Jew or who is called Jewish by others."

Small wonder then that critics and scholars offer varying approaches to Jewish writers and that most of their attention goes to the fiction writers, some of whom have achieved a prominence almost undreamed of by poets. M. L. Rosenthal, himself a Jewish poet, prefers not to be pinned down: "Let me propose a simple definition: a Jewish poem is a poem written by a Jew." He wants to make no "a priori assumptions," because "the truest Jewish poetry will be written out of the inward preoccupations of people who happen to be Jews." While there may be a "lack of explicitly Jewish themes," Rosenthal believes many Jews are influenced by the prophetic tradition as well as memories of the synagogue. However, a Jewish poet may write "about love in a way that does not echo the Song of Songs."

The eminent Scottish critic David Daiches writes that because the Jewish artist feels "an inwardness with suffering," he might have an advantage, since "he can draw on his own traditions of alienation, of suffering, of being on the *other* side of a dividing line, and use his knowledge to investigate and to project the nature of man." He goes on to posit "that there is a sense in which, in the modern world, all sensitive men are Jews." Taking a similar approach, Alfred Kazin claims that to people for whom tension and danger have been so prominent, art may be the only way to create stability.

For some commentators, Veblen's notion of "marginality" is crucial. In his book *The Jewish Writer in America*, Allen Guttman concentrates on the Jewish radical and his "twofold alienation from the society in which he lives." In a famous sociological study, Robert E. Pack concludes that the Jew "was a man on the margin of two cultures and two societies. . . . The emancipated Jew was, and is, historically and typically the marginal man. The first cosmopolite and citizen of the world." In *After the Revolution: Studies in Contemporary American-Jewish Imagination*, Mark Shechner posits a post-Marxist fall, resulting in alienated writers turning to internal forms of radicalism.

The core of Irving Malin's view is that Jewish writers present "the Jewish experience—which is social, religious, and psychological"; however, God is central to their art. "Our writers are trying in different ways to discover and name Him; they search everywhere, attacking pagan deities, and pseudo religions. In a sacred, paradoxical way they give us modern American views of traditional beliefs."

Behind all these approaches is the question of cultural influence. While Abraham Chapman concedes that it is not plausible to equate culture with the unique elements of a writer's art, he believes that "culture may be a battleground of conflicting values and visions" and is therefore "a significant element in the complex of interacting forces out of which a writer creates literature." Like Elie Wiesel, he contends that "the hatred or rejection of a culture is as potent a literary force as the love of, or identification with, a culture."

ALTHOUGH I HAD written poems about Jewishness and several critical studies, I had never conducted a tape-recorded interview before my wife suggested that I interview the "two seminal American Jewish poets, Carl Rakosi and Stanley Kunitz." Aware that both poets had lived into their nineties, she urged me to get their answers to my questions on the historical record.

Her idea appealed to me because it would allow me to meet and speak with two poets whom I admired and respected. My wife even presented me with a precious gift: a tiny minicassette recorder. After some consultation with friends and some practice with the recorder, I realized that I owned an invaluable device that made my project technically feasible.

The next step was to ask the poets for interviews. Happily, they both agreed. I then decided to seek an interview with David Ignatow, because I had written about him as a Jewish poet and edited his selected letters. When I called Ignatow, he not only said yes, he suggested that I interview Gerald Stern. With Stern's enthusiastic agreement, I arranged a cross-country trip to San Francisco, where Rakosi lived, and then back to New York to meet with the other three poets. I had now scheduled interviews with four of the most prominent American Jewish poets.

My remaining task was to create questions. I decided to ask certain key questions of all the poets plus questions based on their individual achievements. For example, I began by asking each of them what is the hardest thing about being a poet and then what is the most enjoyable. I invariably wanted to know if they considered themselves Jewish poets. For me this was a key question, because their answers would help me to explore further what had become a central preoccupation of mine.

The interviews would enable me to continue my research into the phenomenon of being an American Jewish poet. By this time I had four distinguished Jewish poets willing to answer my questions, and I wanted to take full advantage of the opportunity. Many of my questions pertained to issues that I asked myself as I read and thought and studied. I wanted to know how they wrote their poems, but also how they lived their lives and how they faced death.

Excited and encouraged by the four interviews, I decided to do more. Although I admired many poets of various social, ethnic, and religious backgrounds, I chose to stay with Jewish poets, because this was the group that I identified with most closely. Interviews with them would allow me to continue my main work as a poet, critic, and scholar. The interviews would bring me into close contact with poets whom I had read and studied but in some cases had never met.

Since I began with senior poets, I planned to seek out poets at least as old as I whose work I knew and admired and to make sure that women were well represented. Some poets either never answered me or refused to do an interview. This group includes Adrienne Rich, Karl Shapiro, Louise Glück, and Eleanor Wilner. Because I had written about Philip Levine's work in both of my critical studies and admired his poetry, I asked him for an interview, and he agreed. Marge Piercy, Alicia Ostriker, and Irena Klepfisz also agreed to be interviewed, as did Denise Levertov, who, like Adrienne Rich, came from a mixed religious background.

While teaching in England, I interviewed Dannie Abse, Ruth Fainlight, and Elaine Feinstein. I met Feinstein before a reading at the British Library, and she suggested that I interview Dannie Abse as well. Because I had read Sylvia Plath's "Elm," dedicated to Ruth Fainlight, I was anxious to meet Fainlight and was happy when she accepted my request for an interview.

Back in New York I met with Harvey Shapiro, who has written extensively about the Jewish experience. Probably the most challenging of all the interviews was the one with Allen Ginsberg. Unlike the other poets, he had his own office and staff, including his long-time personal secretary, Bob Rosenthal. After dozens of calls, we finally agreed on a date and time, but the interview was canceled at the last minute and had to be rescheduled. As I shall explain later, it's a small miracle that I was able to tape my conversation with Ginsberg.

After four or five years, I had conducted fourteen interviews with distinguished Jewish poets.

I CONTINUE to believe that Jewishness creates a core of meaning and memory to which Jewish poets respond and that this process deepens their art. Poets are not rabbis or scholars; they are lay people seeking to articulate their key insights and experiences through the art of poetry. While much of the Jewish religious and textual tradition is implicit in their secular poetry, the poets both consciously and unconsciously articulate and suggest the tradition by testing, challenging, and changing it, reimagining Jewishness in their own lives as Jewish poets have always done.

MOST OF THESE poets are the children of immigrants, and three of them (Rakosi, Levertov, and Klepfisz) are themselves immigrants to the United States. Like other Jewish writers and poets for centuries, they are citizens of the Diaspora. As a result, they too are strangers in a strange land. Beset by anti-Semitism, they often see themselves as outsiders, even victims. Because of these feelings of alienation and marginality—of living two lives: as Jews and as American or British citizens—they identify as Jews always have, with the stranger, the dispossessed.

Ostensibly they might claim the radical political influence of communism and socialism (Rakosi, Ginsberg, Ignatow, Piercy, and Klepfisz) or anarchism (Levine), but they are also driven by their experience as Jews, who, as an oppressed minority, have always empathized with other oppressed people. Poems such as Ginsberg's "Kaddish" and "Howl," Levine's "They Feed They Lion," and Klepfisz's "*Bashert*" grow out of deep Jewish memories of being the outsider, the victim.

This condition of worldly contingency makes it very difficult for Jewish poets to dissociate from the world around them and to turn inward, as so many late-twentieth-century poets have. Like many of their predecessors, they are committed to reforming the human society in which they and others have been fated to live.

One of the most significant developments in progressive Judaism of recent years has been the emphasis on matriarchal elements in liturgy, Scripture, and ritual. Much of the impetus for this has come from feminists. As Marge Piercy writes in the introduction to her anthology *Early Ripening*, "[A] number of us are engaged with the quest for female godhead, the recreation or creation from scratch, from history, dream, and vision, of a mythology and a cosmology that lead to us, instead of excluding us or sticking us in as an after-thought." Piercy and Alicia Ostriker are among many poets who have written feminist midrash of traditional texts.

A key element in this new reading of the tradition is the Shekinah. According to Howard Schwartz, the Shekinah in traditional texts "designates the personification of God's presence in the world." However, in later mystical sources, especially the Kabbalah and the Zohar, there is the description of a fall from creation in which the vessels of light break open and the divine sparks become scattered in the world. There is also the accompanying myth of the exile of the Shekinah, the feminine manifestation of divinity, from the patriarchal divinity.

For late-twentieth-century feminist poets, the Shekinah represents what Elinor Gadon calls "the renewed experience of God the mother" and the attempt to reclaim a divine female presence that could create a "mystical union with nature." By looking back to the agrarian roots of their ancestors, Piercy, Ostriker, and other feminist poets invoke the Jewish lunar calendar as part of the process of a "rebirth of ecological and matristic values." Elinor Gadon believes that the central figure in this new reading of the tradition is the Shekinah, who represents "the feminization of God and the grounding of faith in a cosmic pantheism."

The Shekinah may also figure, at least implicitly, in the poetry of male poets as well as their female counterparts. Allen Ginsberg and David Ignatow each wrote an elegy for their mother titled "Kaddish." In Ignatow's poem, the mother represents maternal love, but also the energy of the earth. Ginsberg's long poem is an elegy for his mother, Naomi, the mentally tormented woman who holds the mystical key to the universe. In both poems, the mother figure has spiritual significance and may be understood as part of the new feminine reading of God as Shekinah, Mother Goddess, muse, and so on.

JEWISH POETS sometimes present new ways of seeing and imagining the American landscape. In "Psalms," Gerald Stern imposes his Jewish memory on Tennessee; seeing the landscape of hills and cows reminds him of rabbis reciting psalms:

> When I drove through the little bald hills of Tennessee
> I thought of the rabbis of Brooklyn bent over their psalms.
> I thought of the tufts of hair and the bones and ridges
> and the small cows eating peacefully
> out in the open slope or in the shadows . . .

This is a new way of seeing Tennessee that fuses the Jewish and American experience.

Likewise, in "For the Yiddish Singers in the Lakewood Hotels of My Child-hood," Harvey Shapiro writes,

> To be a Jew in Manhattan
> Doesn't have to be this.
> These lights flung like farfel.
> These golden girls.

Again, we have a new dual way of rendering an American place. *Farfel* (noodles shaped like pellets) enters the American poetic lexicon. In "Blessing Myself," David Ignatow describes a man conversing with a wall and evokes the Jewish prayer ritual of davening: "The wall is silent. / I speak for it, blessing myself." Here the poet incorporates Jewish ritual into the implicit shading of the image.

Ignatow's most well known poem puts the bagel center stage in the American urban landscape. Emulating William Carlos Williams's imagistic craft, Ignatow describes a man somersaulting down the street while rolling with a bagel. As Williams's red wheelbarrow symbolizes elements of American rural life, Ignatow's bagel evokes ethnic New York.

Philip Levine's poems often combine rage at social injustice with a corresponding messianic urge for oneness and justice that is rooted in his Jewishness. Only too aware of Hitler's victims, Levine cherishes those Jewish fighters, such as Baby Villon, his tiny French relative and survivor of the Holocaust, who embodies the courage and suffering of European Jewry:

> No bigger than a girl, he holds my shoulders,
> Kisses my lips, his eyes still open,
> My imaginary brother, my cousin,
> Myself made otherwise by all his pain.

Among Levine's other Jewish fighters are his uncle, the tough working man who can quote the Talmud, and his "tiny Russian Grandpa—the bottle king," who causes the young narrator of "Hold Me" to have a visionary experience:

> I am the eye filled with salt,
> his child climbing the rain, we are
> all the moon, the one planet, the hand
> of five stars flung on the night river.

Here, as Levine told me, the child attains independence from the father by becoming part of the universe.

While there is nothing ostensibly Jewish about "They Feed They Lion," the poem articulates Levine's rage at social injustice and oppression. Whether he is capturing his guilt and anger at racial prejudice against blacks, as he said in our interview, or affirming the workers, whom he imagines as embodying the earth's promise and power, and who at the same time are ravaged by the frightening lion, his Jewish identification with suffering and injustice is inherent in the poem's creation.

Although Levine greatly admires the Spanish Anarchists and honors them as heroic freedom fighters, he is always close to his Jewish roots. In the poem "On a Drawing by Flavio," as he stares at his artist friend's drawing of the rabbi of Auschwitz, he recognizes his own face. Even the rabbi's fingers remind him of "our father's hand" and generations of human suffering.

The poems of Gerald Stern show a preoccupation with the victim, the outcast, the stranger. In "Behaving like a Jew," the narrator distinguishes between Lindbergh's cold, stoic, detached response to the general condition of death and the Jew's "unappeased," emotional reaction to the oppossum's death on the highway. The Jew stares as if into a mirror at the image of the dead victim:

> and my eyes are still weak and misty
> from his round belly and his curved fingers
> and his black whiskers and his little dancing feet.

Two of Stern's most focused and compelling poems confront with horror and compassion the martyrs of the Holocaust. In "Adler," the poet parallels the tragic fate of King Lear with the death of Yiddish culture at the hands of the Nazis. While the audience of the great Yiddish actor Jacob Adler, the Jewish King Lear, can leave the theater "and live a while by mercy and innocence," the future victims of the death camps will find themselves in Hell. Although the Jewish audience of Adler's King Lear might weep at Lear's discovery of the dead Cordelia, fifty years later millions of the dead "were dragged from their places / and dumped on the ground or put in orderly piles." The poem ends with a dirgelike lament for the lost millions in language that resembles the saddest of Yiddish songs.

In "Soap," Stern compares with brutal irony the selling of various colored soaps with the Nazi practice of killing Jews and turning them to soap. In the long last passage, the narrator mourns the death of his counterpart born in 1925, who was killed in the death camps. "For him / I write this poem, for my little brother."

"The Same Moon above Us" is one of several of Stern's poems set in contemporary America that concerns the homeless. The poet-narrator comes upon "a man sleeping over the grilles / trying to get some heat for his poor stomach." In his long, elaborate tribute to this stranger, Stern sees signs of himself as poet and by extension as Jew: the victim of misunderstanding, prejudice, and injustice.

In "Hot Dog," Stern's longest and most ambitious poem to date, the poet-protagonist becomes obsessed with a black homeless woman named Hot Dog:

> December fifteen Hot Dog
> was lying on the sidewalk outside the Odessa
> half on cement, half on the metal doors
> of the cellar entrance with her head on the hip
> of her friend and he was lying the other way
> with his head on hers—shoes in a box—

Lying in their sadly vulnerable positions, Hot Dog and her friend resemble the man who sleeps on grilles in "The Same Moon above Us"; however, one is always aware that behind these images of the homeless is Stern's Jewish response to the victims of oppression and injustice. For example, "The Jew and the Rooster Are One," based on a painting by Soutine, describes the slaughtered rooster as "a kind of Jew"; he is "a ripped open Jew," who is "slaughtered" by society's butchers.

A number of short, explosive poems by Harvey Shapiro lament the loss of the law and of the Jewish god along with the loss of millions of martyrs. In "The Six Hundred Thousand Letters," the poet compares the disintegration of the letters of the law with "the blank paper / Being pulled from my type-writer." The narrator of "Ditty" asks, "Where did the Jewish god go?" He provides his own answer: "Up the chimney flues" with "Six million souls." As he indicated in our interview, Shapiro has always seen himself as the immigrant son, shaped by the anti-Semitism that he witnessed while growing up in the United States as well as the German genocide that he fought against in World War II.

As a citizen of England and Wales, Dannie Abse is even closer than his American counterparts to the European anti-Semitism that caused the Jews to be expelled from England centuries before the Holocaust and continues to this day in various forms, including neo-Nazi intimidation. The doctor-poet of "Case History" encounters an anti-Semitic patient, who "praised the architects / of the German death camps." Yet, presumably to uphold his oath of healing the sick, the doctor prescribes for this obnoxious patient "as if he were my brother."

Everywhere there are haunting reminders that the Jew cannot ignore. In "A Night Out," a Jewish couple view a Polish film. With a mordant tone, the narrator describes how the couple, who witness the cinematic scenes of Auschwitz, are too defended against their revulsion to respond emotionally to the film.

> We watched, as we munched milk chocolate,
> trustful children, no older than our own,
> strolling into the chambers without fuss,
> while smoke, black and curly, oozed from chimneys.

At last the couple return to their safe suburban home, and after consulting with their au pair girl, go to bed and make love. They too are Hitler's victims, their psyches too devastated to feel fully alive.

In "No More Mozarts," Abse reveals his hatred of the Nazis. When the narrator travels to Germany, he can't sleep because of the terrible contradiction between Mozart's great music and the death camps. The narrator finds this incongruity everywhere in German society:

> The German streets tonight
> are soaped in moonlight.
> The streets of Germany are clean
> like the hands of Lady Macbeth.

Just as Lady Macbeth can't wash the stain of bloody murder from her hands, the clean German earth "is made of "helmets," and the narrator hears "the far Jew-sounds of railway tracks." For the narrator, nothing, including German high art and cleanliness, can annul the unspeakable crimes, represented by twelve million staring eyes.

The narrator of Adrienne Rich's "Yom Kippur 1984" asks, "What is a Jew in solitude?" She goes on to ask, "What is a woman in solitude: a queer woman or man?" As a lesbian feminist and a Jew, Rich empathizes with the solitary suffering of all oppressed minorities and affirms Judaism's compassion for the stranger. In her introduction to Irena Klepfisz's *A Few Words in the Mother Tongue,* Rich emphasizes the fact that Klepfisz is a Holocaust survivor but also a Jewish lesbian feminist. Stressing this plus the Yiddish element of Klepfisz's writing, Rich places her "in a multicultural literature of discontinuity, migration, and difference."

As a socialist, Klepfisz does not affirm the mystical sources that inspire other Jewish feminist poets, but she does create a new image of Jewish womanhood with a voice that combines Yiddish and English in a bilingual blend. In "Etlekhe Verter Oyf Mame-Loshen/A Few Words in the Mother Tongue," the poet writes of the Jewish *lesbianke*/lesbian, who struggles to keep *Yiddishkayt*/Yiddish life alive. She is a woman who dreams and is afraid, because she is a member of an oppressed minority within an oppressed minority.

Klepfisz, whose father was killed in the Warsaw Ghetto uprising, and who herself survived the war in Europe with her mother, has written poems of powerful witness:

during the war
germans were known
to pick up infants
by their feet
swing them through the air
and smash their heads
against plaster walls.

"Somehow," she says, "i managed / to escape that fate." This is the rage of a poet who as a tiny child in Poland during the war was left with an old peasant while her mother desperately sought help. She captures many of her terrifying memories of the war in her unrelenting poems.

In "A Meditation in Seven Days," Alicia Ostriker's narrator wonders why, if a Jew is someone born of a Jewish mother, Judaism has been such a "violently masculine" religion. Why is the Jewish woman viewed by Orthodox Jews as someone to be feared and distrusted as "if she is / Created to be a defilement and a temptation. / A snake with breasts like a female / A succubus, a flying vagina?"

But Ostriker refuses to give up hope. At the poem's close, the narrator says, "I am the woman, and about to enter." As a participant in the woman's spirituality movement and as a committed Jew, Ostriker believes in "Changing God-language. Women want to worship God the mother, to be able to say God/She as well as God/He. I think all the feminist theologians agree that a God imagined as purely masculine is nothing but idolatry."

In her long liturgical poem "A Prayer to the Shekinah" in *The Nakedness of the Fathers,* the poet prays to the Shekinah to return from her exile and fulfill her promise as the female manifestation of divinity:

> Shekinah bless us and keep us
> Shekinah shine your face on us
> Shekinah turn your countenance
> to us and give us peace.

In this prayerful poem, God the Mother has returned to Jewish liturgy.

For Marge Piercy, Judaism is centered in nature's cycles and the ancient lunar calendar:

> The dark tidal shifts
> of the Jewish calendar of waters and the moon
> that grows like a belly and starves like a rabbit
> in winter have carried that holiday forward
> and back since then.

The poet celebrates her Sabbath in the midst of nature near the sea:

> The great doors of the sabbath are swinging
> open over the ocean, loosing the moon
> floating up slow   distorted   vast, a copper
> balloon just sailing free.

When the Shekinah appears, it is as a bird, a hawk, a sparrow "raising her song and bringing / down the fresh clean night."

Piercy's Jewish poem "The Ram's Horn Sounding" shows how her contradictions as a woman and a Jew are unified in a visionary meeting with the Shekinah:

> Shekinah
> stooping on hawk wings prying into my heart
> with your silver beak; floating down
> a milkweed silk dove of sunset.

In this meeting, a new pattern is created, as spirit and flesh, woman and nature blend into oneness as personified by the Mother Goddess, the Shekinah.

Allen Ginsberg modeled his elegy for his mother, Naomi, after the ancient Hebrew prayer for the dead, the mourner's Kaddish. When the mourner who prays for the departed says, "Let His great Name be blessed for ever and to all eternity," he or she invokes the establishment of God's messianic kingdom on earth, during which a great spiritual awakening, including judgment, resurrection, and immortality, will occur. Through this prayer the individual Jew is joined with the generations of Israel in affirmation of the faith. By basing his elegy to Naomi on the Hebrew Kaddish, the poet links his destiny with the Jewish people and with the God of Israel.

Naomi appears in several guises: a Jewish comedian who sees God in the Catskills and offers to cook supper for him and make lentil soup; a mentally ill woman who, while lying in bed with the scars of her operations showing, tempts her son with incest and terrorizes her family with her violent acts. Naomi is also her son's muse, his Shekinah, his female manifestation of divinity as a Jewish "Communist beauty" destroyed by a terrifying society of machines and technicians.

Although she is scarred and fallen, Naomi inspires her poet-son: "O glorious muse that bore me from the womb, gave suck first mystic life & taught me talk and music, from whose pained head I first took Vision." Learning of his mother's death, the poet refers to Naomi as the biblical Ruth and writes of his quest as "Svul Avrum—Israel Abraham—myself—to sing in the wilderness toward God—O Elohim!"

Then comes Naomi's letter in which she prophesies, "The key is in the bars, in the sunlight in the window." As Naomi shows her son the mystical key to prophecy, Ginsberg aspires to sing like the prophets and psalmists toward God. In "Hymmnn," which concludes the long second part of the poem, Ginsberg comes through his painful ordeal to praise God and his mother in the spirit of the Kaddish prayer: "In the world which He has created according to his will blessed Praised / Magnified Lauded Exalted the name of the Holy One Blessed is He!"

CONCLUSIONS

> A Jew is never *not* a Jew according to Jewish law.
> —J. NEUSSNER

> As the Talmud says, "Every human being is equal in worth to the whole world."
> —LEO BAECK

> His mission was never to make the world Jewish, but, rather, to make it more human.
> —ELIE WIESEL

▪ Judaism and Jewish culture in America, England, Israel, and around the world continue to change, and poetry by Jews reflects those changes.

▪ While each poet is unique and reveals the influence of Jewishness in his/her own way, the experience of Jews in the United States and England continues to show the impact of the Diaspora and such concurrent effects as alienation and marginality. Since the poets whom I interviewed are either children of immigrants or immigrants themselves, they express in various ways the sense of being outsiders, strangers in their adopted country.

▪ All of these poets have been affected by the Holocaust and reflect that horrendous calamity in their poetry. This includes the poets who most strenuously object to being identified as Jewish poets.

▪ Influenced by both a history of oppression and the messianic tradition, many of these poets affirm social and political justice and a prophetic sense of oneness. While Ginsberg and Levine are the most obvious examples, all of the poets see themselves as involved in the events of the world around them; none of them have turned inward to the exclusion of society, nor have they adopted postmodern attitudes and techniques, such as deconstruction and Language poetry.

▪ Although each poet responds differently, each reveals a tension and conflict between Jewish religion and culture and their own secular lives. The result is a synthesis of past and present, Jewishness and national culture.

▪ Each reader is unique. This reader has been moved by the Jewish poems of these fourteen poets and many other Jewish poets. I refer to such poems as Ginsberg's "Kaddish" and "Howl," Levine's "Baby Villon" and "They Feed They Lion," Stern's "Adler" and "Soap," Ignatow's "The Bagel," Klepfisz's *"Bashert,"* Piercy's "The Ram's Horn Sounding," Ostriker's "A Meditation in Seven Days"—poems that show both the direct and the indirect influences of their Jewishness. For me these poems grow out of a core of meaning and memory to which Jewish poets respond and that deepens their art.

▪ I repeat that the poets both consciously and unconsciously articulate and suggest the tradition by testing, challenging, and changing it, reimagining Jewishness in their own lives, as Jewish poets always have.

TO BE A JEW

To be a Jew is to be an enigma
To oneself wandering the human
Wilderness searing to survive open wounds
Screaming your name those murdered
By rationation's butchers suffering genius
Meat and mind driven to excel
Swaying back and forth over this world
Mystical chants and formulas
People of the Book Chosen
To bear God's covenant
And concentration camps

WORKS CITED

Alter, Robert. *After the Tradition: Essays on Modern Jewish Writing.* New York: Dutton, 1971.

Bloom, Harold. *Figures of Capable Imagination.* New York: Seabury Press, 1976.

Chapman, Abraham, ed. *Jewish-American Literature.* New York: New American Library, 1974.

Daiches, David. "Breakthrough?" In *Contemporary American Jewish Literature,* edited by Irving Malin, pp. 30–38.

Guttman, Allen. *The Jewish Writer in America.* New York: Oxford University Press, 1971.

Gadon, Elinor W. *The Once and Future Goddess: A Symbol for Our Time.* New York: Harper and Row, 1989.

Herskovits, Melville J. "Who Are the Jews?" In *Jewish-American Literature,* edited by Abraham Chapman, pp. 471–93.

Kazin, Alfred. "The Jew as Modern American Writer." In *Jewish-American Literature,* edited by Abraham Chapman, pp. 587–96.

Malin, Irving. *Jews and Americans.* Carbondale: Southern Illinois University Press, 1965.

———, ed. *Contemporary American Jewish Literature: Critical Essays.* Bloomington: Indiana University Press, 1973.

Orenstein, Gloria Felman. *The Reflowering of the Goddess.* New York: Pergamon Press, 1990.

Pacernick, Gary. *Memory and Fire: Ten American Jewish Poets.* New York: Peter Lang, 1989.

———. *Sing a New Song: American Jewish Poetry since the Holocaust.* Cincinnati: The American Jewish Archives, 1991.

Piercy, Marge, ed. *Early Ripening: American Women's Poetry Now.* New York: Pandora Press, 1987.

Rich, Adrienne. Introduction to *A Few Words in the Mother Tongue,* by Irena Klepfisz. Portland, Or.: The Eighth Mountain Press, 1990, pp. 13–25.

Rosenthal, M. L. "On Being a Jewish Poet, Memories and Associations." *Present Tense* 3, no. 2 (winter 1976): 27–32.

Schechner, Mark. *After the Revolution: Studies in the Contemporary Jewish American Imagination.* Bloomington: Indiana University Press, 1987.

Schwartz, Howard. *Gates to the New City.* New York: Avon, 1983.

Wiesel, Elie. Foreword to *The Literature of American Jews,* edited by Theodore L. Gross. New York: The Free Press, 1973, pp. xiii–xiv.

CARL RAKOSI

CARL RAKOSI was born in 1903 in Berlin, lived in Hungary, and came to the United States in 1910. He attended the University of Wisconsin, where he edited the *Wisconsin Literary Magazine* and formed friendships with Kenneth Fearing and Margery Latimer, and the University of Pennsylvania, where he received a degree in social work. For many years he practiced social work and psychotherapy. He is the sole surviving Objectivist poet; his fellow Objectivists included Louis Zukofsky, George Oppen, and Charles Reznikoff. In the thirties, his poems appeared in magazines and in the Objectivist issue of *Poetry*. His early volumes, *Ere Voice* and *Ex Cranium Night*, were published by New Directions. Recent publications include *The Collected Prose of Carl Rakosi; The Collected Poems of Carl Rakosi; Poems 1923–1941;* and *Carl Rakosi: Man & Poet*.

I FIRST saw Carl Rakosi at the National Poetry Foundation Summer Conference in Orono, Maine, during June of 1993. There was something preternatural about this ninety-year-old man, as if he had found a way to live beyond clock time. He was short, slight, with huge, luminous eyes and a long mane of white hair; and he moved so gracefully and spoke so graciously that he reminded me of a Prospero with a hidden magic wand. When he read his poetry at a reading with Allen Ginsberg, he spoke barely above a whisper, but the packed house was hushed, listening to every word of this poet who seemed an adored father figure to Allen Ginsberg and who had earned a place in literary history as one of the Objectivist poets of the thirties.

When I mentioned during my interview with Ginsberg that I had seen his reading with Rakosi in Maine, he praised Rakosi's *Collected Poems* and called him "our greatest poet, Jewish or non-Jewish." And yet despite such praise from Ginsberg and his association with the Objectivist group of Louis Zukofsky, George Oppen, and Charles Reznikoff, Rakosi has hardly been treated like a leading American poet. He has not won any of the major national prizes or a MacArthur grant, he is not widely anthologized, and his poetry has not been addressed closely by leading critics and scholars.

Rakosi may well be partly responsible for his lack of recognition. After establishing himself as a poet in the twenties and thirties, he stopped writing poetry for twenty-seven years to devote himself to his family and his profession. Also, as a person of the political left, he had grown disillusioned with the limited role of poetry in bringing about social change in America. It was only after his retirement, when he was in his sixties, that he returned to poetry and wrote many of his best poems.

In addition to his long exile from poetry, Rakosi has not been a man who courts fame through his writing or his lifestyle. He is a very private person—modest, polite, self-effacing—who writes of the quiet, contemplative, playful moments in his life. He eschews the sensational, and he refuses to discuss his poetry in anything but the most simple, straightforward language. When I asked him to speak about his poetics, his approach to poetry, to the writing of the poem, he was terse and direct. "I really don't have much to say about that, because in a way I work organically. I don't have any fixed ideas about style or form. When the impulse comes and I have an idea or a perception, I let it take me wherever it will go. The form follows that."

Although Rakosi has little to say about the Objectivist poetics of Louis Zukofsky and seems skeptical about literary terms and theories, his poetry is often subtle and sophisticated, especially in its language play. The Language poets and other avant-garde poets, critics, and scholars have begun to give Rakosi his due as an innovative poet who if not ahead of his time was in the forefront of it.

The central figure in a number of the poems in the "L'Chayim" (To life) section of *The Collected Poems,* which the poet cites as his favorite section along with "Meditations," is a grandfather who admires his granddaughters. This grandfather has a sensuous eye and a kind and loving heart. In "Services" the narrator prays for, among other things, his grandchildren and himself:

> and let their children, Jennifer, Julie and Joanna
> be my sheep
>> and I their old shepherd.

But he is not without thoughts of "a pale cocksman." This poet of the gentle, comic, grandfatherly demeanor and pastoral tone and setting is always close to the sexual impulse.

Few of Rakosi's poems are free of the poet's presence. The poem that he cites as the sole example of objectification in his work is "The Lobster" because, he says, "I'm not into it except through my perception. . . . What made it possible in that poem is that there are no people in it."

I believe there are other Rakosi poems that fit the objectification criterion established by Zukofsky. An example might be "The Avocado Pit." Turning the

avocado pit over in his hand and in his imagination, the poet sees it from a
magical timeless perspective. It is

> a complete earth
> > hard as stone
> the size of a plum
> > Pompeian red,
> darkened and faded
> > like an old Roman mural

The poem ends with the poet imagining the avocado pit from a cosmic
perspective,

> as if the earth
> > had cracked with age
> or we were looking
> > at the rivers
> from a satellite.

The poem shows the avocado pit through the magical lens of a poet who uses
his imagination to see through and beyond clock time.

·

ON FRIDAY, December 8, 1995, I interviewed Carl Rakosi in his San Francisco
apartment, its walls covered with paintings and prints by, among others,
Chaim Gross, Walkowitz, Ben-Zion, and Raoul Dufy. On the table in front of
us and on the mantle over the fireplace were striking sculptures by his late
wife. In the middle of the large living room was a high-powered stereo set with
giant speakers. Large picture windows overlooked the picturesque structures
on the poet's block in San Francisco's Sunset District. Carl Rakosi had, like
Stanley Kunitz, sketched in some answers to questions and used these texts
during the interview. He later revised a number of his answers from the origi-
nal transcription.

GP: For you, what is the hardest thing about being a poet?

CR: In my early years and for part of my middle years, it was finding the time
to write because I was always working, first as a social worker and then as a
psychotherapist, and the only time I had for writing was at night. It was a
struggle, however, because once I got going, my ideas would keep me up all
night. After I got married and had children, it became impossible because my

free time was gobbled up by my responsibilities to them, and I stopped writing altogether for over twenty years; but after I retired, I had no trouble picking it up again and had a burst of energy, particularly in Mexico, where my wife and I used to spend five months out of the year. I still write but allow myself to get distracted by endless little distractions, probably what Otto Rank, who was a poet himself before he joined Freud's circle, called the counterwill.

There is also in the back of my mind an uneasy awareness that poetry is a marginal occupation and is viewed as having no recognizable utilitarian function. We're in a strange kind of limbo. Our work is honored by those who read us, but very few people do, and government feels almost no responsibility towards us. This is a drag, but I can't claim that this stops me from writing.

GP: Carl, why do you think it is that poetry is not acknowledged in this country? Why are people not interested in it? Why don't they read it?

CR: I don't think a poet can answer that question satisfactorily; his self-esteem is too dependent on the answer. Besides, only people who might be expected to read poetry and don't, can tell us. An opinion survey might be helpful.

To be honest, however, we have to ask ourselves whether it is reasonable to expect that more public recognition and more institutional support should be given to poetry when the overall society is so single-mindedly commercial, when our potential reader lives a daily life perilously competitive in a dog-eat-dog, every-man-for-himself atmosphere, which leaves him exhausted at the end of a day, with a need to relax and be entertained, not to get into the concentration required by poetry. Furthermore, what can you expect when commercial publishers bring out only a trickle of poetry books because they lose money on them and when the large bookstores no longer stock them because they need the shelf space for books that sell faster?

Despite all this, I see signs that poetry is inching its way out of its marginal state. This began, I think, with public readings, which immediately pulled in a larger audience because the poet now was a performer, an actor, and that was theater; and people who would never go to the trouble of reading poetry will go to the trouble of observing and listening to a performance of it because that's a live person there performing, and that's drama, not just a book. This has been facilitated by the fact that poetry has become more like prose. In fact, I find it impossible sometimes nowadays to tell the difference between a poem laid out as such and the same thing laid out as prose. This change, of course, has made it easier to follow poems at a reading and has made them viable in that medium.

Add to this, that technology, which poets ordinarily decry, has suddenly catapulted us into an entirely new arena and medium, one which no one could have predicted and which we had no part in creating. I'm talking about the Internet. This new medium is wide open and loose. For the first time in history, poetry has become instantly accessible there without cost to the reader and without his having to move one inch from his computer, to anyone and everyone anywhere in the world. The prospect is dizzying. We have leaped from the margins to the whole globe. And there are startling, new opportunities. For one thing, since the person who has called up a poem on the Internet can enter into a dialogue with the poet on any subject that interests him—nature, the environment, social ills, whatever—it becomes a public discourse. This takes poetry out of its ivory tower and propels it into people's consciousness as another, equal voice in the discourse. To that extent, it constitutes a potentially big presence for us in the world at large.

The odd thing about this is that at the same time that this is going on, the experience of the Internet user is between him as an individual and the written poem he is reading . . . that is, person to poem, as it is between a reader and a book. A surprising mix of the most distant, mechanical impersonality and intimacy. I would expect this kind of activity eventually to receive considerably more public attention and support, but I hope that in the doing of it, poetry does not lose its soul, which is aesthetic and elusive, not expository. I don't have to say that poetry is not just public discourse.

GP: What is the most enjoyable thing about being a poet for you?

CR: Maybe not exactly enjoyable, but there is an excitement in it which reaches a high point when I think that my imagination has discovered something. And then there's a cooling off when the discovery becomes familiar and I've had a chance to assess it. And then, if after a while it still looks like a discovery, I am deeply elated. There is also, of course, as for other poets, the sheer pleasure of writing. But then, I've never had a romantic view of the poet.

GP: When did you first meet the other Objectivist poets—Zukofsky, Oppen, Reznikoff, Niedecker, etc.?

CR: Zukofsky I met in the early 1930s in New York when I was working there, and for five years we saw a great deal of each other. We were at an age when our creative juices were popping up all over the place and we had a great time exploring each other's ideas, confirming each other's likes and dislikes, and so on. This was a time when everything looked possible and exciting to us, when there was never a cross feeling, so it comes back to me now in a glow. Essentially what it did was to confirm where our talents lay.

Reznikoff I didn't meet until the early 1970s. It was at his apartment in New York, and he chattered away like a sparrow about little things in his life until it was time for me to leave. When it was over, I knew some things about him, but he didn't know any more about me than when I came in because it had not really been a conversation.

It must have been 1969 that I met Oppen. I was in San Francisco for a reading at San Francisco State University, and he asked me to stay at his house because he said the campus was too dismal to be around. We had already corresponded and seen each other's work in different magazines. In fact, he (and Duncan) was one of the reasons I moved to San Francisco after I retired to get out of the cold winters in Minnesota, and when we settled there, Leah and I and he and Mary were constantly in each other's homes, until he passed away. I have written elsewhere of the deep identity we felt with each other.

Basil Bunting came to a reading I gave in Newcastle, and we talked a bit but nothing came of it to make a relationship.

Lorine Niedecker I met late in 1968. I was writer-in-residence at the University of Wisconsin in Madison at the time, and she lived about an hour's drive from there in a tiny cottage on the shore of a lake. I found her very plain and homespun, with a fresh, country kind of simplicity that was immediately engaging. It was comfortable being with her, and we chatted away merrily, sounding each other out on all kinds of subjects. Then when we reached the point where she felt that we were completely in sync, she became very serious and declared, "Of course, you agree that Zukofsky is the greatest living American poet." The look she gave me showed that she thought that was so obvious a fact that if I didn't agree, I was not the poet she had taken me for from my close association with Zukofsky. I wasn't ready to appraise him *that* highly, but I didn't want to knock him either. I mumbled something ambiguous. I could see, however, that I had fallen in her esteem and that there was nowhere to go from there, so I excused myself to visit with her husband, who was puttering away at his work bench in their garage. I left, feeling that if I wanted a relationship, I would have to believe that Zukofsky was the greatest. Our paths never crossed after that.

GP: Now these people, outside of Niedecker and Bunting, were Jewish. Did you identify with each other as Jews?

CR: No, not at all. At no time. In fact, in the many contacts I had with Zukofsky, it finally struck me that we never talked as Jews with each other, and I said to him at one point, "What does being Jewish mean to you as a poet?" He said, "Nothing." That didn't seem believable, so I said, "Come on, it must mean something." He said, "Absolutely nothing." It was clear that he didn't like the question. I felt at the time that he was hiding something, but it was also possible, of course, that he simply didn't see any connection between those two things.

Reznikoff was so unmistakably a Jewish writer that you just took that for granted and had no need to discuss it as such when you were with him.

Oppen and I didn't talk with each other as Jews for a different reason. His father had had an altercation of some kind with his rabbi and had stopped going to services. As a result, Oppen had never been inside a synagogue or even been bar mitzvahed. But you'd never have known it. He had warm, open feelings about his Jewishness. A charming incident that happened to him in New York bore this out. I could tell that he had gotten a kick out of it. As he told it, he was sitting on a park bench in Washington Square, taking in the sun and chatting with William Bronk, who is not Jewish, when they were approached by a couple of rabbinical students, perhaps from a nearby seminary. On a hunch, one of the students asked George whether he had ever been bar mitzvahed, and George, without minding in the least that his privacy had been invaded or that there was anything unusual about such an invasion, said no, whereupon their faces lit up, and they asked whether he would like to have it done now, and George said, "All right," Bronk looking on, somewhat at a loss. So they bar mitzvahed him on the spot and departed in great glee. Here they were, only students, and they had already saved a Jew from being absorbed into the surrounding population and disappearing. They acted as if they could hardly believe their good fortune. As he told it, he was amused at the incident and said he had agreed because he thought it would be an interesting experience.

GP: Continuing along the same lines, but somewhat paradoxically, you were all, along with so many other poets, influenced by Ezra Pound, who obviously flirted very seriously with Fascism and even Nazism during the Second World War and wasn't shy and bashful about it. Were you aware, even during and after the war, of the paradoxical influence of Pound on you as Jewish poets? Whether you identified with Judaism or not, you still knew, obviously, that Pound was anti-Semitic and you were Jewish.

CR: I have to preface what I have to say with the fact that when I was young, anti-Semitism was so prevalent in this country, both in the general population and in the universities, that I had to face it as a given and go on from there. Not only were Pound, Eliot, Cummings, and probably Stevens, infected with the bug, but I know of only one writer of that generation who was not, Sherwood Anderson. Even Williams, who had a Jewish grandmother, was not altogether clear of it. So, yes, of course I was aware of Pound's anti-Semitism. But if you're going to single him out, Eliot and Cummings, in my opinion, were worse offenders. What they did was stereotype the Jew as a coarse, loud merchant type, physically loathsome, and then derided that stereotype. So under the circumstances, it wouldn't have made sense for me not to get the most I could out of their work despite their prejudices.

In addition, I have to say that I found no anti-Semitism in Pound's earlier work. When we get to his maniacal rantings on Italian radio in support of Mussolini and Fascism, we're into something quite different. Here he stepped out of his activities as a poet and became a citizen activist, subject to the consequences that go with that. He didn't have to, as you know, but in my opinion he should have been tried as a traitor. A man has no license to vomit his bile in the cause of Fascism just because he's a celebrated poet. But one has to keep his life as a poet separate from his life as a citizen activist. Otherwise we would be forced to judge poetry by the character and actions of a poet. Besides, once poetry has been published, it's out in the public domain and has become public property. It should not be contaminated or confused by considerations outside of its own turf.

GP: Well, I can understand your position, but there is a lot of anti-Semitism in *The Pisan Cantos,* which he wrote, of course, while he was incarcerated in a stockade in Pisa. Let's go on, though, to a question about Objectivism. What do you think is the most important thing that Objectivism stands for, either in its aesthetic program as articulated by Zukofsky, or in the actual poetry of yourself and the others?

CR: To answer that question I have to go back to the beginning of this thing. Pound had been after Harriet Monroe, the editor of *Poetry,* to get some fresh, original talent into the magazine because it had become sterile, imitative, sentimental, dead on its feet. He nagged her endlessly about it in letter after letter. She didn't, naturally, quite go along with his judgment, but she finally did agree to his proposal, reluctantly, and Pound chose Zukofsky as the person on the scene, since he was in London and couldn't know what was going on here, to locate and edit the best new work to be found and present it in a special issue of *Poetry.* This he proceeded to do and that's how Oppen, Reznikoff, and I found ourselves together for the first time in published form in that February 1931 issue of the magazine. Any idea of a movement, however, was so far from Zukofsky's mind that he wanted to include the work of poets of Pound's generation, but Pound quickly killed that notion.

A problem only arose because the editor insisted on calling the contributors to that issue by some name, having in mind probably that the magazine would get some mileage out of the publicity that would go with introducing a new generation of poets, approved by Pound behind the scenes. But Zukofsky hated the whole idea. It showed, he wrote me, that she didn't understand what it was all about. It was ridiculous, preposterous, but he was in no position to be adamant about it. He was young and just beginning a career . . . so he did what she asked. He invented the term *Objectivist* (not *Objectivism*) and took great pains always to put the word in quotation marks, suggesting subtly thereby that the term was not quite what it claimed to be and that certainly no movement was to be implied by it. This put him into an untenable position, however, because if there were Objectivists, it was illogical to claim that there was no such thing as Objectivism. But it was the best he could do under the circumstances.

He invented the term *Objectivist,* checking it out with me, as I assume he did with Reznikoff and Oppen, to see if I had any objection to it. I didn't. He had needed some model on which to base a name and had chosen Reznikoff, apparently because he admired particular qualities in his work: his unmistakable sincerity and his ability to extrovert his experiences in such a way that they became objects outside himself. The term could be said to apply to Oppen and myself too but not to Zukofsky. What appeared as an introduction to us in *Poetry* turned out to be a hermetic, elusive encapsulation of what was taking place in his own work and at the same time was a test of what he thought poetry had to be in order to be good enough. He himself had taken off in a different direction, however, not ours, towards a destination in which there were more and more ellipses in an effort to compress everything to a kind of final lingual state, and more and more contortions in an effort to get closer to a state of music.

So your question has to be rephrased, I think, as "What is the most important thing that the Objectivists stood for?" And that question can be answered, for Zukofsky too. We stood for getting rid of all insincerity, all cant, all pretense, all phony, puffed-up content. I'm sure I left something out but that's all I can think of at the moment.

GP: You favored Reznikoff among the other three Objectivists. In fact, it's interesting, as different as Oppen and Zukofsky and you are, all three of you really seem to like Reznikoff. So why, in your case, did you like Reznikoff's poetry so much?

CR: I think it's because he had a trait that none of us had. He seemed to have complete trust in himself, so that he could be the most natural, the least forced, the least puffed-up, the least rhetorical, the most honest in his poetry. He didn't seem to have to need to struggle against all the disabilities that the rest of us have to contend with. He was just a precious innocent.

GP: You're always associated with the Objectivist movement, the Objectivist poets, but obviously you've been writing poetry for generations and have made your own discoveries. You've written in your own voice, in your own way.

What would you say about your poetics, your approach to poetry, to the writing of the poem?

CR: I really don't have much to say about that, because in a way I work organically. I don't have any fixed ideas about style or form. When the impulse comes and I have an idea or perception, I let it take me wherever it will go. The form follows that.

GP: Do you have any favorite poems of your own? Can you tell us which they are and why, and is there anything you can think of that they all share in some way, shape, or form? Is there a quality about them that particularly pleases you?

CR: Yes, there are two groups of poems that I personally favor. One group is my meditative poems, and those, I think, come in the first part of my *Collected Poems.* Another group is my simplest, personal poems, having to do with my daughter, my son, my wife. They're in the section called "L'Chayim." Also, the poem "The Clarinet." Why do I favor them? I don't know. Maybe because there seems to be the best match in them of cadence, thought, feeling, and form.

GP: Who influenced you the most among your contemporaries, among older poets, or poets of earlier eras? Obviously you were influenced by Oppen, Zukofsky, Reznikoff, Pound, Williams, I suppose. Are there others, maybe, that you could think of?

CR: No, I can't say that my contemporaries influenced me at all. I was too busy, as the other Objectivists must have been too, working out my own character in poetry. I did learn immeasurably, however, from Pound's critical essays, and when I encountered the poetry, first of Eliot and later of Stevens, they cast such a spell over me that I wasn't aware they had entered my work and it was an agony to exorcise them. From Williams and Cummings I got the form that felt most natural for me. The strongest influence of all was Eliot's *The Waste Land.* That poem completely turned me around. Having said all this, however, I have to add that a poet is influenced by everybody that he reads and for me the list is very long: Shakespeare, Chaucer, Blake, Baudelaire, Rimbaud, Cendrars, Ponge, Machado, D. H. Lawrence, Sandburg, and so on. I picked up something from all of them.

GP: Do you have anything to say about things like rhythm, music, free verse, meter, the craft of the poem?

CR: A little, and that is this: Because I write in free verse, I need some form to satisfy myself that the poem is not shapeless, that there is something there that makes it an artifact. That something for me is a beginning, which is nearly always a title, a middle, and a closure. Closures are particularly important for me because usually my strongest line is the closure, which brings the poem full circle back to its title.

GP: What has poetry taught you about language? You've been writing poetry for a long time, and of course poetry is a highly concentrated language art. Has it taught you some things over the years about how you and others use language, or how to better use language?

CR: Well, poetry does show that language can be elevated to a very high point through imagination and skill.

GP: What can America learn from its poets? We've already touched on the fact that this is a country that does not, as you said, provide the poet with high status. Nevertheless, this country has hundreds and hundreds of poets, including some great ones. What could this country possibly learn from all these people who write poetry in their privacy?

CR: Maybe this: that there is in poetry a world of rich imagination and great perception, a world free from self-interest, a world simply not available in the workplaces of the world, a world which can enrich a reader's life if he gets himself to it.

GP: Does poetry add to life's meaning? I guess we could ask that for both the poet and the reader. And can the writer or the reader build a faith, a way of life around it? Wallace Stevens talks about poetry as the supreme fiction, and I guess some folks think that that may in some way imply that poetry can be the central myth or provide the central myths of our culture.

CR: The question, as you put it, is much too grandiose for me, and when people talk about something becoming a central myth of our culture, I become very uneasy and go deaf. Yes, Stevens says poetry is the supreme fiction, but he is simply saying that it is the highest form of the imagination, but the way he carries on about it, it becomes a flight into abstraction, but not a myth. Could a way of life be built around truth? It sure could. Does poetry tell truth? It can and sometimes does. But to conclude from that that a way of life could be built around poetry is to jump into myth.

As I said before, however, the rich imagination and deep perceptions of poetry can enrich a reader's life. Whether it has something special to say about the meaning of life, I haven't yet discovered.

GP: There was a long period of time, something like twenty-five years, I believe, when you wrote no poetry. Can you talk about that long hiatus?

CR: The main reason I stopped writing poetry for so many years was that once I was married and had children, I didn't have the time or the energy to do both. Social work is very exacting . . . there weren't enough hours in the day, and what there was had to go to my family if I was going to be any kind of a husband and father.

Also, at the time this happened, the Communist party was big in New York and I was a believer, but found myself confronted by the fact that the kind of lyric poetry I could write was anathema to them, which made me lose confidence in it and shrink back. In order to stop writing poetry, however, I had to stop reading it, too, in order not to be tempted. The first two years were almost unbearable. I was sick for six months, and the thought flashed through my mind that it might do me in, but eventually social work and psychotherapy filled my life and I was able to live without poetry or pain.

GP: In the poem "Men At Work," you refer to numbers as part of that "timeless order which is bilk to poets." Yet you yourself have written about not only numbers but music and ideas—in other words, abstractions, even though you have described yourself as primarily a visual poet. Do you go against your own grain and that of other poets when you write of numbers, music, ideas, etc.?

CR: The point in that poem is that numbers, another term for mathematics, are an integral part of all industrial and scientific work, as well as of the mind itself. They are as far as you can go in the absolute. One can't do without them. Yet they are "wholly without heart or humor" and therefore "bilk to poets."

True, I am a visual poet but I am also satirical at times and often meditative and those three sometimes clash, but that's just being a human being.

GP: You've said that the poem "The Lobster" is your only Objectivist poem. So my question is, does it then demonstrate the sincerity and objectification that Zukofsky, who coined the terms, has written about?

CR: Not sincerity, because that doesn't come up in the poem, but objectivity, yes, in the sense that it's outside my self, my psychology. I'm not into it except through my perception, which is not true of my other poems, where I think I'm always in them in some way. What made it possible in that poem is that there are no people in it.

GP: So what you suggest, then, as the essence of Objectivism is that the poet's personality and even experience are not part of the poem? The subject matter that the poet's talking about, in other words, is not personal?

CR: Not exactly, because the personal can be objectified too. One just has to know how. In any case, you can only objectify so far; to go further would wipe out the poet entirely. But if you don't objectify, you wind up with a sloppy, inchoate text.

GP: What inspired you to write translations of Hebrew poems?

CR: Many years ago I came across a selection of these medieval Spanish Jewish poets in a translation by the Anglo-Jewish novelist Israel Zangwill. They were simply dreadful translations. The language was dead, but despite that there was something in the work that touched me deeply. So although I don't know Hebrew, I tried my hand at translating what I thought was underneath that deadness, and I had in my ears the music of the Song of Songs and Job.

GP: What was the impact of Hitler and the death camps on your work, on you?

CR: It was a massive, unbelievably horrible experience for me and for every other Jew that I know. But it was always too enormous a subject to tackle. I just didn't know where to begin. And also, since I was not personally an observer or a victim, I thought I'd better stay away from the subject.

GP: What kind of impact has Israel, the modern Jewish state, had on you, if any?

CR: When it became official that after centuries and centuries the Jews would be reunited and have their own nation, I felt a wild burst of excitement and joy, and when Israel was in danger from the Arab armies, I rushed to help it financially. It had the effect of making me more Jewish and it continues to support that identity.

GP: So do you now consider yourself a Jewish poet, or an American Jewish poet?

CR: In a sense, neither. I am, of course, a Jew and an American but any poem that's worth its salt, no matter what its subject matter, expresses human experience, and human experience is not ethnic or racial. A good poem is simply a human poem. Was Celan a Jewish poet? No poet had more Jewish content. He was obsessed with the Holocaust. But being a poet, he reduced his experience to such a quintessential point that it ceased being Jewish. It was universal. This applies even to Reznikoff's biblical poems and Jews-talking-to-Jews pieces. If it didn't, you'd have to conclude that non-Jews couldn't have his experiences, and nobody would say that.

GP: How does one face death? Can poetry help? Or can Judaism, or can any other source that you can think of?

CR: Not many people actually have to face death, as such. There are exceptions, of course. If you're facing a gun leveled at you or in an airplane that's lost control, the thought may flash through your mind that this is it, death rushing up at you. But I was in an airplane once when it flew into a sudden storm, with lightning circling the plane, and dropped a thousand feet, yet as it was plunging, I was so preoccupied with the experience of wondering what the plane would be able to do about it that I wasn't thinking that I was going to die. Ordinarily death steals up on us over the years so gradually that we are spared the ordeal. At the same time I know from personal experience that there is such a thing as facing death, under certain circumstances. My wife, Leah, after suffering through three years of treatment for cancer, finally had become bedridden at home. As time went on, she ate less and less and became weaker and weaker until finally she was down to liquid food. We could observe death little by little stealing up on her. One day she asked to speak in private with my son, who is a doctor. They were together for a long time, and when he came out he told us what she had wanted to know was whether she was really going to die. She knew he wouldn't lie to her. As soon as she knew, her whole body seemed to give in to the knowledge, and she went peacefully into death. Which suggests that people can face death when they are told truthfully when it is going to happen.

I don't know enough about Judaism to know whether anything in it can help. All I have heard from rabbis are the usual bromides. Buddhism might be closer to helping. Even closer, it seems to me, is the Indian's view of man as an integral, inseparable part of nature in which all things eventually die, man along with all the other creatures and vegetation on the earth, simply sinking back into nature.

Poetry? I can't see anything there. A terminally sick person is too preoccupied with his illness to read poetry. But, of course, in the end, I don't know any more about this than anybody else.

GP: You've obviously lived for a long time, and you continue to be productive, to thrive. I know you're not a philosopher or sage, but do you have any advice, particularly for younger people, as to how to survive, how to go on, how to enjoy life, how to live a long and productive life? There's a lot of talk today about how unhappy especially young people are in this country, and about how cynical they've become. Do you have any thoughts about (I guess one could call it) metaphysics, life's meaning, at this point in your existence?

CR: The bookstores are full of books by psychologists and would-be therapists that tell you exactly what to do to, as you say, survive, go on, enjoy life, whatever, but you can read them all and not be one bit happier. The only thing that will have happened is that you will have a placebo effect for a while and your head will be full of rules and you will become anxious when you fail to observe one of them. No, unfortunately happiness doesn't come that easily, by prescription. As for people being cynical, people have good reason to be. It will stop only when the political leaders of the country stop putting money interests ahead of human interests, with a sanctimonious air to boot, and hoodwinking and lying about it all the time with upper-middle-class civility.

Life's meaning? What do you mean? If you mean for what purpose we were created, only people who believe in God have an answer. But must we assume life has meaning other than the experiences we have? Granted we crave more. But what? What is that what? Are we in a cloud-cuckoo land when we ask that? This is poet's country as much as the philosopher's or the theologian's, where it is assumed that the answer lies within the possibilities of language and we are in hot pursuit of it.

I have no advice that would be helpful to young people. They will find out as they go along what they need to do to make the best of a bad situation. They need their cynicism to protect them from being tricked.

GP: What place do you most identify with? I guess I'm thinking of a physical, geographical place.

CR: I've been in San Francisco long enough now to begin to feel like a San Franciscan and to find the tremendous ethnic and racial diversity and mix here exciting and exhilarating, but a part of me is still in the Middle West.

GP: What is the most amazing thing about life?

CR: To me, it's that the mind and the imagination do not deteriorate with age. When I was young, most people thought that poets were finished by the time they were in their thirties and forties, that their lyric impulse and their imagination would run out. Thank God that's a fiction.

GP: What do you think is the most amazing thing about your life?

CR: I wouldn't exactly call it amazing, but what is perhaps surprising is the extent to which accident has shaped it. I'm constantly surprised by that.

GP: Does maturity give you a new, fresh perspective or vision, or do you think that your view of life has pretty much not changed over the years, that it has remained constant?

CR: I can't say that age, as such, has given me a new or fresh perspective, and I was never a visionary, God forbid, but of course the world has changed fundamentally since I was young and my view of some things has changed along with it. One of the changes, not connected to that, has been, I think, that I have become more tolerant of ideas not my own and less sure of mine, and I know now that some things just don't work, and that my abilities are limited.

What has remained constant is the nature of my poetry. When I resumed writing after some twenty-five years, the first poem I wrote was "Lying in Bed on a Summer Morning," and it was unmistakably apparent that it had come out of the same imagination and personality as the earlier poems. It was as if there had been no break in the writing.

GP: What do you think of postmodernism and the language-centered poetry that gets so much academic attention today?

CR: I don't know what is meant by *postmodernism.* The term seems to me to wipe out the meaning of *modernism.* As for the Language poets, they made some bold experiments, and if they had left it as such, I would have had no problem with it; but the claims they made for it and their rationale, and the connection they posited with Marxism, were hard for me to take. But these things come and go. Personally, I found these poets to be as sharp and intelligent as they come.

It's interesting to note that the Surrealists, in a way, paved the way for them by dehumanizing the imagination, and the Language poets followed and took it further by dehumanizing the language. But they will have a place in literary history because experimentation is, after all, a history of how poetry changes.

GP: There's a movement today which is quite interesting. Lots of people, particularly young people, are getting together in bars, nightclubs even, to perform their poetry for each other. And in addition there's a lot of emphasis on the oral performance of poetry in general. Do you have any thoughts about this approach to poetry?

CR: I've already commented on this. My problem with it is that there isn't time for my mind to fully absorb a poem when I'm listening to it by a performer, and meditate about it, as I can when I'm reading a poem, because by the time I'm through listening, the performer has moved on to another poem. But it *is* a new, widening medium, and I don't quarrel with it.

STANLEY KUNITZ

ALTHOUGH HE was born in 1905, Stanley Kunitz's poetry was largely unrecognized until he won the Pulitzer Prize in 1959 for his *Selected Poems*. In 1979, at the age of seventy-four, he published *The Poems of Stanley Kunitz: 1928–1978*. And in 1985 he published a new volume of poems and essays, *Next to Last Things*. Then in 1995, at the age of ninety, he received the National Book Award for *Passing Through: The Later Poems, New and Selected*, his ninth collection of poetry. He has also translated Russian poetry and published several collections of prose writings. He is now at work on new poetry, translations, and essays. In 1993 he received the National Medal of Arts from President Clinton at a White House ceremony. He was appointed Poet Laureate of the United States in 2000.

LIKE WILLIAM BLAKE, Stanley Kunitz glorifies the role of the poet in the modern world. In our interview, I began by quoting his statement to Bill Moyers that "poetry is the most difficult, the most solitary, and the most life-enhancing thing that one can do in the world." When I asked him to elaborate, he replied, "The experience of love and the creative act are the supreme expressions of the life force. They do more than express it; they refresh and renew it and give it back, magnified."

It is a testimony to the lights of love and poetry that Stanley Kunitz is so energetic, vibrant, and creative in his nineties. In my time with him, I began to feel that every word he used in speech or in writing is meticulously forged and crafted to be the best word possible. Nothing less would do. Our interview went through at least three drafts over several years. The finished document is very different from the original.

Small wonder that Kunitz is not a prolific poet. In our interview, he said that the hardest thing about being a poet is writing the poem and "making it right, in sound and sense; making it whole and true." For many years he was one of the finest practitioners of complex, intricately wrought formal verse. However, with *The Testing Tree* (1971), the reader senses a new, more open and free approach.

For Kunitz, form is not "an end in itself, only a means. Only a means to gain control over language, to make it more sensitive to the modulations of one's thoughts and feelings, to improve its precision so that one won't have to tell lies." Having been schooled in traditional rhyme and meter, he has turned to the sharply chiseled language of common speech to speak directly of his passionate responses to life and death.

The poetry of Stanley Kunitz is Jewish in only a tangential way. In fact, his Jewishness can hardly be separated from other cultural forces behind his verse. Yet it is tempting to link Kunitz's sense of loneliness and of being the stranger, an outcast upon the earth, with his Jewish heritage.

He begins his poem "The Flight of Apollo" with the memorable line "Earth was my home, but even there I was a stranger." The space voyage only increases his earthly alienation, which he equates with the Jewish Diaspora:

> I was a stranger on earth.
> Stepping on the moon, I begin
> the gay pilgrimage to new
> Jerusalems
> in foreign galaxies.

For Kunitz, Jewishness provides neither the poem's subject nor its theme, but it may be an underpinning that is essential to the poet's inner life that lies behind the poem.

Part of the poet's implicit tie to Jewishness is in his imaginary quest to rediscover his father. In "Father and Son," he longs to know the "Gemara" of his father's "gentleness" that fate had taken from him. In "An Old Cracked Tune," he lays claim to his Jewish heritage through his father's name. "My name is Solomon Levi," he declares, and "the desert is my home." Once again he links himself with the Jews' exodus and the long and lonely search for a homeland. While he too is a stranger, who has no father, he is also a survivor, who has learned from his mythic past and dances "for the joy of surviving."

■

ON TUESDAY, December 5, 1995, I interviewed Stanley Kunitz in his spacious Greenwich Village apartment crammed with books and plants and works of art. Although he is short and frail, Kunitz has large, brilliant eyes, speaks forcefully, and moves around gracefully. One quickly forgets his chronological age. He had just returned from a reading in Cambridge but had found time while on the train to write some answers to my questions, and he referred to these texts during the interview. In the spring of 1997 we had a follow-up discussion that led to a number of revisions and additions.

GP: Stanley, you have said to Bill Moyers that "poetry is the most difficult, the most solitary, and the most life-enhancing thing that one can do in the world." Can you elaborate, especially about what makes it such a life-enhancing activity?

SK: The experience of love and the creative act are the supreme expressions of the life force. They do more than express it; they refresh and renew it and give it back, magnified.

GP: What have you found the hardest thing about being a poet? You're obviously saying that it's extremely important and beneficial, but I'm sure there are hard things about it.

SK: Being a poet is more or less easy, but writing poems is difficult.

GP: Are you talking about the formal challenge? Are you talking about finding just the right word?

SK: Making it right, in sound and sense; making it whole and true.

GP: Are you the person who determines that? Do you feel that you, finally, are the person who knows whether the poem works?

SK: In the long run I do. I try very hard not to be self-deceived.

GP: What is the most enjoyable thing about being a poet for you?

SK: The knowledge that there is nothing else I would rather do or be.

GP: Here we are, almost at the end of the twentieth century with all these incredible technological changes, most significantly in the modes and process of communication. Is there any future for poetry in the new age?

SK: The relevance of poetry is to the history of civilization, not to the progress of technology. Poets today can hope to do precisely what poets have always done, that is, tell the story of the human adventure, express what it feels like to be alive in this particular time, this particular place.

GP: What does a poet need to know about craft, and are rhyme and meter still important enough to be part of a young poet's training?

SK: I am never satisfied that I know enough about craft. I am still learning. But I think that it's important to stress that craft is not an end in itself, only a means. Only a means to gain control over language, to make it more sensitive to the modulations of one's thoughts and feelings, to improve its precision so that one won't have to tell lies.

GP: You are someone who has written poetry of note, both in traditional forms and in free verse. Do you think free verse can be taught, and is there anything coherent and plausible that one can say about writing free-verse poetry?

SK: In the first place, I don't think free verse is free. It has rather indeterminate principles, but at the least it must connect and cohere and establish a defining rhythmic pulse. As to whether traditional form is still essential, all I can say, out of my own experience, is that my early discipline in metrics and rhyme has been invaluable to me, even though I no longer tend to write in strict metrical patterns and prefer subtler internal harmonies to the click of rhyme. Incidentally, there were no graduate writing programs in my youth. I learned my craft by studying the poets around and before me.

GP: What do you think inspired you to be a poet, and as part of that, were there poets who made you want to write poetry?

SK: When Henry James, toward the end of his life, reflected on his long creative voyage, he identified his point of embarkation as the port of his loneliness. That is true of most of the poets I know. "A poem is solitary and on its way," said Paul Celan, the poet of the Holocaust. What sets it on its way is the search for a community.

GP: Do you identify with any of your contemporaries in particular? Of course one thinks of Roethke and Lowell. Are there others?

SK: I feel close to a whole tribe of poets, young and old, but in the act of writing a poem, I have always felt alone.

GP: Do you have any favorite poems of your own? Which are they and why?

SK: A new poem is always the one I feel closest to, if only for a while.

GP: "The Wellfleet Whale" is different from most of your other poems. Was your writing process in that poem different from your usual procedure?

SK: "The Wellfleet Whale" had a long gestation period. I knew from the beginning, in September 1966, when the whale foundered in Wellfleet Harbor, that it was a significant experience, and I experimented through the years with various ways of conveying what I saw and experienced. All of them were failures. During that interval, I had an opportunity on Cape Cod to study other beached whales, went out on sightseeing watches, and read whatever seemed to me even remotely pertinent, until I began to feel I was part of the civilization of the whale. Fifteen years after the event, I was able to pull it all together and write the poem.

GP: You succeeded in converting all that information into a significant action. Can you comment on your guiding principle of organization?

SK: In the end, I turned to Greek drama—specifically Sophoclean tragedy—to help me solve the problem of the poem's architecture. Jane Harrison's *Prolegomena* clarified for me the main structural elements in the development of the action, from agon to recognition scene. It's a poem that wants to be read aloud, preferably in the open air. I guess I'm really thinking of an ancient amphitheater.

GP: You have translated Russian poets. How did you come to the Russian poets?

SK: I came rather naturally to them. After all, my parents were raised in Eastern Europe. My mother's forebears, who were fugitives from Spain, wandered through central Europe until they settled in Lithuania at the time of the Inquisition. Despite this heritage, I never heard Russian or any foreign language spoken in our household during my childhood. My connection with the Russian poets dates from the early sixties, when Patricia Blake, then a correspondent for *Time,* and the Oxford scholar Max Hayward, the outstanding Slavist of that period, persuaded a number of friends and acquaintances to undertake translations of Andrei Voznesensky's poems for an edition in English of his *Antiworlds.* This was the book that made Andrei famous in the Soviet Union and eventually everywhere else. There were six of us in that list of translators, and none of us, including Auden and Wilbur, knew a word of Russian, but we felt confident that we could rely on Max's literal versions and, if needed, his interpretation of the text. I felt the same way a few years later, when Max and I collaborated on the poems of Akhmatova, an exceptionally important book for me.

GP: Did the intimate contact with Akhmatova's poems affect your own work?

SK: I hope I learned something from Akhmatova about the management of an open style and the possibility of breaking down the barrier between the public and private poem. Perhaps I learned something more from the passion and humanity of her voice.

GP: You recently won the National Book Award for poetry with the publication of *Passing Through,* the poems of your later years, including your newest work. Thirty-six years before, in 1959, you received the Pulitzer Prize. Did that earlier recognition have a significant impact on you and your career as a poet?

SK: One doesn't write poetry for prizes, but I have to admit that the Pulitzer Prize actually changed the course of my life. It gave me self-confidence at a time when I needed it sorely. The manuscript for my *Selected Poems: 1928-1958* had been rejected by more publishers than I could bear to count before Atlantic accepted it. I had been through a bad period and I was tired of being called a "poet's poet." That sudden turn of the wheel did wonders for my morale.

GP: In regard to the poetry intrinsically, do you have any themes, concerns, subjects that matter a great deal to you and enter frequently into your work?

SK: Actually, I never think about themes when I am writing my poems. In the usual course of events, my poems spring from the occasions of the day, something perceived as beautiful or terrible or true. When that perception attaches itself to language and rhythm, I know I am on my way, but not with any foreknowledge of my destination. Whenever I yield to the temptation to explicate one of my poems, I am astonished at all the secrets I find buried in the text. Poets are characterized less by their subject matter than by their tone of voice, their ground of feeling. When I was still at school, I picked up a volume of Keats's letters and discovered the passage in which he spoke of "the holiness of the heart's affections." More than seventy years later, those words still light the way for me.

GP: As I look around your apartment, I see many striking works of art, including several by your wife, Elise Asher. You have written about some of your artist friends. Would you comment on that relationship?

SK: Like so many other poets, past and present, I have a feeling of kinship with painters and their art. During my youth in Worcester, my favorite haunts were the woods, the public library, and the local art museum, and it seemed almost inevitable that I should eventually marry into the world of painters. When that happened in the fifties in New York, I inherited Elise's friends and soon felt very much a part of the emerging generation of Abstract Expressionist painters just as they were preparing to step in the limelight. They were wonderful company—lively, articulate, ambitious, hard-working, hard-drinking, gregarious, outrageous, and ready at any hour to argue about anything. Eventually, of course, success and fame and hypertension took their toll. I'm thinking, in particular, of Rothko, de Kooning, Guston, and Kline—all of them gone now. But in the early years, they seemed to embody Blake's dictum that "energy is eternal delight," and their élan struck me as irresistible and contagious. Painters, I think, have a special gift for friendship.

GP: Have you done any artwork yourself?

SK: I am never happier than when I am working with my hands. In Provincetown, where we spend a good portion of the year, my toolroom and garden compete for attention with my study. If there's any odd job that needs to be done around the house, I treat it as a challenge. There was a period when I produced a number of collages and assemblages and wire sculptures, but that was when I could make a bit of free time available. These days I seem to be busier than ever.

GP: Dante is a presence in your work. In "The Illumination," you address his apparition as "my Master and my guide." What is the source of your connection?

SK: My conversation, so to speak, with Dante began very early. Thanks to my immigrant parents, our house in Worcester was the only one in the neighborhood, as far as I knew, that could boast of an extensive library. It was there that I first encountered the plays of Shakespeare, each in a separate volume, bound in red cloth, with a critical preface and an appendix of historical sources. Other well-thumbed books that I recall were complete sets of Tolstoy, Dickens, and Thackeray; the poems of Browning, Tennyson, Wordsworth, Longfellow, and Whittier; a multivolume set of classic histories, including Plutarch, Gibbon, Grote, and Prescott; the *Century Dictionary,* unabridged; Spinoza and Maimonides; and the Holy Bible, leather-bound, both Old and New Testaments, with red-ink passages and marginal glosses. But the book that enthralled me most in that library was a folio edition of Dante in Cary's translation, with the Gustav Dore illustrations. Those visual images of Hell took possession of my imagination. I used to sit in that library with this enormous folio on my lap (I was twelve years old or so), terrified by that vision of the underworld. I had nightmares. So Dante was with me at a most impressionable stage. Later, at Harvard, I studied the *Divine Comedy* with C. H. Grandgent, the famous Dante scholar.

GP: The poet Gregory Orr, who has written about you, says the suicide of your father shortly before you were born is the central fact of your imaginative life, "that from which all else flows." Do you agree?

SK: Certainly the most traumatic event through my formative years.

GP: The poem "The Knot," which I find mysterious, does that have symbolic associations for you, and how did you come to write it?

SK: The poem's origin is quite simple, nothing mysterious about it. Over a period of years, in our place on the Cape, I couldn't help but notice a great swirling knot that kept bleeding through several layers of paint on the lintel of our bedroom door. And the more I studied it, the more I marveled at its persistence, as though it still had a buried life, a will to grow, to become branching pine again "out of the trauma of its lopping-off." As I lay in bed, only half-awake, it did not seem far-fetched to imagine flying into its boughs.

GP: All right, another deep, difficult poem, "King of the River." What kind of disintegration takes place within the narrator? "You would dare to be changed, / as you are changing now, / into the shape you dread / beyond the merely human." Are you writing of madness there, or are you writing of some other kind of transforming experience?

SK: "King of the River" deals primarily with the aging process. The Pacific Northwest salmon gets done with it in only a few weeks. For humans, death is the most definitive of a long series of gradual transformations. That thought adds to the complication of feelings when I say in a later poem, "The Layers," "I am not done with my changes."

GP: Is "An Old Cracked Tune" in some way suggestive of Jewish alienation and suffering for you?

SK: The very first line, "My name is Solomon Levi," is borrowed from an ugly, anti-Semitic street song recollected from my college days. Coincidentally, Solomon was my father's first name. According to what I have learned, he was a Levite, and so am I by inheritance, descended from a tribe with a priestly function. Obviously, "An Old Cracked Tune" has some connection with my heritage. As for alienation and suffering, I believe that the people of the Diaspora carry the memory of exile in their blood. But don't forget that the singer of this poem closes it with a dance.

GP: You were obviously raised to be conscious of Judaism as a religion.

SK: I was raised in a Jewish community in Worcester. In our household the emphasis was never on religious practice, but on the ethical tradition. And so it still remains for me.

GP: A tough question: Do you consider yourself a Jewish poet?

SK: My sense is that the noun "poet" does not require a qualifying adjective, either "Jewish" or "American" or "modern."

GP: Didn't the Nazi death camps of World War II have a large effect on you?

SK: Of course! Even Dante's vision of Hell hadn't prepared me for that monstrous reality.

GP: It doesn't seem to enter into your poetry directly.

SK: It's there, nevertheless, deep in the substratum of my poems. The one poem that seems to me great and terrible enough to evoke the smell of evil, the delirium, of the death camps is Celan's "Todesfugue." Only a survivor of the camps could have written it, one whose borrowed life ended in suicide. My most explicit approach to the genocidal horror of the Hitler years is my poem in honor of Dietrich Bonhoeffer, that true Christian, whose failed plot against the Führer led to his death by hanging—yes, in an extermination camp. I call it, "Around Pastor Bonhoeffer."

GP: How would you characterize your faith? Is it an artistic faith, is it a religious faith?

SK: I am a nonbeliever, but with strong religious impulses and yearnings.

GP: Has the Bible influenced your poetry?

SK: The Bible—Jewish and Christian, as I've already indicated—was one of the first books that I studied, page after page.

GP: Here's a big question. How does one face death, and can poetry help?

SK: One lives and dies simultaneously. It happens bit by bit, every day. I have tried to report that dialogue. In my childhood I dreaded going to sleep, because I was terrified at the thought of losing consciousness. I am less fearful of death in my nineties than I was in my teens, for the natural cycle has its own

reasons, even its own dark beauty. I consider myself lucky to have been given
this life.

GP: America doesn't seem to listen to its poets. If America listened to its poets, what could it learn?

SK: Our American culture has no poetry written into its origin. We inherited our poetry—mostly hymns and heroic couplets—from England, and we've tended, since the onset of the Industrial Age, to regard the medium itself as superfluous or frivolous, if not dangerous. Whitman clearly perceived that our myth, our great national myth, has to do with power, success, money; and he attempted to supersede it with a myth of Democracy and of himself as Democratic Man. And the truth is that he died unhappy, believing that he had failed, that his country had rejected him. We still need to understand that a nation that alienates itself from the creative imagination has already begun to wither.

GP: You seem to agree with your mentor, William Blake, that the genius of the poetic imagination is the most important gift. What do you hope to still accomplish?

SK: Oh, how do I know? I want to record whatever I feel most deeply. And I have plenty of unfinished business.

GP: What is the most amazing thing about life?

SK: Life itself is the most amazing thing in the universe!

GP: What is the most amazing thing about your life?

SK: Maybe it's that here I am, at this age, still loving this life as I did from the very beginning, and wanting more.

GP: And finally, while many of your poems have an elegiac tone, you have survived and lived a long, rich life. Have you found light within the darkness?

SK: Love and poetry are lights enough.

DAVID IGNATOW

Born in 1914, David Ignatow did not begin to receive national recognition for his poetry until his volume *Say Pardon* was published by Wesleyan University Press in 1961. In 1965 he received his first Guggenheim Fellowship and the Shelley Memorial Award of the Poetry Society of America. After teaching at various universities, he was appointed poet-in-residence of York College, City University of New York, in 1969. He continued to publish poetry books throughout the years, including *Rescue the Dead,* for which he received the Bollingen Prize, and several omnibus collections, plus his latest books *Shadowing the Ground, Against the Evidence: Selected Poems 1939–1994,* and *I Have a Name.* In addition to his *Notebooks,* his prose collections include *The One and the Many: A Poet's Memoirs, Open between Us* (reviews), and *Talking Together* (letters). Several collections of his poetry have been published since his death in 1997.

Like his mentor, William Carlos Williams, David Ignatow found poetry in commonplace, everyday experience, and he wrote about it in language so straightforward, simple, and unpretentious that even he described his style as antipoetic. He produced neither an original masterpiece, such as Eliot's *The Waste Land* or Ginsberg's "Howl," nor a poem of epic proportions, such as Pound's *Cantos* or Williams's *Paterson.* Instead, over a sixty-year period, he created hundreds of short poems that taken together serve as an intimate record of his life, spoken in a voice that remained constant throughout his career.

Until he was in his fifties and began to teach at universities, Ignatow was a harried businessman struggling to establish a literary reputation. In his *Notebooks,* he wrote of the loneliness, pain, and despair that he experienced while trying to succeed at two conflicting careers and raise a family. Although much of his poetry is bleak, there is a compensating comic spirit that flashes in the darkness of Ignatow's world.

Ignatow's humor is revealed in the inflections of his voice and in the strange twists and turns of thought and feeling rendered in simple, highly expressive language. Skillfully using the Yiddish comic voice in "Nice Guy," the poet captures the conflict of the businessman who wants to go to his friend's funeral but can't leave his business:

> I had a friend and he died. Me.
> I forgot to mourn him that busy day
> earning a living.

Somehow this poem about death and conflicting loyalties is funny because of the speaker's blunt, expressive mixture of Yiddish and English speech:

> He was a good guy,
> he meant well, only he had lost his teeth
> and had to swallow whole.
> He died of too much.

There is something of the schlemiel in Ignatow's comic persona, the man who has a proclivity for losing and being awkward about it.

Beginning with the volume *Rescue the Dead,* there is a subtle but substantial shift in Ignatow's art. The earlier poems picture the self as protagonist surrounded by other selves via images of realistic urban scenes. By the poem's conclusion there is usually an epiphany, a hint of meaning and even hope. In the later poems, the protagonist as self becomes almost inclusive, surrounded not by other people and a realistic setting but rather by a dreamlike ambience. Instead of meaning that derives from objective experience, the chief artistic mode becomes not the visual image but the rhythms of the mind's besieged music. The deeper he goes into his psyche, the closer the poet comes to confronting the contradictory forces in his life.

I ALWAYS identified with David Ignatow's poetry. Besides publishing him in my magazine, *Images,* and writing an essay about his poetry, I edited *Talking Together,* his selected letters, and along with Sandy MacIntosh interviewed him on local cable-access television on Long Island. I was also one of the poets who read at the poet's eightieth birthday celebration at Guild Hall, East Hampton.

It wasn't easy getting to East Hampton to interview him. The poet told me to take the train from Jamaica, Queens, to East Hampton, but when I got to Jamaica, Queens, there was no weekend train to East Hampton. My only alternative was to take a train as far as Patchog and then ride a taxi the rest of the way. When I got to my motel, Ignatow was waiting for me and agreed to "share my pain." We split the $80 cab fare.

■

On Sunday, December 3, 1995, I interviewed Ignatow at his home. Because he was suffering from Parkinson's disease, he shook and his voice was muted, but there was no mistaking his lively intelligence. We sat at a table in his writing room, which was also his bedroom and kitchen. There was also a blue chair and his father's old oak desk in the room. Ignatow typed his poems on an electric typewriter—his only concession to post–World War II technology. Next to the desk was a tarnished gray filing cabinet and next to that was a small refrigerator. The room also included a bed, dresser, dining table, television and radio, and several bookcases as well as a small kitchen area with a sink and cabinets. Near the desk was a green office chair once used by the poet's father. It was quite rickety and off-kilter.

GP: You are often seen as a disciple of William Carlos Williams, and yet you have questioned and even criticized his influence. What's your feeling now about Williams's impact on you?

DI: My impression of this is that you stated the problem incorrectly. I haven't criticized him. I've just simply distinguished the difference of myself from him as a person, as a poet, temperamentally and aesthetically. I based myself upon his theories of imagist writing, which I'm absolutely in agreement with, and they have been the basis of my style.

GP: Okay, but it seems like in your later poetry you've gone away from that imagistic poetry to something else. Maybe there you had to question Williams.

DI: That's not in disagreement so much as a change in temperament on my part or a need for my experience to find other outlets, larger outlets. Now you have to remember one thing about Williams. When he wrote the Paterson poem, he knew that he was creating a symbol and he always was against symbolist writing. But he conceded to me that yes, this is a symbol. Now, what I did really was to continue further. As far as he went with it, he did a very good job with *Paterson*. But I had to find, I had to use symbolist writing also but for my own purposes, my own personal interpretations. Williams does it more sociologically, I say, or in terms of the culture in which he is living and observing. I have to do it in terms of my individual life and being, which may amount to finally a statement of cultural importance. It may be. But there's the difference between us, see. Generationally and the fact that I lived a much harder life than he did and he had many more advantages than I did, psychologically, financially, and culturally.

GP: Let me ask you about another influence. You met Robert Bly in the fifties in New York. Now how did he change you and vice versa?

DI: He struck me as being exactly what I was looking for in terms of writing. His symbolist writing struck me right away. I was very much interested in it, and I realized that it was just the kind of encouragement I needed. And I turned more strongly towards that kind of writing than ever before. That's really the essence of his influence upon my work. But the hard thing is that in turn he seems to have become influenced by my writing.

GP: How so?

DI: Well, he wrote about his parents in a way which people have said to me reminds them of what I wrote in my study of my parents. The darkness, you know, and the light, whatever light was capable of coming through. The poems about his father are very good: the darkness, the drunken guy, the dark guy on the stairs? And then the poems about his father's wife reach out full of pathos towards the mother. But, of course, I based myself on symbolist poetry that he was writing. And he was the first poet I met and spoke with who called me up out of his own good will to say how much he admired my writing. So it just kept me going.

GP: Do you think he made you a more political poet? During the sixties, he led the anti-Vietnam War movement in poetry.

DI: No. I was a political poet myself then. I'm supposed to write an essay, a 45-minute essay for a lecture on how I began as a poet. Well, I began with Shelley. Shelley, an extraordinarily marvelous political poet. And this was during the deep Depression, and there was Shelley denouncing the wealthy and the arrogant and those who were indifferent to suffering, you know. He was extraordinary for me. It was a great encouragement to write that way, and I did. I wrote many poems like that, a good many. My first book has about four or five of those poems where you thump away at the moral.

GP: How would you characterize the contribution of Charles Reznikoff as an American poet? Did he or other Objectivist poets influence you?

DI: Very much so, very much. I recognized that he turned a realist moment into a moment of interpretation, which is one way of writing the symbolist poem. In other words, he created, he did something that is unusual and is done only by the very best writers, in fiction and in poetry. They take the reality before them that's observed, and they interpret it according to the values and the experience in their own lives, so that without losing the sense of the reality they are observing and portraying, it also offers a point of view, which is intimated between the lines. And this is Reznikoff's technique. I adapted that also.

I took that very seriously and used it. So I've written many poems—take for example the poem about the bagel. There is an example of what I'm talking about, where I take an incident of having dropped a bagel onto the ground and suddenly I turned it into something very different from an ordinary experience of having to pick up an object from the ground.

GP: Do you see yourself as part of a movement, school, or tradition of poets?

DI: I guess I belong to more than one school, to put it truthfully. I'm in the Reznikoff school and I also like to write in a way that creates a symbol, removed from the actual event itself that inspired the writing of it. And often I like to create imaginary things, imaginary situations with no basis in fact that never did exist except in my mind. But I create a reality about them. That's yet another way I write. That would be, for example, the prose poem "The Diner." It's a totally invented experience. It never happened. Yet to a lot of people it sounds and reads very convincingly. And I've done quite a few like that. Well, I'm at a new stage of writing now, where I write very short, precise sentences. You would think I was writing generalities, words that aren't themselves precise or imagistic but which in the tight sentence structure I give them take on a certain resonance. And this is a different way of writing now entirely.

The language doesn't attempt to be metaphysical or metaphorical. It's straightforward, conversational, perhaps nearly a highly cultivated newspaper style, like in a feature story possibly, where language is used economically, without emphasis on style, but to the point.

GP: How is it different from your earlier poetry?

DI: The thing is that I've returned to it but on another level, of which I was not capable or conscious that it was there to use at that earlier time. For example, "Reality is the other person. / We are all imagination / on whom the other intrudes / to give us pain and sorrow / of our unfulfillment / in the other." It's the kind of writing that only a certain experience in living can eventually produce: on one hand keeping to the ordinariness of the language, which is to symbolize the day-to-day life lived, and on the other hand it is shaped with an emphasis on thought that has come with time and age and living the day-to-day life. The style was there to use, as I did years earlier, but not with the sobriety of accent on insight. The earlier style, also concentrating on the language and pace of conversation, emphasized the narrative or the action in which the poem found itself responding to and, as in Reznikoff, translating this action as meaning. In my new version, it is action of thought, pervasive thought.

GP: So have you come full circle?

DI: Yeah, I'm returning to this kind of straightforward writing.

53

DAVID IGNATOW

GP: But you've learned a lot about life and death since you wrote those very early poems.

DI: Which adds to that kind of—what would be called generalities, words that have generalizations in themselves, such as this poem: "It'll surely be eight o'clock, / however I wait for it, / and then at eight I can prepare / for ten arriving, whether I live / for it or accidentally die. What / am I then, if not important / to my hours?" You notice it's not metaphorical. I wouldn't call it metaphorical. It's written in the Objectivist mode, the kind of writing which was done to perfection by Oppen, George Oppen. I felt his presence, too, as a poet, but I had to do it my way. When he wrote, you know, he just lobbed a few phrases. He wanted the reader to amplify them in his or her own mind to what exactly was being insinuated or intimated in those few phrases. That kind of writing could be a product of the Chinese technique, you know, of saying a few things with the barest number of words, in fact barely suggesting the thought, with the reader left to guess or fill out the rest of it. It implies. The method implies, is resonant: a few simple lines that you can supply with your own thoughts.

GP: What can this country, what can America, learn from its poets, poets whom it really hasn't celebrated very much in this century?

DI: This country has nothing to learn from its poets. It feels it has to learn from its own self-destructiveness. That's the only way it'll ever learn. It starts to destroy itself and it catches itself up, just barely in time. Perhaps we're doing it now, perhaps, by suddenly deciding to go to Bosnia. We're really asserting that we are a nation committed to humanitarian life. Maybe. Before that it was all money, money, money, and power. And all of a sudden, out of the garbage and the dust and the destructiveness with which we've been living, the phoenix bird rises, the bird of liberty and humanity rises again. That's Whitman coming to life again, you see. Whitman keeps coming back, all the time. You have nothing else; you have no other center. Well, you've gotta give Clinton credit for doing the right thing against the anger and indifference of the rest of the country. They want to pursue the money, they want to pursue their self-satisfaction, you know, and self-aggrandizement. But he said, no, we have to do something else.

GP: In your poem "Rescue the Dead," you seem to touch on a theme such as you've just articulated. I mean, it's a very deep poem. But it almost seems as if the poem says that you have to give up worldly power and money in order to love. Am I close?

DI: You're right, you're right. They don't mix.

GP: It's a terrible choice, in a way.

DI: But if you really love with your whole being, if your being can't exist without love, then naturally you live that way. You live without money, you live with love. There's no other choice.

GP: Are the lovers free or are the power-hungry people free, because one of the lines of the poem says, "You who are free, rescue the dead"?

DI: It's irony. In a sense, statement of irony. Those who think they are free.

GP: So the only freedom finally is in love.

DI: That's right.

GP: And in order to love it's as if you have to give up almost everything of worldly significance.

DI: You don't become a beggar, no. You live according to principles which don't confuse you, which don't entangle you in graft and greed and power.

GP: Why did you write the *Notebooks,* where you really concentrate on pain and suffering?

DI: It was the only way I had, other than a therapist, and I couldn't find a therapist and I didn't have the money for a therapist, and I knew I had to write or otherwise I would go crazy. There was so much pressure on me from many directions. So I wrote, and I figure much of it got out on paper, and I allowed myself to write that way because I felt that there was light, that I would see the light at the end of the tunnel. The more I wrote, the more light I would find coming into the dark.

GP: Can we say, then, that poetry, art, which brings light, must come from the darkness of suffering?

DI: That's not an absolute. But those who have suffered, who find their lives are just a ball of suffering, have no choice, no choice at all. But when you think of a Molière, who could laugh and be satirical, or George Bernard Shaw—you know, they wrote beautiful things, too. Suffering doesn't have to be all there is to life, by no means. And if you're living with love and by love and for love, you don't see it that way. You don't see suffering as an absolute. You see it as a possibility, but you don't emphasize it. You emphasize the freedom you find in love.

GP: For years your poetry was centered in New York City, and then you began to write about more internal, subjective experience. Do you see an overall direction in and toward which you have been moving?

DI: Well, the fact of the matter is that I was writing internally even while living in New York City. That really is a fact. If you look through my work, you'll find that I was looking into my shortcomings, looking into the kind of life I had to live in New York, you know, becoming associated with New York. I really internalized the whole problem of New York for people who had to earn a living and had to live on the edge all the time, you know, near bankruptcy and near failure. That sort of thing. So I did live an internal life. When I moved to East Hampton, it took on a whole different aspect because, while I found silence in East Hampton to be very soothing, it forced me back upon myself in a way that I never anticipated. I mean, I had no stimulation from the world around me, and the stimulation had to come from myself with which to find a way to live and enjoy my own presence. And then I began to associate, recognize that I had some relationship to the trees, believe it or not. I felt, here I am, the trees are stuck out here, well, I'm stuck out here, too. And the two connections I made made me realize that trees were just as human as I was in some ways.

GP: What did you mean when you said that energy is the god we are looking for? Is the energy in nature?

DI: The energy is in nature, that's true. I was, I recognized I was, part of nature. I may—in New York City I may have felt I was just part of New York City. But when I began living out in East Hampton, I had to acknowledge that one is part of nature. You're surrounded in every way by everything that represents nature at its very basics.

GP: Let me ask you this. The statement reads, "Energy is the god we are looking for." So are you talking about the god of science, of physics, when you say that?

DI: If there is a god, then god would have to be energy. Because energy manifests life. Life we know of as something which moves and acts and has the power to act upon others, other people and other things. Where there's no energy, things remain completely still and void. But I don't think of energy, literally. I don't think of energy as god at all. But I was just replying to a question as to whether I believe there is a god. I don't believe there's a god, but I do believe that energy is the controlling element in our lives, the dominant element in our lives, that which gives us our life and keeps us alive as long as energy is part of our body, is in our body.

GP: You grew up as a Jew, your parents were Jewish, you were Jewish. Did Jewish culture and religion influence you?

DI: Oh, considerably, I would say. Yes. Jewish culture through Russian culture. Yes, my parents both were Russian, let's say Ukrainian, but Ukraine was influenced by the Russian culture. So there was that element, that melancholy element in their Jewish Russian culture, which I suppose I inherited in ways. And also this melancholy wasn't only for oneself, but there was a melancholy which settled over the entire world for a Russian Jew. That is, the whole world became part of the whole Russian Jewish problem. And there was sympathy, there was a great amount of sympathy that you could feel for others because, as a Jew, you didn't consider yourself to be exceptional.

GP: In "Europe and America," the poem, you say, "My father brought the emigrant bundle / of desperation and worn threads, / that in anxiety as he stumbles / tumble out distractedly." So you are a product of the Jewish immigrant experience in America. Probably your most famous poem is "The Bagel," which certainly has a Jewish flavor to it. Do you think of that as a Jewish poem? You know, actually, Robert Bly says somewhere that it's your good-hearted tribute to the Jewish people.

DI: I never read that.

GP: Do you think of it that way? Or is it a poem about Jewish food?

DI: No, strangely enough, the poem began as a sad revelation to myself that I was living a very limited and quietly desperate life, you know.

GP: How do you get liberated in that poem?

DI: Here's what happened. In other words, I was really doing the melancholic thing, and feeling my own limitations, you know, my potentials weren't really being developed as I had hoped. So I don't know how the idea of the bagel struck me. But it did come all of a sudden and hit me that I could write about it. But it wasn't intended to be humorous, strangely enough, when I wrote it. I was going to make all these somersaults, not necessarily to humor myself, but they meant something else. I couldn't know what they meant, but I decided to write them anyway.

And when I finished, I felt that I had sort of revealed my inner longing for a wider life, a much more expansive life, a much more varied life, a much more hopeful life. I felt satisfied about that. I think that's what really got me to write. Then when I read it to an audience, they laughed. They saw humor in it. I didn't realize how much humor there is to it. I saw it as a way, a token of my hope for a larger life, a bigger, more varied life. A more open life.

GP: One thing we can say about it is you took your symbol from Jewish culture.

DI: Yeah.

GP: Bagel. There hadn't been many prominent poems about bagels before you wrote this one. It might have been the first.

DI: It is the first.

GP: It can be read in a number of ways. I've read it in a Jungian way as saying that the bagel symbolizes the female anima. In other words, that the person, the man, becomes happy because somehow he gets into touch with his female archetype. Going into the unconscious, there is a wider range of human experience there because man comes into contact with his female consciousness. Another Jewish poem is the one called "Blessing Myself." In the poem you say, "I believe in stillness, / I close a door / and surrender myself / to a wall and converse / with it and ask it / to bless me." There you seem to conjure a picture of a man davening, of praying to a wall, as Jews have done for centuries. Were you aware of that?

DI: No, I wasn't aware of that. I honestly wasn't aware that I was thinking of the sacred wall in Jerusalem. No, it didn't occur to me at all. When I thought of the wall it was as the limitation to our lives. You pray to the limitation to our lives, you know? About ways we have been limited, not by us but by circumstances. And I meant by prayer to it to let it open itself up and become a help, some sort of a help. But then I finally realized that it's silent; therefore, I had to find the help in myself. I had to find faith in myself.

GP: All right, now let's talk about another of the Jewish poems. It's one of your most beautiful poems. It's called "Kaddish." It's an elegy for your mother, right? And it's based, the title, of course, is based on the Kaddish, the Jewish Kaddish prayer for the dead, which is spoken at the funeral and of course every year at the memorial date. Well, you chose the Kaddish prayer to title that poem, so you must have been thinking Jewish in some way, shape, or form.

DI: Unquestionably.

GP: But it's interesting that it has this other aspect of your faith in it, I think. I don't know if we can say god of energy, but god of nature; in other words, the mother becomes the earth mother. "Earth now is your mother, as you were mine, my earth, / my sustenance and my strength, / and now without you I turn to your mother / and seek from her that I may meet you again / in rock and stone. Whisper to the stone, / I love you. Whisper to the rock, I found you. / Whisper to the earth, Mother, I have found her, / and I am safe and always have been." So in a way it seems to be a prayer to mother earth. But you gave it the Jewish title.

DI: Well, since I buried my mother, she became part of the earth. So I'm praying to her mother and to her new being; her new sense of being was in the earth.

GP: So your faith is not in heaven or hell but in the earth.

DI: Well, I was just thinking the other day: This world, this earth, is an accident, you know. It's an accident of the collision of different elements in the cosmos. The earth, being an accident, therefore, the law of accidents will apply to this earth and will totally destroy it at one point, accidentally. So therefore that's as far as I think we can have faith in the earth, as just for the time being, and that's about all we can hope for.

GP: Of course, the time being could be for millions of years.

DI: But I think that eventually it will disappear.

GP: Each individual human life, of course, ends in death, and you've written a lot about death. How does one face death, and can poetry help?

DI: No, the connection isn't very strong. To face death means to acknowledge your limitation and acknowledge your aging or your weakness or that you're coming to an end, because you have seen for many, many years all around you things coming to an end. To a calm end, many things to a calm end, some to a violent end, but an end it is. Everything, people and things, comes to an end. And having seen all this all through your years of living, as a child, as a youth, as a grown man, as an aging man, you have to consider yourself part of the phenomenon of death, the phenomenon which creates death. And you accept it.

Poetry would mean, therefore, if you were to write about it, when you write poetry as a Jew and as a person who must die, you offer another vision, a vision of revival; it's a token of energy. Poetry is a token of energy which demonstrates to you and maybe to the rest of the world that while there is death, you can leave behind that token of energy; there is energy, too.

GP: This is the energy of language?

DI: The energy of your imagination, of creativity, the energy of creativity, which is the other side of death; death and creativity share the world between them.

GP: So in a way, your faith is in the poetic imagination, the ability of the human being to create in the face of darkness and death.

DI: Yes, but at the same time he draws from the natural energy of the world. And he finds it in himself. He mustn't ever consider that he isn't part of the universe. Once he realizes he's part of the universe he knows he has that energy that the universe has. He has a token of its energy, and this is demonstrated in your creativity as a poet.

GP: You like the prose poem, which is almost the other end of the continuum from the sonnet, let's say. What does the prose poem offer you, and is it prose or poetry or both?

DI: It's poetry. The emphasis, of course, is on the style with which you want to make poems for yourself. When I say prose, it's because I acknowledge that all my experiences are rooted in reality, in my reality, and prose is a form, a way of indicating reality. The prose style means, it's a prose life, we live a prose life. We don't live an elevated life, as Shelley would wish us to believe is possible. It's not possible. We live a life, an everyday life. And we can take the everyday life and its technique is the prose, is prose, but when we look into it more deeply, the everyday life, we see that it's not everyday in the sense of come and go. It exists for all time for every place we live in, for all history, past and present and the future. The common life is the life of the universe. This is what I try to indicate. But you mustn't lose the fact that it's a life lived every day, and the prose style indicates every day.

GP: In your poem "Rescue the Dead," you almost imply that you have to die to all that routine in order to find love. Where are these people going to find love? They want it, but where are they going to find it?

DI: I don't know. This poem doesn't help with that.

GP: You have written mostly short poems. Any reason for that? Is it just the way it comes out?

DI: I once thought it was because, working long hours in industry many, many years ago, I could only find the strength with which to write a poem of a dozen lines at the most, maybe even less—eight, ten lines at the most. And I learned how to compact and condense. And that I think was one stimulus to writing symbolically and writing with a precision which I may have learned from Reznikoff.

GP: Have you written long poems? The one that I think of is "The Rituals" poem. Have you written other poems of that length that haven't been published?

DI: Yeah. One that I didn't publish in this book but was published in Israel, a four-, five-page poem.

GP: But the most recent ones in your new manuscript are short, very short.

DI: Most of them are short, some are two and a half pages in length.

GP: One of your really affirmative poems begins with the line "How good it is to feel the joy at last." Do you remember that?

DI: Yeah.

GP: Why is it night when the joy takes place? Why not in broad daylight?

DI: The poem explains the reason, because lights are on, there are lights.

GP: There are lights in the world?

DI: No, the poem talks about lights. "How good it is to feel the joy at last / of oneself. It is like the full moon, / shining down upon the dark trees. It is / like lit trains sliding by in the dark. . . ." It explains itself.

GP: The light is always there.

DI: There's always a light there, always a light.

GP: The light of the imagination.

DI: That's quite right, yeah. The light of joy the imagination can give you, joy in the sense of belonging, of accepting yourself in the dark.

GP: Let's go back to a previous concern. Were you raised to be conscious of Judaism as a religion?

DI: Well, it happened, it just happened organically, so to speak; since I did attend the synagogue with my father on the High Holy Days, naturally that whole thing became embedded in my consciousness. I've never really lost it, but I really don't know how to use it, and I don't think I can use it.

GP: Has Jewishness and maybe even the Yiddish language entered into the language of your poetry? I think it has in certain ways.

DI: You'll have to tell me how.

GP: In the rhythms of some of the poems. You were talking about a lilting melancholy just now. The humor of your poetry almost seems Jewish, you know, little sparks come out of the darkness. And also you meditate on questions from different angles and points of view, in almost a Talmudic fashion.

DI: That's both Talmudic and it's philosophical at the same time. Philosophy starts and ends with questions and you never find answers. That is to say contemporary philosophy has no answers, it has questions.

GP: So do you consider yourself a Jewish poet, then?

DI: Not in the sense that you mean it. The prophets, to me, were very important. And the prophets led me to Shelley. So Shelley and the prophets formed an enormous impact of energy for me, and I used it in my youth. Very early in my life I wrote many poems where the prophets and Shelley dominated the work. But then I knew, that is after awhile, that living and working in the city began to make Shelley and the prophets virtually ineluctable to me. They did not relate to the city because the city lived by routine, routine which for some people meant wealth and happiness and for other people meant misery and a short life. The Shelleyan and prophetic apostrophe to good and evil did not apply here. People lived out their lives almost by pure habit of suffering or in affluence.

GP: You've been writing poems for sixty years. What's the central thing you've learned in that long period of time, writing poetry?

DI: As a poet, you mean?

GP: Yeah.

DI: You've gotta write what you wish to say and not what you think will appeal.

GP: So you're not writing primarily to an audience, then?

DI: No, I'm writing to reveal myself to myself and I'm also looking for the wholeness in the world itself. Could I find any hint of wholeness in myself? You see, the book I'm publishing next fall (1996), titled *I Have a Name,* is based on the division in oneself. Not only myself but everyone else. The division between death and creativity. It takes destructiveness, depression, negativeness, relationships that go awry, huge number of divorces, many, many divorces, inability to stay in love with anyone or love of oneself, as a matter of fact. Death has many sides to it. Creativity, if it's of the highest order, you must write as you think, as you really feel within. Otherwise, as a poet, you'll never be happy with yourself or your poems.

   If you're that serious about writing, you are writing to give your life some equipoise, some balance. The balance is to be found in that creativity which satisfies you, at least temporarily, for the time being as you write, until other questions arise needing answers. You have to answer all your questions honestly and that's what makes a poet do good work. It's honest, authentic poetry. And when that's done, then you balance death, you have death—-your balance between death and creativity is well kept, and you can live a life of, not contentment, but a life of salvation. Let's put it that way. It's a life of salvation from depression and it's a life which anticipates death, because it also has to accept creativity. There can't be one without the other.

GP: The test of creativity is in the poem, then, as opposed to the critic's judgment of the poem?

DI: Yeah. I don't know what you mean by a critic's judgment.

GP: Well, there usually has to be some kind of worldly receptivity to the poem in order for it to get published, for example.

DI: Well, a poem should be recognized for what it is by a critic who's familiar with the poetry and is experienced with poetry and has lived a life of his own, honestly. He comes across a poem like "Kaddish," for example, and he should be able to recognize it instantly, that this is not my experience alone. I'm really calling upon the experience of healing and that's part of nature, too. Nature heals itself. After it becomes destructive, it heals itself, and when you have a death in the family, you have to heal yourself after that. And that's what the poem does authentically. The poem is an absolutely authentic portrayal of how a person like myself, for example, has learned to make the best of things and by appealing to the very nature of life itself, which is creativity, which is energy, and to be found in nature. I am nature, you are nature, we're all nature. But we have to point to nature in its other forms, forms of stone and mountains and earth. That's where we find our balance, our revival, and our interest in life after great loss and great grief.

Well, I personally continue living because it's a challenge to live with all the ills of age, old age, a lot of challenge. And I think I look at Stanley Kunitz. I admire him, how he does it. I know he's not impenetrable, but he acts as if he's impenetrable to calamities and to aging itself. He's got the vivacity in his life and his being and his poetry. I say that's something really to model yourself on. He expresses creativity. He knows he's coming to an end, but he expresses creativity as the only answer to death, the great answer.

GP: What do you think is the most amazing thing about your life? Is it your creative imagination?

DI: I still have my intelligence at this point. I'm still capable of being objective, I can still reason with myself and reason with other people, reason with my life, and find my place in the world. Still find my place in the world. I don't feel at a loss. I'm losing energy, I'm losing, but I feel I'm holding on to my own presence. I know I'm conscious of my presence. As long as I'm conscious of my presence, then I'm satisfied that I'll continue living as I always lived, for the issue of a good poem.

GP: Your *Selected Poems 1934–1994*, a sixty-year retrospective volume, has a poem in it called "Against the Evidence," which is central to the book. It says in the last few lines, "I set a typewriter on its surface / and begin to type / to tell myself my troubles. / Against the evidence, I live by choice." So what you've just been talking about is similar to what you say in that poem, isn't it?

DI: Yeah, right.

GP: Against the evidence of all the ills in the world and in yourself.

DI: I affirm that the other side to all our ills is our ability to live with these ills and make a life for ourselves, which is to be distinguished from destructive-ness, to be distinguished from unhappiness, from depression, from self-abne-gation, and it's interesting therefore to live for that alone. It's interesting that you can maintain it, that you are interested in maintaining it. Your curiosity gets the best of you and can make you see how long you can maintain this quality, you know.

GP: Do you think love is possible in this life, love between two people?

DI: Yes, it can be done; of course it is. Two people have to really work at it, because it doesn't just flow naturally, you know. People can be attracted to one another, but that's only the start of a relationship. A relationship to me means that two people have decided that they will single themselves out from the rest of the world and be to each other a wholeness, a wholeness to each other, and that's what they've always felt and sought for, a sense of com-pletion. If you're completed in a love relationship, if there are two people who have acknowledged that this is what they lacked in their life, this is what they want to contribute to the relationship, a sense of wholeness between them.

GP: How do you see your place in American poetry?

DI: I have a place.

GP: In what way?

DI: I've affirmed all the important goals, that which makes life lasting. My work shows that I've done two things: I've gotten to the bottom of the pit of hell, and life can be hell, and I've also found that I've come out of hell, and I'm looking down into the pit, I'm looking down into where I've come from. And I look around me, and I see that not only have I come out of that pit but lots of other people have come out of that pit. But this is talking subjectively. I don't know what it means to be a poet, I really don't know. It means to affirm your-self, for one thing, to affirm yourself in the universe. That you're not only a speck but you're also a spark. That's nature. Nature is a spark. So you and na-ture, you've affirmed nature in yourself and in the world. To do that, I suppose, is to be a poet. In other words, reaffirming life as it is and always has been and always will be.

DENISE LEVERTOV

DENISE LEVERTOV'S background was certainly varied and unusual for a major American poet. She was born in 1923 and raised in Ilford, Essex, near London. Her Welsh mother was descended from the Welsh tailor and mystic Angel Jones of Mold, and her father, who was related to the Hasid Schneour Zalman, "the Rav of Northern White Russia," converted to Christianity. He became a priest of the Anglican Church and sought the unification of Judaism and Christianity.

The poet was taught at home and never attended any school or college, except ballet school. However, she met prominent religious people, artists, writers, and scholars, who visited her house. T. S. Eliot wrote her a long letter praising some of her earliest attempts at poetry.

During the war, Levertov lived in London and worked as a civilian nurse. After the war, she and her husband, Mitchell Goodman, lived in France, where she met Robert Creeley and through him Charles Olson and Robert Duncan. But the main influence on her early work was William Carlos Williams. It was Williams who helped Levertov develop "from a British Romantic with an almost Victorian background to an American poet of any vitality."

By the time of her death in January 1998, Denise Levertov had published over twenty volumes of poetry. Her work is represented in most anthologies of twentieth-century poetry in English. Her work also includes several volumes of essays and translations, and her posthumous collection *The Great Unknowing: Last Poems* appeared in 1999.

IN OVER twenty volumes of poetry, Denise Levertov created a large body of work in which she wrote clearly and suggestively about everyday events as well as their connection to beauty and spirituality. Although she took many of her sources from the Judeo-Christian tradition, she wrote neither as a traditional Jew nor as a Christian, but as a poet who followed what she referred to as her muse or her gift to capture moments of revelation, when she saw with a mystical sense of oneness and joy.

What she wanted to do was "To stand on common ground," to write about the objects and events of everyday life, but in a language "not 'common speech' . . . / but the uncommon speech of paradise." It is as if the words of the poem are a bridge, or "what Whitman called / 'the path / between reality and the soul.'" In several of her poems she used the symbol of Jacob's ladder stretching between earth and heaven to show her attempt to create poems that mediate the everyday and the eternal.

In Levertov's poetry, love often communicates the merging of flesh and spirit, body and soul. Her love poems often contain biblical allusions and are written with a sensuousness that suggests the spiritual:

> It is leviathan and we
> in its belly
> looking for joy, some joy
> not to be known outside it
>
> two by two in the ark of
> the ache of it

While these lines from "The Ache of Marriage" are erotic, they convey a religious longing as well for something more lasting as suggested by the biblical allusions to Jonah in the whale's belly and the Ark of the Covenant. Even in "Song for Ishtar," where the lovers are compared to sows—"we rock and grunt, grunt and / shine"—it is significant that the poem's last word, "shine," symbolizes a purity beyond the sensual.

■

OUR INTERVIEW began in 1997 with the poet's response to my question "What have you found the hardest thing about being a poet?" Levertov wrote, "I can't say I've found *anything* hard about it." Underlining anything conveys confidence, if not brashness. She went on to say, "I consider myself extremely lucky to have the gift." In her poem "Writer and Reader," she said, "I feel awe at being / chosen for the task."

Because of the interview's written format, I was not able to ask follow-up questions, so I could not question the poet further about her answers; they imply a belief in what Coleridge called "the esemplastic power" of the creative imagination. Nevertheless, because Levertov's answers were so brief, I still wonder what she meant by her experience of the gift. None of the other poets whom I interviewed, not even Ginsberg, spoke with such assurance about the challenge of creating poems. And none was as romantic and mysterious.

During the Vietnam War, Levertov became known for her poems of protest. "Life at War" is one of a number of poems in which the poet expresses her outrage at America's military effort in Vietnam. It is as if her religious sensibility will not tolerate man's inhumanity to man in war, certainly not America's inhumanity toward the Vietnamese: "these acts are done / to our own flesh; burned human flesh / is smelling in Viet Nam as I write." At times the language of these poems conveys an antiwar doctrine through the language of passionate invective: "we shall thirst in Hades, / in the blood of our children."

The best of Levertov's poems are love poems, whether they describe erotic love or a mother's love for her son or the poet's love for nature. Her ultimate desire was "to taste and see," to experience as much of earthly life as possible. In the forest as well as on city streets, she found hints and clues of "a beauty / not to be denied." In her poem "Primary Wonder," the last poem in *Sands of the Well*, she marvels at "The mystery / that there is anything, anything at all, / let alone cosmos, joy, memory, everything, / rather than void."

Questions and answers were submitted in writing.

GP: What have you found the hardest thing about being a poet?

DL: I can't say I've found *anything* hard about it!

GP: What is the most enjoyable thing about being a poet for you?

DL: I consider myself extremely lucky to have the gift. And I'm also lucky in having received a lot of positive response, all my life, for simply doing what it is natural for me to do. I've also been criticized, of course, but some negative criticism is salutary, and the positive responses have outnumbered the negative.

GP: Are we at the end of the long journey of poetry? What can a late-twentieth-century poet hope to accomplish?

DL: We may, if we continue destroying our environment, be at the end of our journey as a *species!*—but as long as the human species exists so will poetry, I believe, because it is a human characteristic. I don't have an answer to the second part of the question; or perhaps I do: Poems can serve to remind people of many things they don't notice, and to reveal the extraordinary within the ordinary, and to stimulate imagination and intuitive knowledge, and by being beautiful, moving, powerful—just as poems have always done.

[A later addition to this answer:]

At this tail end of the twentieth century, one of the things about which poetry can nudge people is matters of ecological consciousness and conscience. Because poetry has traditionally dealt with "Nature" anyway (especially poetry in English), it is well placed to do so. "Consciousness raising" is certainly part of poetry's range and is what links it to prophecy (though poetry and prophecy are not identical).

GP: What does a poet need to know about craft? Are rhyme and meter still important enough to be part of the young poet's training? What is free verse? Can it be taught?

DL: Of course, a poet needs to develop craft (although it is of little use without inborn ability). A poet needs to perceive and recognize the craft elements in other poets' work—though not necessarily to adopt them. The function of rhyme and meter, along with other technical devices, can be (and needs to be) learned, but can be absorbed through attentive *reading*—they don't *have* to be taught in school. What *does* have to be taught (today, in America, anyway) is reading. And attention. "Free verse" (a name loosely applied to various "nonce" or nontraditional forms as well as to loose *vers libre*) is no different in this from any other mode, though it demands yet closer attention.

GP: What do you think inspired you to be a poet?

DL: I started to write as a young child. The ur-impulse is a native special relation to language (as for a musician to musical sounds or for a visual artist to color, form, paint) and *not* to subject matter. (For a writer of fiction the ur-impulse is probably more related to storytelling than to language as such.)

GP: How did Williams Carlos Williams influence you as a young poet? And do you still feel his influence?

DL: William Carlos Williams became an influence in my mid-twenties, by which time I had published my first book. His influence helped me to free my diction and rhythms from received habits, and to survive undiagnosed culture shock at the same time! I think I *absorbed* his influence a long time ago, so I don't actively feel it today—but I know I would not be who I am without it (even if I'm not sure if he would have approved my work of later decades).

GP: How did you meet Creeley, Duncan, and Olson? Have they and you learned from each other? Do you believe in the breath unit, projective verse?

DL: I met Creeley through my husband (they had both been at Harvard). Duncan introduced himself to me with a poem-letter. I only met Olson a couple of times and did not correspond with him. NO, I don't believe in the "breath unit." To me, "projective verse" meant the possibility of a much more inclusive kind of poem ("composition by field") than the discrete focus of a more "bijou-like" poem prevalent in the fifties; and also the necessity for a good poem to follow its trajectory without stopping to "load the rifts with ore" (as Keats had said) because it would have no rifts. This may well not have been exactly what Olson meant. In any case, it was good advice as I understood it—though not particularly original.

GP: In "Illustrious Ancestors," you write of your dual ancestry and how it has influenced your poetic aspirations: "Well, I would like to make, / thinking some line still taut between me and them . . ." Do you suggest that your religious vision comes from the Rav and his people? Can you address your father's impact upon you as a writer?

DL: I don't imply that it came to me more from the Rav than from Angel Jones of Mold—I was claiming them both as ancestors, equally.

GP: In "The Third Dimension," you say "a simple honesty is / nothing but a lie." Is the third dimension something hidden in nature that only language can capture? Is this a mystical notion?

DL: "The Third Dimension" was a poem about falling in love with someone, although I still loved my husband, and about the inexplicableness of this. It wasn't "mystical." It was just about how complicated life is. (Incidentally, as is well known, I stayed married for many years after that and wrote love poems clearly addressed to my husband, as well as some to other people.)

GP: In "Stepping Westward," were you conscious of the pregnant pauses and rich sounds of the lines "There is no savor / more sweet, more salt / than to be glad to be / what, woman . . ."? Or did the sounds flow spontaneously in the writing? Do you think of the poem as a feminist poem? Is there a controlling metaphor for you in the poem?

DL: I was both conscious *and* spontaneous. No, it's not feminist in any ideological way, nor have I ever been an active feminist. I'm not sure what a "controlling" metaphor is.

GP: You refer many times to Jacob's ladder (Gen. 28:15) as well as Jacob's wrestling with the stranger (Gen. 32:28), after which he is known as Israel (For you have striven with God and with men, and have prevailed). Your epigraph re the ladder quotes Buber: "Even the ascent and descent of the angels depends on my deed." How do you interpret your fascination with Jacob? Is this not evidence of your Jewishness?

DL: Many non-Jewish people have been fascinated by the story of Jacob and the Angel! So I don't think my interest constitutes "evidence of Jewishness" at all! I do think arguing with God (or "God wrestling") is a (delightful) Jewish characteristic—but though I have poems expressive of doubt or the sense of disconnection, I'm not, I think, particularly apt to argue with God. My friend David Shaddock wrote a wonderful series of "God-wrestling" poems a few years back, for which Arthur Waskow wrote an introduction (unfortunately the book was only published in a *very* limited edition . . .).

GP: Have you been aware of the impact of the Song of Songs and other biblical poetry on such poems as "Song for a Dark Voice," "The Ache of Marriage," and other love poems by you?

DL: Yes, of course I perceived the biblical influence on the poems you mention, and others. I was brought up hearing the King James Bible.

GP: In "In Memory of Boris Pasternak," you write of the great Russian poet's profound effect on you, as if you aspire to "fulfill / what he had written." Have you been drawn to the Russia of your father and to Pasternak in particular because of his and your Jewish-Christian roots? Did you ever meet him? You show this Jewish-Christian interplay as well in "A Letter to William Kinter of Muhlenberg."

DL: Yes, I'm sure my love of Russian literature was not altogether unconnected with certain proprietal feeling. But not because of the Jewish-Christian roots. Russian (not Hebrew or Yiddish) was my father's first language, and despite his perfect German and virtually perfect English it remained the language in which he dreamed. I did not meet Pasternak but I did have that one wonderful letter in which he wrote, "I feel that we shall be friends." He died not long after, though. The letter is now in Stanford's Special Collections. I called William Kinter "Zaddik" because he stood in that relation, I felt, to his students—and at that moment, to me too. (Later on he sadly seemed to become more and more eccentric and got involved with flying saucers I believe. I don't know if he's still alive.) I was reading "The Tales of the Hasidim" a lot at that time, too.

GP: Can you speak of the impact of the Holocaust on you? Do you remember what prompted you to write "During the Eichmann Trial"? Have your reactions to the Holocaust changed since you wrote that poem?

DL: My parents and my sister (nine years my senior) were heavily involved in helping refugees get out of Germany and Austria and so before I was ten I knew a bit about the persecution of the Jews by the Nazis. By the time the camps were liberated I knew a *lot* more than the average English person. The *New York Times* coverage of the Eichmann trial, with the many bizarre things he said, prompted me to write that poem. I don't think my attitudes about the Holocaust have changed since then—however, I don't have the poem with me here in Beloit and don't remember it very clearly. I know I later felt the peachtree part was not well written—all that Mr. Death stuff—slack language.

GP: What's the religious impulse if any behind "O Taste and See"? Do you suggest a belief in an earthly paradise?

DL: I was pretty much an agnostic at the time of "O Taste and See." It doesn't imply an earthly paradise but that (as an earlier poem said) "If we're here let's be here now"—a sentiment reechoed in many a later poem. See for example "A South Wind" in *Sands of the Well.*

GP: This leads me to your psalms. Are they part of an evolving series or are they separate poems to you? You seem to want to affirm earthly experience as holy. "To worship *mortal*"—"without hope of heaven." To affirm "somber beauty in what is mortal." Is there a Jewish influence here from the Hebrew Psalms, etc.? In "A Psalm Praising the Hair of Man," you affirm the body, sexuality, earthly love as holy. Again, this strikes me as biblical, but you may think of it differently than I.

DL: Some poems have just felt like psalms to me. They are separate poems. I agree with you about their expressing a sense of the sacred in the earthly (the ones you mention).

GP: "The Psalm Concerning the Castle" is more elusive than the other psalms. Why a castle? Kafka? Can the castle be within the speaker?

DL: The poem was inspired by a Han Dynasty pottery watchtower in the Boston Museum of Fine Arts. These were funerary objects. The poem describes it and also articulates what I felt to be its symbolic significance. (Not perhaps its intended significance but what it meant to *me.*)

GP: There's a paradox in "City Psalm": "I saw paradise in the dust of the street." How does bliss emanate from the violence of the streets?

DL: It doesn't say "emanates from" and it says "dust," not violence—though it does speak of violence too I expect; of ugliness anyway. It is testifying to the paradox of bliss, the sacred, the ecstatic, being present ineffably *every*where . . .

GP: When in "A Cloak" you speak of "breathing in / my life, / breathing out / poems . . . ," you make me think of Muriel Rukeyser. Did you know her well? Did she change your poetry, your life, in any way? She has a great sonnet ("To be a Jew in the 20th century / Is to be offered a gift . . ."). The poem is included in an anthology of Jewish American literature edited by Abraham Chapman, which includes a selection of your poems as well.

DL: I knew Muriel quite well (and as you probably know we went to Hanoi together—with Jane Hart, wife of the late Senator Philip Hart of Michigan, in 1972.) She was a great human being but no, her poetry did not have any influence on mine. Nor did she "change my life" except in the degree that every single person one knows has *some* effect on one's life, unmeasured and indeed immeasurable. I've read the poem you mention but am not familiar with the anthology.

GP: What madness do you write of in "Mad Song"? How is the madness dear to the speaker?

DL: I was (again) madly in love. I knew that was a hopeless and stupid infatuation but—as one does at such times—continued to cherish it.

GP: Can you speak of your involvement in the anti–Vietnam war movement? Has the Jewish prophetic impulse toward social and political action had an impact on your political poetry? If not, what did inspire you to write these poems?

DL: Again, my social conscience, which caused me to become active in the antiwar movement, was stimulated even in childhood by that of *both* my parents and my sister. Since my active involvement was a condition of my daily life, I naturally wrote poems that arose from my concerns and experiences. I have always tended to reflect in my poems the places and the experiences of my life.

GP: Is "Prayer for Revolutionary Love" a feminist prayer for you?

DL: A former student, who was also a political comrade of mine, and his girl-friend were going to have to live in two separate cities, he because of his commitment to a local printing collective, she in order to take a nursing training course which was *also* a political commitment, like his. The poem was written for them. It's not specifically feminist—it addresses their *equal* rights.

GP: Were you raised to be conscious of Judaism as a religion? And has the New York Jewish culture that you experienced had an impact on you as a poet?

DL: Of *course* I understood that Judaism was a religion! And that it was the religion of all the first Christians, and that Jesus was a Jew. (Also that there were lots of Jews who did not believe or practice any religion, as well as those who, like my father, were Jews by inheritance but Christians in belief.) I never attended a Jewish worship service, however.

I don't think "New York Jewish culture" had *any* impact on me that I can think of, except to learn a few terms like "meshuggener," "shiksa," "oy veh," and the very useful word "kvetch"; also to eat lox and bagels and cream cheese. The usual superficial New York jargon for which, as the rye bread ads used to say, "You don't have to be Jewish." Many of our artists friends were Jewish but entirely secular and, as you know, painters and poets form their *own* subculture. My in-laws were pretty typical Brooklyn working class or petit bourgeois. They were lovable people, but I didn't spend much time with them and felt stifled when I did.

GP: Do you consider yourself a Jewish poet? If not, why not and if not, how do you see yourself as a poet re your essential beliefs and influences?

DL: As you already know, I *don't* consider myself a Jewish poet. Nor do I consider myself a Welsh, English, American, New York, Massachusetts, Californian, or Seattle poet, nor a Catholic poet. I cannot be categorized except as a mishmash.

GP: Does maturity give you a fresh, new perspective?

DL: Age increases or decreases certain preoccupations and opinions and modifies certain convictions—as does the passage of time at *any* stage of one's life, in fact—but it doesn't (in my experience so far, some weeks before my seventy-third birthday) suddenly introduce entirely new perspectives. Of course, new ideas and experiences continue to be encountered, but one's basic way of meeting them is long-established.

GP: How does one face death? Can poetry help?

DL: With awe. With hope that one's faith is not illusory. With the desire to be spiritually ready for it when it comes. Yes, I think poetry probably can help in that preparation.

GP: What has poetry taught you about language?

DL: I really can't think of a response to that one. It's almost like asking, what has breathing taught you about air?

GP: What do you wish to still accomplish?

DL: I hope to continue to write well and to surprise myself in each poem. I also hope to deepen my spiritual life and to manifest this in my dealings with others.

GP: Do you have hope for the world's future, for America?

DL: I don't have much reasonable hope but I also have trust in the unpredictable—the possible as distinct from the probable.

GP: What place do you most identify with?

DL: England has so changed in the Thatcher (and now Major) years that I no longer feel the same attachment to it that I used to—nevertheless there are certain things about rural England and even dear old London that have not changed and which I have a special emotional response to. But I have never really "belonged" anywhere, and therefore in some degree am at home anywhere. Perhaps among well-filled bookshelves and galleries full of great paintings as much as anywhere.

GP: If you could live your life again, what would you do differently?

DL: I wouldn't want radical differences in events, I think—not the major settings and events of my history. But I'd like to have been kinder and wiser—doesn't everybody?

GP: What is the most amazing thing about life?

DL: That anything exists at all, rather than a void.

GP: What is the most amazing thing about your life?

DL: I'm so grateful for *all* the amazing good things in my history (not that it has not had its dark times) that I can't possibly specify a single one. Though I suppose I could say, Well, I've never led a boring existence, have wonderful friends, etc., etc.—not ever forgetting that I was born with a definite gift—but you see how it immediately becomes a *list*.

DANNIE ABSE

BORN IN WALES in 1923, Dannie Abse has pursued a career
not only as a medical doctor but also as a man of letters. He is
the author of some twenty books, including four novels and a
dozen volumes of poetry. In addition, he has had a number of
his plays produced in London and elsewhere. He has edited *The
Hitchinson Book of Post-War British Poets* and other antholo-
gies. He is a Fellow of the Royal Society of Literature and of the
Welsh Academy. *Be Seated, Thou: Poems, 1989–1998* is his latest
book of poems.

DANNIE ABSE is a man of many parts. A Welshman from Cardiff, he contin-
ues to live part of the year in Wales, but he still resides in Golders Grove to the
north of London, where he practiced medicine. Besides being a man with two
national allegiances, Abse is a Jew who is well aware of the history of anti-
Semitism in Europe and in Britain. He is also involved, as both a medical doc-
tor and a poet, in the two worlds of science and the arts. Both ways of
perceiving, analyzing, and imagining the world enter into his poetry.

In "The Grand View," the narrator questions mystics and mysticism but
acknowledges that as a poet he, too, is "spellbound by the grand view." Al-
though he lives with skepticism and doubt, he is of the earth and the earth is
holy:

> My littleness makes but a private sound,
> the little lyric of a little man;
> yet, like Moses, I walk on holy ground
> since all earth is, and the world is round
> I come back to where he began.

While he is not a mystic, he compares himself to Moses the prophet and, play-
ing on "littleness," once again affirms the human scale of his imagination:

> There are moments when a man must praise
> the astonishment of being alive,

when small mirrors of reality blaze
into miracles; and there's One always
who, by never departing, almost arrives.

It is the small miracles of life closely and lovingly observed that Abse the poet affirms.

As a doctor as well as a poet, Abse has no romantic illusions about beauty:

I have seen red-blue tinged with hirsute mauve
in the plum-skin face of a suicide.
I have seen white; china white almost, stare
from behind the smashed windscreen of a car.

Because he has seen death constantly and up close, Abse sees beauty from a perspective seldom imagined by poets. "Pathology of Colors" shows how death and beauty are fused in the poet-doctor's imagination.

Since he lives two professional lives, Abse knows two visions, two ways of seeing the world: one is imaginative, inclusive, and emotional; the other is rational, analytical, and detailed. Nevertheless, the two ways of responding to the world that Abse practices as poet and medical doctor sometimes cohere.

As he shows in "Song for Pythagoras," Dannie Abse has worn both the white coat of the professional doctor and the magician's purple coat, which symbolizes imagination and irrationality:

White coat and purple coat
    can each be worn in turn
but in the white a man will freeze
    and in the purple burn.

Despite the duality that Abse knows well in the conflicts that he has faced in his dual careers as poet and doctor, he has been able to affirm "the astonishment of being alive."

•

THE INTERVIEW took place in the late morning of November 1, 1996, at Dannie Abse's home in Golders Grove. Although the Sabbath had not yet begun, I saw many Orthodox Jews walking on the main street. Abse greeted me at the front door as I arrived at his house. The interview took place in the living room in the front of the house, which was also his study. The room contained many art books and several paintings. His wife, Joan, is a prominent art historian and the author of an acclaimed biography of John Ruskin. Abse spoke in an animated way and with rich, resonant Welsh intonations. His boy-ish features and tousled hair belied his years.

GP: What have you found the hardest thing about being a poet?

DA: Writing the poems. I write poems with difficulty. I've found I write prose pretty easily. I write poetry uphill, and I write prose downhill, but my ambition is, as I've said many times before, to write the next poem and then the one after.

GP: What is the most enjoyable thing about being a poet—which I suppose isn't the same as what's the easiest thing—what do you enjoy the most?

DA: I enjoy being a poet about six, seven, or eight times a year, when I've fin-ished a poem to my own satisfaction. In between times, one isn't really a poet, as I think W. H. Auden said. But there are occasions when I've finished a poem and I'm excited about what I've written. Then I feel good for a week or two.

GP: What does a poet need to know about craft, I suppose especially a young poet, and are rhyme and meter still important enough to be part of the young poet's training?

DA: Well, I think so. I use rhyme and assonance and, you know, regular meters sometimes or syllabic poetry. I find it's very helpful. As the Welsh poet Vernon Watkins said, without having that kind of discipline it's like playing tennis without a net. With regard to young poets: I know in America, at the moment, there's a new formalism. Some of the poets there are more, much more, like British poets. Here, there's been so much translation of poets, some Eastern European poets for instance, and some of them are very good, but many young poets are too influenced by this poetry, for what happens in translation is that the music is lost. What I find sad about the new poetry that's being written is that it isn't very musical. But there is some very good stuff. Dylan Thomas once said that poetry was an accident of craft.

GP: Do you write free-verse poetry? Is some of it free verse, and if so, how do think of free verse? How is it different from meter?

DA: Well, I've just, as I said, concluded rather a long poem about David and Bathsheba by an imaginary scribe. You know, the scribes are actually men-tioned in the Bible, but presumably there were other scribes whose texts never made it, as it were. I invented a scribe, one that had two voices, and what I did was to make one write in free verse, and the other with rhyme and so on. What

I also did was to try and make the rhyming voice more colloquial so that there was a tension set up between something that appeared to be old-fashioned and that which had a more contemporary diction. With the free verse I reached for a more dignified language, such as, for example, I'd say T. S. Eliot used.

GP: You write deeply about duality, and in the poem of that title, you describe a divided person filled with conflict and tension. Can you discuss this conflict and tension in your poetry, perhaps in you, between realism and mysticism, science and religion and art, and how you feel about it? Of course, that's a big question, isn't it?

DA: Yes. That's the sort of question you respond to with "Golly."

GP: Well, let me go on with it. The poem "The Grand View" seems a major statement of skepticism toward mystics, mysticism. As opposed to the grand view of the mystic, your persona says, "My littleness makes but a private sound, / the little lyric of a little man; / yet, like Moses I walk on holy ground." So you belittle yourself and then claim your own holy ground. Of course, you could be ironic there, I suppose. At the end you say, "a man must praise / the astonishment of being alive, / when small mirrors of reality blaze / into miracles." So, actually there are two things: a duality and also you are able from time to time to affirm, to have a faith.

DA: Well, forgive me if I repeat myself, because you know over the decades obviously one gets interviewed from time to time, and you get sometimes quite actually the same questions and sometimes you press a button and then out comes the same answer. What was the question?

GP: Okay. That's what Gertrude Stein said to Alice B. Toklas. You want it again?

DA: Yeah, only the last bit will do for me.

GP: All right. Well no, let's start with the duality.

DA: Well, "Duality" is a very early poem. And perhaps reflects that time when I was a medical student, had a book published, and wondered whether I should give up medicine, go one direction, not another. I talk about a man with two masks, and I had read Rilke's prose book *The Notebooks of Malte Laurids Brigge*. And in it, Rilke describes a woman whose chin is in her hands and whose elbows are on the table, and her name is called loudly, and she, utterly surprised, turns her head, say to the left, leaving her face in her hands. I was excited by that image, and I thought it was a way for me to write existentialist poems in those youthful days. But those, those were very early poems. You mentioned the poem "The Grand View." That is quite an early poem. It is an affirmative poem, and I am pleased, because, and this is what I was going to say earlier, it's easier to gather the images of despair, more difficult to say yes and to affirm. So when one does write an affirmative poem, then I'm delighted.

GP: Well, certainly that rings a bell. The beautiful poem you wrote called "The Smile Was" . . .

DA: Before you leave that point about duality . . .

GP: The duality theme, to me, does seem to run through your poetry, because in the poem "Prescription" you advise the young poet, at least implicitly, to go for vision as opposed to a stuffy view of craft, and yet the narrator still has to wait, or is it write, in his dull room of urine flasks, etc. It does seem like medicine is sort of always there. Then you've got the poem about the white coat and the purple coat. But then we were talking about affirmations, and in "The Smile Was," you write of creation and of birth. The mother's smile is "an uncaging / a freedom." Medicine does seem to bring you a grand affirmation in that poem.

DA: Yes, that was another poem which did strike that affirmative note and again I'm grateful for it, as it were, because most of my medical poems tend to be on the whole grim, unfortunately.

GP: In the latest book, you affirm Blake. But there you seem to be affirming the visionary prophetic bardic poet, whereas in others of your earlier poems especially, you seem quite skeptical of that kind of visionary imagination, or at least the mystical religious kind of imagination. Like another poem I was going to ask you about, where you question orthodox Jews, but you don't feel quite as badly about doing so, because you question the fundamentalist Christians as well.

DA: You know, of course, I contradict myself. I contain multitudes. I contradict myself greatly from time to time. The way this conversation is going makes me think of how, not quite recently, I looked at the poems that I've written over the last four years and realized I've nearly got a book ready—well, perhaps in a year—and how often these poems could be almost compartmentalized. You know, there are medical poems on one hand. There are poems that have a Jewish undertone. There are poems with Welsh coloration. And there's a miscellaneous group. I could actually put them into groups. I don't set out to do that; it happens, I also remember one of the Ks—it was Kierkegaard or Kafka—who said that one shouldn't be afraid of repeating oneself. He's right, because repetition makes a style.

GP: Do you identify with William Blake?

DA: Well, we're back to Blake, I mean, back to my poem called "Talking to Blake." When *On The Evening Road* was reviewed, somebody in *Poetry Review* while being quite nice about the book was antagonistic towards that particular poem, "Talking to Blake." English poets are not very pleased to read a poem deflating English poetry.

GP: What don't you like about recent English poetry?

DA: I've already said something about how many young English poets have no musicality and have been too influenced by translations. I do think that I come from, after all, a background in Wales where, especially in the early days, the Old Testament was known to orators and to political speakers and to soapbox preachers and where the language was quite rich and oratory generally florid, and they were unafraid of verbal coloration. In England the Bible was less an influence. Certainly the language is much more tame, I think. Though I've been affected by the English ambiance, I'm still aware of the richness of Dylan Thomas and Glyn Jones and Vernon Watkins, even though some of their poems I don't necessarily think are wonderful, though Dylan Thomas at his best was.

GP: Have you been influenced by or are you particularly interested in any of the American poets? Like Williams, for example, who was a doctor-poet?

DA: Well, I came to people like Wallace Stevens and Carlos Williams pretty late, and I enjoyed reading them, but I don't think I've been influenced by them. I think you're influenced, you know, when you're young. And then what happens is that you shed off these influences, and you try to find your own voice, whatever that may be.

GP: In the poem "The Abandoned," you have in part two a superb villanelle, which is an eloquent atheist's statement. You say, "Dear God in the end you had to go, / we keep the bread and wine for show." And yet you have many midrashic poems based on Jewish texts, tradition, and tales. Is there an inconsistency in your rejection of religious Judaism and your, on the other hand, embrace of the tradition's literary texts?

DA: I don't think there's a contradiction. I've also called on Greek mythology. It doesn't mean to say I have to believe in the Greek gods. I am a secular Jew, but I'm also aware of the richness of the Jewish tradition, and I'm very happy to call upon it and use it because that's what writers do. They use things and use their experiences. They use everything, I think, they can. And I do that with Welsh medieval poetry as I do with midrashic texts or whatever. Or Jewish legends.

GP: The poem "The Red Balloon" is an unusually personal, painful portrait of a victim of anti-Semitism where your wit and humor are held in abeyance. How and where did you receive such treatment?

DA: Right, now it just goes to show that poetry is fiction. There was no real anti-Semitism in Wales when I was a boy. I think there was a pogrom in Tredegar in south Wales in 1911, but that is a singular occasion. But what I wanted to talk about I think in that poem, and it is a very early poem, is the sexual nature of racialism.

GP: You have a poem called "After the Release of Ezra Pound." Ezra Pound, whether we despise or like him, of course, has had a tremendous impact on poetry in this century. What's your feeling about Pound, and what has been his impact, if any, on your poetry? Have you been, for example, a follower of Objectivism and other Poundian principles?

DA: I loathe the politics and absurd economic theories of that sensitive Fascist, but his poetry, particularly his pre-*Cantos* poetry, I have enjoyed ever since I was very young. I think what has influenced me is rather some of his statements about poetry, his "Don'ts." When I taught at Princeton for a year, I remember putting on the blackboard "The Don'ts of Ezra Pound." And I think in teaching poetry that's what you can do best, say what you shouldn't do generally. I am sympathetic to his emphasis on the concrete, too, I suppose.

GP: What has been the impact of the Holocaust on you as a person and on your poetry? Some of the effects can be seen immediately in poems like "No More Mozart," where you write strongly against what the Germans did. And then there's the bitter irony of "A Night Out." Any thoughts about the impact of the Holocaust on yourself and your poetry?

DA: Absolutely. I, you know, I'd be a different person, as I think we all would if there had been no Holocaust. It's just not possible not to be aware of what's happened to Jews in Europe in this century, and of course it's affected one and makes one fearful for our grandchildren simply because of what's happened in history.

GP: You had mentioned Dylan Thomas. Did you ever meet him? Did you know him?

DA: Yes, I met him on one occasion. I've written an autobiography called *A Poet in the Family,* and I describe in that book my meeting with Dylan Thomas, and how he fooled me and how I thought he was extremely courteous, when in fact I was being sent up. I was a student, and I was having a drink in the Swiss Cottage pub. Shall I relate, would you like me to relate it? I was having a drink in the Swiss Cottage pub, and I was sitting around by myself at a table, oddly, I don't know why. But in came Dylan Thomas with somebody else, and that somebody else was buying him a drink, and to my amazement Dylan sat down at my table. I recognized him simply from his photograph. I had heard from my cousin, a sculptor who is seven or eight years older than I, called Leo Solomon, who lived in Swansea, that he was a great friend of Dylan Thomas and how Dylan had visited his house and so on and they were quite close. So after a while, I said to Dylan Thomas, "I think you know my cousin, Leo Solomon in Swansea." Well, first of all, I had said, "You're Dylan Thomas," and he said, "Yes." And I said, "You know my cousin Leo Solomon in Swansea?" And he said, "No." And, of course, I felt really embarrassed and didn't know quite what to do. I wanted to say, "I write poetry too and I've just had a book accepted," but I didn't do that. And I thought actually I'll go, and I just said goodbye, and he stood up very courteously and said, "Goodbye, Mr. Solomon." And I thought he was being extremely courteous actually, but of course later on I got to know many of Dylan Thomas's contemporaries, friends, all of whom knew Leo Solomon well, and they said, "Of course he knew Leo. Of course he knew Leo." And when I wrote *A Poet in The Family,* I still thought he was being courteous, so it was only post that book when people, when friends of his, read it and told me that "You know he was having you on."

GP: Well, I want to get back to medicine, to the point that it does seem to contribute positively to your poetry in many ways, giving you a sharp angle of vision, as in the poem "The Pathology of Colors," where you see both death and beauty converging in nature in the moment. And in "Song for Pythagoras," you speak of wearing two coats, purple and white. What's the purple coat?

DA: Well, the purple coat is that of the magician, the coat of irrationality, as it were. Mesmer, for example—who incidentally was a doctor, Franz Anton Mesmer—used to wear the purple coat. He was a showman who wore a purple coat. I see the purple coat as one that is, as I said, related to irrationality, and science, theoretically, which is supposed to be rational, to that of the white coat.

GP: One more question along this line. It just crossed my mind. We've had so much trouble, so much conflict between the arts and the sciences. Do you think there can ever be a convergence, one unifying vision?

DA: Well, I know that there are those people, usually not scientists, who want to make some kind of synthesis. But in actual fact, for example, if I take the *British Medical Journal,* there's such a specialization that I can't understand quite a lot of it. I'm trying to say scientists can't understand scientists. I think science is a much more analytical way of thinking; poetry is much more intuitive.

GP: So that, let's say, the vision of Einstein and the vision of Blake are different in kind, you think?

DA: Well, I was just thinking of the meeting of Freud and Einstein where they got on very well together because Freud didn't talk about mathematics and Einstein didn't talk about psychoanalysis.

GP: Now as a doctor and a poet how does one face death? For our purposes, can poetry help?

DA: I once came back from a radio BBC program where somebody asked me, "What's your view of death?" Staying with me at that time was William Meredith, the American poet. Do you know William Meredith? Anyway, William said, "I expect you said, 'That's for other people!'" I think poetry can be a consolation, of course it can, and you know I think I've related somewhere how, on one or two occasions, I've found a book of my poems next to a patient, but I don't know what consolation they've got from it. But it appears that poetry, in moments of great stress, evidently is required by people more than prose works are.

GP: What has poetry taught you about language?

DA: Writing poetry has taught me to sort of kneel down before language. It's just extraordinary.

GP: Can you speak about your prose at all, and how that experience, that writing experience, has been different from poetry?

DA: Well, the first prose book I ever wrote, called *Ash on a Young Man's Sleeve,* was published in 1954, and I'm glad to say it is still in print. So it has been, in some ways, a most successful book. It's a book which has got too many adjectives, but I'm still proud of it really. Now, when I wrote that book, I was interested in how one could use heightened language and mix it with colloquial dialogue. I was hoping that that would set up a certain kind of tension. I discovered, in fact, Dylan Thomas had already done it in *Portrait of the Artist as a Young Dog.* Because of that, Dylan's book was a negative influence. Because of it, I accentuated the Jewish dimension in *Ash on a Young Man's Sleeve.* Dylan didn't have that, though we had very much a common background in many ways. At the same time, I also emphasized a political background, which again is not present in Dylan Thomas's *Portrait of the Artist as a Young Dog.*

GP: Let me ask you about something else. You've written novels, right?

DA: Yes.

GP: The notion of a plot or an action in a novel or even a story seems to be different from coming at a lyric poem. What about that? In other words, when you write novels, or even your plays, do you think of an action? Do you think of a plot, or does it just sort of happen like poetry, intuitively?

DA: Well, I can't really talk about how the plays arose, but I do know what my feelings were. If you write about people in poems, they're really one-dimensional. People become silhouettes rather than rounded characters, and I found a great pleasure in trying to make characters relate to each other and to show them in a wider perspective. There is a great pleasure too in writing humorous dialogue, which is easier to do in prose than in poems. But finally, of course, I'm interested in the dramatic impulse in all the forms. Henry James kept on his desk the slogan "Dramatize, dramatize," and that's what you do in poems, in plays, and in fiction.

GP: All right, so what's the essence of "dramatize," then? Do you mean conflict? Resolution? Character?

DA: Well, all that.

GP: Joyce Carol Oates, I remember her writing, "All art is autobiographical." One ordinarily thinks of lyric poetry as being autobiographical, but perhaps not fiction. How does it strike you? In other words, are your fictional characters projections of yourself? I guess in some way they have to be.

DA: Well, to go back to *Ash on a Young Man's Sleeve*. I actually used my uncles, who were eccentric enough to be written about. I got great pleasure in redrawing them and putting them in situations that they might have been in in real life. So it's autobiographical in that sense, without necessarily being about one's self. One's self is there as a spectator, as an observer.

GP: I remember recently reading an article, actually from a book to be published by Joseph Brodsky, the Nobel laureate who died recently, where he was touting poetry as a way to learn how to read. And he felt that it taught one concision, concentration, and sophistication with language. Do you feel, too, that it's the highest of the literary forms?

DA: Yes, I do. I do, and of course the concision interests me a great deal because one of my brothers who was a member of Parliament is a very great orator. And I can see that the difference between oratory and rhetoric in poetry has very much to do with economy, really. It's true that in Walt Whitman you get some lines which could be actually spoken by a politician on a soapbox.

GP: He was very interested in oratory and the opera as well, of course. What place do you most identify with? I mean, writers often identify with their childhood places most, but you've not lived in Wales for a number of years now.

DA: I have a home in Wales, and I spend a great deal of time there. In fact, I go there regularly. I have a season ticket to the Cardiff City Football Club. My home is at Ogmore by the Sea. I was born actually twenty-three miles farther away in Cardiff. I certainly have a great identification with that south Welsh locality, and indeed I've just edited an anthology of Welsh poetry, twentieth-century Anglo-Welsh poetry, which will come out next summer. So I'm very involved with Welsh literature, Welsh life and Welsh history.

GP: How is Welsh literature different from English? I know that must be a tricky question, but will you try?

DA: It's a good question because it's one that has preoccupied me while I was doing this anthology, in fact, and I needed to say why the anthology that will be coming out next year will be different from an English anthology. Many years ago, when I was interviewed on the Welsh radio, I said that a Welsh poem was only Welsh insofar as it was about locality, that a poem about a blackbird singing in Wales, is no different from a blackbird singing in London, but I can see that that response was rather overly simple. Some of the difference has to do with language, and I have already spoken earlier about the Bible's influence in Wales and the richness of the language in Wales, the fact that many great or-ators in Parliament have been Welsh, a large majority, from Lloyd George to Neil Kinnock to my brother, if I may add him. There's also I think a greater display of emotional content. I'm speaking in generalizations—but I think on the whole, the Welsh are less afraid of emotion than some English poets. And you know, Browning once said, "Be unashamed of soul." Well, you never have to say that to a Welsh poet.

GP: Who are some Welsh poets whom we should look out for, besides yourself and Dylan Thomas?

DA: Well, there's always R. S. Thomas, of course. He's a miserable fellow; he's a pessimistic Welsh nationalist, but he's written some very good poems. And there's a neglected poet by the name of John Ormond and there are women poets coming to the fore now. There's one young one called Gwyneth Lewis, whom I recommend. And then there are poets such as Tony Curtis, Robert Minhinnick, and Duncan Bush. There's a whole lot of poets who are not well known enough in England, never mind in America.

GP: Who publishes these people?

DA: Well, there's a Welsh publisher, there are several Welsh publishers; the main one is Seren Books. It started off as Poetry Wales Press, it's now called Seren. *Seren* is Welsh for "star." And they publish most of these poets. Some are published by English publishers, but the fact that others are published by Welsh publishers is one of the reasons why they're not better known in England. In the USA, Dufour Publishers distributes the Seren books.

GP: A sort of retrospective question. If you could do it again, what would you do differently, as a man, or as an artist?

DA: I don't know. I think we're compelled by our needs, and I probably would do the same thing.

GP: I'm going to come back to the poem "The Smile Was," which really struck me in reading through your poetry as a superb affirmation of birth and of cre-ation. I think there you broke through the kind of conflict or duality that you write about often to affirm creation itself, and medicine got you to that point.

DA: Well, the poem in fact is about duality that you find in the ambivalence of people's smiles. A Yiddish author by the name of Itzik Manger, a great Yiddish writer, was very drunk one time when I was a youth. He came up to me, said very flattering things about my work, and then he hit me in the jaw. And I realized how much ambivalence there is in all human beings, even in smiles, so that the surgeon's smile can be very different from the pure smile of a woman who just hears her baby cry for the first time. So I think in a curious way that that poem was about the duality of ambivalence. It's a poem I'm pleased I wrote because oddly enough one remembers Auden's remark that "Poetry makes nothing happen." Well, I'm very proud of the fact that the great pianist Alfred Brendel told me that as a result of reading "The Smile Was" he went to watch his baby being born. So there you are, it makes things happen, even if it makes you go into the hospital.

GP: That's great. In a poem called "A Salute on the Way," dedicated to Peter Porter, there's a line saying, "Who believes / these days in a second edition?" And I was thinking, in a way you might be touching on a problem that all poets face, the problem of the marketplace, or the lack of a marketplace. Do you have any thoughts about the condition of poetry in the English-speaking world?

DA: Well, I think I'm being more metaphysical in talking about the second edition. I was thinking beyond the evening road into the next world. I was talking just a bit more about mortality. But as you know, sometimes a book goes into a second edition, sometimes not.

GP: Do you think poetry has a place, and will have a place, in a world which seems to be changing so much with the electronic media and the predominance of pop culture, young people especially turning more and more to film and tapes and seemingly everything but books?

DA: Well, that's a question really for, you know, prophets, not poets. One doesn't become an expert about the future because one writes poetry. My next-door neighbor can make the same prediction or hazard a guess as I can. I like to think that as long as there are sentient human beings there will be some, at least a small, readership for genuine poetry.

GP: What is the most amazing thing to you about life?

DA: Life. I suppose . . . life.

GP: What is the most amazing thing about your life?

DA: Well, I suppose the fact that we exist at all I think is extraordinary.

GP: So are you a Jewish poet?

DA: When I was a medical student in lodgings in the Swiss Cottage, I had my first book of poems published, and I saw it soon after in the local book shop. It was in the window, and underneath it, it said, "Local author." And I thought to myself I didn't want to be a local author, I wanted to be an international author.

GP: One more once. Are you a Jewish poet?

DA: Well, I am first of all a poet. But if there were a new anthology of Jewish poets and I were not in it, I would feel very bad indeed.

HARVEY SHAPIRO

Born in 1924, Harvey Shapiro is a graduate of Yale and Columbia. He was a gunner in a B-17 in World War II, receiving the Distinguished Flying Cross and the Air Medal with three oak-leaf clusters. From 1975 to 1983 he was editor of the *New York Times Book Review* and is now senior editor of the *Magazine.* His most recent poetry volumes include *Selected Poems, A Day's Portion, The Light Holds,* and *National Cold Storage Company.*

When I referred to Harvey Shapiro as a soldier-poet, a World War II hero, in our interview, he seemed shocked. "Not a hero. Come on!" I replied, "Holder of the Distinguished Flying Cross and Air Medal with three oak-leaf clusters." I asked him if he recalled the events that resulted in the medals. He said that flying thirty-five combat missions was such a powerful experience that he was still working through it.

War is a subtext to many of Shapiro's poems that do not directly touch on the war. The soldier performing his dangerous feats becomes the embattled middle-class family man and the walker of bleak, threatening, big-city streets. If there is an affirmation in Shapiro's dark world, it is in the imaginative act of shaping the poem, in creating something of substance, beauty, and order in words that will last.

Shapiro's life was significantly shaped by the immigrant Jewish experience. Both of his parents came to this country from Russia. In our interview, the poet revealed that "the immigrant experience formed me when I was very young, sometimes in ways that were injurious to me. I never felt that I was an American. I always felt that I was a guest in this country."

Shapiro has always responded deeply to his status as a Jewish immigrant son in America, and he has utilized his knowledge of Jewish texts in his poetry. Some of his poems read like laments for the loss of the Jewish tradition and the resulting chaos: "Jews, departure from the law / Is equivalent to death."

Shapiro writes of his life in America with an ironic awareness of the spiritual vacuum behind such secular symptoms as alienation, angst, and nothingness that he documents on the realistic surface of his work. Consciously or not, he may be warning us of imminent danger in our lives.

In addition to the Jewish content of his poems, Shapiro has known and been deeply influenced by such older Jewish American poets as Charles Reznikoff and George Oppen, two of the Objectivist poets of the thirties. Reznikoff's short imagistic portraits of immigrant life in New York as well as his biblical narratives are reflected in Shapiro's poems. Oppen influenced Shapiro by his example as a father figure and a poet.

For Shapiro, writing poems provides a way of dealing with life's violent conflicts that can be satisfying and sustaining. "There's a certain life-saving, safeguarding element in art that permits you to take language, which is after all a very ephemeral, evanescent thing, and draw a line around it and keep it fixed in place, so that it can last through centuries." Despite life's difficulties, the poet sees a redeeming beauty at key moments that strikes him as "a series of miracles."

■

ON SATURDAY, March 22, 1997, I interviewed Harvey Shapiro in his Brooklyn apartment, which is a block from the waterfront. The apartment was old and uncluttered. We sat at a table in the living room. One wall was lined with books from floor to ceiling and another wall faced the street. There was a large plant in a pot near the window facing the street. In addition, the living room contained a crowded coat rack, a television, a tiny chair piled high with books, and a few knickknacks. Shapiro, a short, stocky man with a goatee, spoke in a deep, resonant voice. He had seen the questions beforehand, but he spoke without notes.

GP: What have you found the hardest thing about being a poet?

HS: I suppose the hardest thing about being a poet in America is the unreality of what you do. That is, you spend most of your creative time doing something that society for the most part has no use for. That lends a certain air of unreality to the whole enterprise. And that's true, I would think, for most American poets. There are those few favorite poets who get a reaction from the world when they write and publish, who are told that they exist and that they mean something. But most of us work in, if not total obscurity, pretty near total obscurity. It's not the kind of obscurity that someone like Charles Reznikoff labored in for most of his life. He was a poet who couldn't find a magazine to publish his poems or publishers to publish his books. George Oppen once told me that Reznikoff almost went crazy out of that absolute, annihilating neglect. But there is a relative kind of obscurity that can sap energy and diminish your feeling for what you're doing. And what fights against it, of course, is your own belief in your work and your own pleasure in the process of writing poetry. I suppose that's not quite as true for those poets—and that would be about ninety percent of them now—who go into the university and who work as teachers of poetry, because the poetry that they've written becomes part of their credentials. But for those of us who make a living doing something totally different, I think what I said applies.

GP: I suppose you've answered the second question—which is "What is the most enjoyable thing about being a poet for you?"—when you talked about the process of writing poetry. But is there anything you would want to add about the most enjoyable part of being a poet before we go on?

HS: The most enjoyable part of being a poet is the joy you get out of the work done and, you know, that joy tends to diminish with age. With age you begin to see a body of work build up, and you can begin to trace the outlines of a career in writing. On the other hand, that pure pleasure of finishing the poem, typing the poem, seeing it in its objectified state is not as great when you're seventy-three as it is when you're twenty-three.

GP: You've already talked about the obscurity of the poet. What can a late-twentieth-century American poet hope to accomplish?

HS: Everything. There's no question in my mind that the kind of mainstream poetry that I grew up with has been pushed to the margins of the mainstream culture in my lifetime, and that the poets who were important in my early years occupied a much larger space than any of their counterparts do today. On the other hand, the whole world of poetry is changing. I have no notion of what's going to happen with the resurgence of oral poetry. The multicultural movement with the poets that it's produced, who speak directly to their own communities and for their own communities, has unlimited potential. I have no way of knowing where that's going to go. Forms change. It's perfectly true that there was a period when the novel didn't exist. These things are not immutable. There may be a period when poetry as we know it ceases to exist. There may be some poet right now sitting down at his desk who's going to write a poem, which I would recognize as a poem and something that I would admire, that is going to absolutely capture the imagination of the American reader, as the late Allen Ginsberg's poetry did when he came on the scene, and institute a whole renaissance.

GP: What is free verse and can it be taught, or do you have any kind of coherent way of talking about free verse?

HS: There's a lot of junk said about free verse. Every trade has to produce some mysterious jargon. It's a way of credentializing itself. I think those practitioners and teachers of free verse in the universities, in order to earn their keep, do some of that. I remember in a manuscript group that I belonged to—that is, a small group of writers, where we would bring the poems or stories or novels we were working on and read them and then pass them around for comments—somebody said to me about a poem of mine that he didn't see much in the content of the poem but the line breaks were beautiful. The notion of looking at a poem and thinking just the line breaks were beautiful was kind of amusing to me.

The problem with free verse is, how do you put down words on a page, so that they stay there and so that they make an object and so that they're not just free-flowing speech? Every poet has his own devices, from Allen Ginsberg's rhetoric and repetitions and sound echoes and his kind of chant line, to the way Williams breaks the line on the very unimportant word like "and" or "the" but makes this absolutely solid, Brancusi-like image that you know isn't going to slide off the page but is going to stay there. Certainly there's a technique. I don't know how much can be taught in the training of the ear. That's basically what a poet has to do: to train his ear. When I grew up, there were no poetry workshops in any university. You'd develop an ear by reading great poems and by writing. Because the bulk of English poetry is formal, most of the poetry you read was formal. When they came to write their own poems, most of the poets in my generation went through a process of writing formal verse first and then, being heavily influenced by Williams and by the need to break out of what we felt were the confinements of formal verse, began to experiment with free verse.

GP: What inspired you to be a poet, and do you remember when you first started writing poetry?

HS: I remember being interested in writing itself when I was a kid, and I certainly wrote some poetry when I was in grade school as well as short stories. I don't think I had a notion of writing poetry seriously until after the Second World War. I'm not quite sure how or when I decided that's what I wanted to do. When I went into the war, I'd had one year at college and was an international relations major. I have no notion now of what an international relations major means or what I planned to do. But during the war I read all these little cheap military editions. They were free books that the army gave us, particularly overseas. I remember spending a lot of time with Whitman. In any case, when I came back to college after the war, I knew that I wanted to be a poet and to write poetry seriously. I was a gunner in the Fifteenth Air Force in Italy, and in a B-17. It could be there was a kind of clarifying chill flying at high altitude and on each mission facing the prospect of death that helped me understand what it was I wanted to do. Sometimes it takes a crisis to make you figure out who you are and what you want to be. In any case, when I came back from the war, I knew I wanted to write poetry. That's been a constant in my life and, in fact, the only constant in my life since 1945. My first book came out in 1953.

GP: Do you see yourself as part of a movement, school, or tradition of poets?

HS: I don't see myself as a part of any formal school, and I don't identify with any contemporary poets. I did feel very close to the Objectivist poets—to Charles Reznikoff and George Oppen, in particular. George was a very close friend and lived only a few blocks from me in Brooklyn. Charles's work meant a great deal to me probably because of the image that he projected in his poetry, that image of an urban man, a city man, making his way through the labyrinth of the city, a sort of worn, used, somewhat antiheroic image of a man looking about him, trying to figure out what the proper way of living was. Someone with a kind of almost religious insight into the urban experience. I identified with that. I may also have identified with the Jewish nature of Charles's work.

What was very important for me, looking back on my life, is the fact that I was firstborn in my family in this country. Both my mother and father were immigrants. They came here separately at different times in their lives, met here, but they both came from Russia. My father from a town near Kiev and my mother from a shtetl in the Ukraine. This is by way of a long digression. They never talked about the old country. I had very few details from them about their life there, even though my father came here as an adolescent, because they were so busy, clambering aboard the American ship. They were so busy becoming Americans that like many immigrants in their day they turned their backs on where they had come from and their early lives.

I've lived in this section of Brooklyn for about forty years now, and one of the interesting things about it is that on my daily walks I look out across the bay to the place where my mother and father first came to this country. I look out at Ellis Island and Castle Garden, and it's as if I've gone back to their starting point. I'm wrestling with the question that their lives and my life revolve around: Why am I here and what am I doing? It's not to identify me in any formal way but it's to identify me ideologically.

The immigrant experience formed me when I was very young, sometimes in ways that were injurious to me. I never felt that I was an American. I always felt that I was a guest in this country. When I went to Yale, for example, it never occurred to me to protest the fact that I couldn't join any of the fraternities or any of the clubs. As a Jew I was excluded from that whole side of campus life. I recognized that as a reality of being a Jew and an immigrant son in America. I remember when I was a kid and I'd get into fights with the Italian or Irish kids in the neighborhood, my grandmother would come out and start screaming at me not to fight back. It was part of the immigrant ethos that we don't like to talk about much. It was the notion that came out of experiences in the shtetl when a Jew was told, well, you know, if you fight back, it will bring down massive retaliation. I could see in myself that mentality, the way Chekov said he had to fight off the slavery in his soul through his life and through his writing. That's a long way from your question of what kind of poet I am, but that's the kind of question that I think has formed all my work.

GP: You write of knowing Louis Zukofksy and George Oppen in your poem "Borough Hall." Have they influenced you as poets? I know Reznikoff has.

HS: I've read a lot of both Zukofsky and Oppen's work. I'm sure parts of "A" have influenced me, but I would not consider myself a Zukofsky disciple, and my poetry is certainly different from George's, just as my personality is different from his. He influenced me in that he became a father figure for me for a number of years. And he became the image of the poet for me: the seriousness with which he wrote and spoke; the intensity and the focus of personality that he brought to his poetry were terribly important to me. That he was writing poetry made the enterprise of poetry mean something to me, made it valuable—that this man could spend his time doing this enhanced poetry for me. I've certainly learned from his letters; I've learned from his conversation.

On the other hand, I certainly can't say that my thinking about poetry jibed then and jibes now completely with his. There was a world of poetry that he did not care for, poets like Lowell, that I read with pleasure. He had a very strict canon. At the same time he had a great love of the tradition in English poetry, and he made contemporary poems out of the sounds of sixteenth- or seventeenth-century poems that he loved. Wyatt was a poet he read as much as any contemporary one. I remember once talking about a little urban poem that he had written. He said to me he was trying to get Wyatt's sound in that poem. Where George was very important to me was in answering a question that divides poets today: Do words point to something or not; is there a world out there or not; does language point to language or does it point to something that precedes language? George's poetry is all about the thereness of this world, about the fact that words point to a reality. It is all about, as he says, not the miracle of our being here but the miracle of the world's being there—that the rough deck is always there.

GP: Unlike most poets who earn their living in academia, you've been at the *New York Times* for many years now. How has that environment worked out for you as a poet?

HS: Certainly there's been an interchange between what I do during the day and what I do at night, between the 9 to 5 job I've had most of my adult life and my writing at night and on weekends. There would have to have been some kind of interchange, although I saw the lives as quite separate. In fact, my career as a poet certainly got in the way sometimes of my life as an editor at the *New York Times.*

I remember at one point, after my book *Battle Report* came out in 1966, I was offered a Rockefeller Foundation Fellowship. It was a fellowship you didn't apply for; the foundation had a board of poets who selected other poets and wrote to them inviting them to take a year off at the foundation's expense and write poetry. I went to the then Sunday editor of the *New York Times,* whom I worked for, and I showed him the letter and told him I wanted to take time off. He fought it all the way and didn't want to give me the time off. I needed to have a job to come back to. I didn't have any money other than the money that I earned at the paper, and I was married and already had one son, and jobs were not easy to come by then.

Finally I realized that one of my problems was that he would have to go to see the editor of the paper and explain to him that his articles editor wanted to take some time off to write poetry, and he found that so embarrassing and demeaning that he wanted to avoid it at all costs. Anyhow, I did finally get the time off, but sure the careers have fought each other.

Also, as an editor at the *Times* I don't fit the romantic image of a poet. Americans have trouble seeing a poet who has that kind of job. So it hasn't added to my glamour as a writer. Because the university world does control poetry, for good or ill in our day, it has kept me out of the network and certainly has kept me from the people who run writing programs and who edit the anthologies and who invite the writers to read in colleges. They are the people who have the power, who in fact are making the canon in our day. I was never part of that world because I was working for a newspaper.

That's the minus side. The plus side of working at a newspaper is that I learned early on that one could move language around. That is, if you're working with somebody else's composition and it's your job to get it into printable shape and give it its maximum force, you see that the first paragraph is throat clearing and that the lead is in the second paragraph or perhaps in the last paragraph. You learn to move paragraphs around. You get a kind of freedom that's very important for a writer to have with materials and manuscripts.

When I first started to write poetry, the poems came to me as if they were engraved, chipped into stone. The way they came to me was the way I put

them down. I could hardly imagine moving language around. I learned to have
that freedom as an editor, and I also learned to write out of editing. That is, my
process for many years was to come back from work, have dinner with the
family, and go up to my study about eleven o'clock. I would always help myself
out with a little bourbon to get the necessary elevation, put an edge on things,
and I would start writing in my notebook. I would make myself write every
night. I've been keeping notebooks since 1966. There'd be periods when I
would feel that something that I was writing related to something I had writ-
ten the night before. I would start to trace back through the notebook and ac-
tually through editing, that is, simply looking at what was probably a sort of
free-flowing, associative language exercise, begin to cross out lines. I'd begin to
discover a poem developing from, say, three weeks back that would come into
existence for me through a process of editing, that is, through a process of
deletions.

I should also say that being at the newspaper kept me in the city. It kept
me in touch with the world in a way that other professions and other jobs per-
haps would not. It gave me some poems that I certainly wouldn't have had liv-
ing another kind of life. Some of the poems that I've done have come directly
out of my experiences during the day at the paper. For example, my poem "Na-
tional Cold Storage Company," which is about the assassination of John
Fitzgerald Kennedy. I'd spent every day working on articles about the assassi-
nation. That Friday night I was walking down on the Brooklyn waterfront to-
wards the bridge and looking at the National Cold Storage Company, which
sits there by the bridge, and all those thoughts that I'd had during the workday
began to coalesce into a poem that I wrote in my head.

GP: What was it like to be a poet and the editor of the *New York Times Book
Review*? Did you resent all the attention to the best-sellers and the commercial
books that obviously take up a lot of space in that powerful and important
publication?

HS: I was the editor of the *Book Review* from the fall of 1975 to the fall of 1983.
Being a poet and being an editor of the *Book Review* presented me with a cou-
ple of problems. I understood how difficult it was to write, how hard it was to
spend five or ten years working on a book and what that can mean to you. It
made me take my job seriously. Also, as somebody who had been writing for
years, and when the world of poets was much smaller than it is today, I did
know a lot of the poets, so when it came time to review their books that some-
times was a problem for me.

When you're editing a section like a Sunday book review, you are partly
editing it from the culture's point of view. You have to do several things: you
have to think of the reader of the paper; you have to think of the culture itself;

and then, if you want to be an interesting editor, you have to think of your own appetites. So that if a book was important in terms of the culture of the period . . . if Norman Mailer published a novel and it might not be the novel you were particularly interested in, you knew you had to give that novel some space. At the same time, when George Oppen published his *Collected Poems* or when a great anthology of Chinese poetry came out, you had to give that some space, because otherwise you'd be denying your own self.

Once you begin to deny your own self, there's no way you can be an effective person and you can't be an effective editor. It's a very fulfilling job because you're able to find works of literature and bring them to the attention of readers who would not necessarily find them for themselves. To put a novel on the front page of the *Book Review* (in those days the front page of the *Book Review* was wisely used to promote one book), to find a work by a writer that no one had heard of that you loved and tell the world about it—that was a real high. And to call attention to a poet whose work deserved attention was exciting for me.

Of course, I had problems. You go to a reviewer whose opinions you can't predict, but you know the reviewer will have some interest in the book. Otherwise why go to him or her? Occasionally I published reviews that were critical of some poets whom I knew and sometimes they held me personally responsible for those reviews and indeed would threaten me. The world of poetry is sometimes not a very pleasant world, as you must know; you've been in it enough. I would get letters from poets who would say, I'm going to make sure that you're never in any anthology I edit and you will never come to any university where I have any say. In fact, that did happen to me.

I remember once my friend Phil Lopate, who was then teaching down at the University of Texas, said to me when he came up to New York, you know, Harvey, I've been trying to bring you down to Texas to read. But this poet on the faculty, who got a review she didn't care for while you were editor of the *Book Review,* when I bring your name up, says, Over my dead body. So yeah, there were problems.

GP: Let's talk about your poetry. You characterized the grandmother in "Death of a Grandmother" as a witch. Life and the American dream don't seem to go well for the two principal characters in the poem. Why is America so difficult for its people, particularly its immigrant Jewish people? Here's a quote: "I sing her a song of praise. / She meddled with my childhood / Like a witch, and I can meet her / Curse for curse in the slum heaven where we go / When this American dream is spent— / To give her a crust of bread, a little love."

HS: This is my Yiddish-speaking grandmother, my mother's mother, who lived with us during my growing-up years. She never spoke any English. She spent her days listening to Yiddish programs on the radio. She was probably a figure of fear for me. She represented the nightmare of Europe to me as she must have even to my parents—that world that they'd escaped from. I spoke Yiddish before I spoke English, according to my mother. But I certainly have no facility in Yiddish and our communications were probably limited. Yet in some ways she represented a reality for me which was as strong as the reality of the American dream. That's what the poem is about partly, and that her condition may be in fact my condition. It's a very early poem. It was a very important poem to me, because I had been writing a lot on Jewish themes.

I was a Jewish poet at one point in my life. I certainly am not a Jewish poet now. My poetry grew totally out of Jewish material. I published only in Jewish publications. All my poems appeared in either *Midstream* or *Commentary*. I had a lot of crazy myths going through me. I remember as an adolescent I thought if I learned Russian, maybe I would become a great poet, because Russia was where my parents were from. It was a totally asinine notion, since my parents didn't know a word of Russian. They were Yiddish-speaking shtetl Jews. I also had the myth at this point of my life when I was writing and publishing in Jewish publications that I was writing for a Jewish audience that other poets hadn't tapped and that these poems were for them.

When Alan Swallow published my little book *Mountain, Fire, Thornbush*, which was all on Jewish themes, I told him to take out small ads in *Midstream* and *Commentary*, because those were the people who would buy my book. When my book came out, he took out small ads in those two publications, but nobody responded, which taught me that there was no Jewish audience for my work. That the audience for my work was the audience for any other poet's work. But to come back to "Death of a Grandmother," most of the poems in that little book are in a dense rhetoric. I take themes out of the Bible and put them in poems of thick texture. And they're poems that don't use the word "I." In those days I found it almost impossible to use the pronoun "I" in a poem.

When I came to write "Death of a Grandmother," I had to try out a new rhetoric for myself. I wanted to use the word "I," and I wanted to use my grandmother's Yiddish speech, so that poem became a real breaking away for me from the work that I had done before.

GP: Are there specific Midrashic sources behind the poem "The Feast of the Ram's Horn," or are you drawing on general associations between the sacrificial lamb and the New Year's celebration?

HS: "The Feast of the Ram's Horn" is a poem about the High Holy Days. All the themes came out of my reading of Agnon's *Days of Awe*. I had worked through that book because at the time I was writing a libretto for a cantor. He was a very famous cantor who was giving a cantorial concert for a synagogue in New Jersey. It was all based on High Holy Days liturgy, and he needed poetic bridges between the music and poetic explanations of what the prayers were about, so I spent a lot time with that book by Agnon and that's where the themes are from.

GP: In the poem "ABC of Culture," you say, "So the angel of death whistles Mozart" and you describe "The Jews of Auschwitz, / in the great museum of Western Art." How do the death camps reflect Western art, besides being instigated by Nazi Germans, who were of course part of Western Europe?

HS: That poem, "ABC of Culture," is a play on Pound's book *ABC of Reading*. Some of the other poems I wrote about the Holocaust in that period—for example, my poem that begins, "Where did the Jewish god go?"—are poems in which I want to say very strongly that this destruction of the Jews took place in the twentieth century of Christendom. This is A.D., after the death of Christ. Of course, in the poem "ABC of Culture," I was describing Mengele, who went around the camps whistling Mozart. This has been commented on many times. There were men who ran the concentration camps who went back at night and read Rilke. There were men who would go back at night and listen to Mozart, but it didn't stop them from killing Jews. I felt that the death camps were not just an aberration, that they were really part of the Museum of Western Art. If you were going to do a museum that would show the art of the twentieth century, you would have to include the death camps.

GP: The art of Christianity?

HS: I don't mean religious art. I mean Christian culture, Christian anti-Semitism. Goldhagen's book demonstrates this. Part of it comes out of my own childhood experiences. I can remember as a kid I went to a public school that was right across the street from a church and parochial school. In the late thirties when Nazism was coming into power in Germany, I remember one day the kids from the parochial school marching out led by nuns (we were playing in the playground across the street, mostly Jewish kids), and they were chanting, "Kill the Jews." It's a very strong, sharp memory of mine. Now that's not to say the church is an engine for Jewish destruction. The role of the pope during the Holocaust has been controversial. But that Christian culture contributed to what happened in Nazi Germany seems to me inescapable.

GP: In the poem "The Six Hundred Thousand Letters," the Jewish law is in chaos. Does this represent for you something like the unraveling of Judaism?

HS: No, I don't think that was my meaning. That poem is simply about the chaos of my own life. I was working with the Jewish belief that there are 600,000 letters in the law, actual letters in the Torah. It's just a poem that says A does not precede B and C doesn't follow B. In my life right now, there seems to be no order and no logic. The law is scrambled, as if you took all the letters of the law, all the letters of the Torah, and you threw them up in a heap, and they all came down in a pile.

GP: Do you agree with Harold Bloom that to have Jewish poets in Protestant America is not possible because Jews can't identify with what he considers the great Protestant father poets?

HS: I don't agree with Harold. I don't agree with his basic feeling that you have to identify with a great father poet to begin with in order to write. If I read Milton, he's my poet as much as he is anybody else's. I feel that very strongly. It doesn't matter where your cultural roots are. You're creating your own culture. It's part of what we do in America. If I want to make Milton my major figure, I'll make Milton my major figure. If that's where my soul and my body gravitate toward, I'll make him mine, and I'll use him the way Ginsberg, for example, used Blake. Blake was the great figure for Ginsberg and helped him to produce magnificent poetry. He didn't have to identify with every facet of Blake's life but there was enough there to make that identification real for him.

There are American Jewish poets who've meant a great deal to me and I can identify with if I need to. There is George Oppen. But I find that whole father/son-in-literature argument of Harold's somewhat specious. It's true, for example, in Delmore Schwartz's poetry and in the poets of an earlier generation there was some sense that in order to write poetry you had to dress up a little. You had to sound like the poets in Palgrave's anthology. Delmore Schwartz is a case in point for me. In Delmore Schwartz's prose, in those stories in *The World Is a Wedding,* I found a city rhetoric and a Jewish rhetoric that I could really respond to. It's not the rhetoric of his poetry. In his poetry the voice is strained. He's turning his back on everything that is his native gift and he's becoming an English poet.

GP: Must Jewish poets write out of the tradition of Jewish texts, as again Bloom and Robert Alter suggest, or are there other ways to suggest and express Jewishness in poetry?

HS: I don't know if that's a goal for any poet—to express Jewishness in poetry. The goal of a poet is to write good poems, to write as well as he can about the world. If part of his world is Jewish or if part of his world is reading Jewish texts, then it's for him to use. I don't think there are any rules or any prescriptions for this kind of thing. Lots of poets have done very well digging back into Talmudic texts and certainly some of the poems that I've done in recent years have come out of my attendance at a seminar held at the Jewish Theological Seminary called Genesis Seminar.

It started ten years ago, and we spent five years on the book of Genesis. Mostly a group of writers with some Jewish scholars and Protestant scholars, people from the Jewish Theological Seminary and the Union Theological Seminary down the block, getting together and talking about text. I've certainly written poems that derive directly from some of those discussions, but I have never programmatically, except in that very early period we talked about, gone to Jewish material in order to write Jewish poems. If I'm writing about who I am and what I'm doing in America, the Jewish experience has got to be reflected in it. Because the shock waves of my father and mother's arrival in this country are still in me and they're going to appear in my work.

GP: You said a few minutes ago that you used to consider yourself a Jewish poet but that you don't anymore. I'm wondering why you make that distinction.

HS: If you look through my work, you can see that Jewish themes keep running through it just the way writing about the war does. I'm a Jewish American poet, and I've gone to conferences for Jewish American poets, and if you have to label me that would be a label. But there was a point in my life when I was building a kind of ghetto for myself, when I was writing the poems that are in *Mountain, Fire, Thornbush*. I certainly don't live in that ghetto now. I also have the feeling that we're creating a new kind of Jewish life in this country and that life has yet to come into being. Certainly suburban Judaism can't mean much to any thinking man—what passes for normative Judaism in this country. Those of us who work with Jewish themes, whether we want to or not, are helping to create a new Jewish culture and are changing the shape of what Jewish belief is. To think that Jewish culture and Jewish belief after the Holocaust can be the same as Jewish belief and Jewish culture before the Holocaust seems to me foolish.

GP: In the poem "Riding Westward," you say, "Jews, departure from the law / is equivalent to death," which is similar to the other quote that I called attention to from "The Six Hundred Thousand Letters." Do you wish to be taken literally on this? Because obviously you're a secular Jew like most Jewish poets. Yet I find it hard to read irony into this.

HS: It's partly a poem about my father, so there is some awe in it. I say, "Shades, we greet each other," meaning we're all dead; we're all shades in the world of death greeting each other on the highway. It's meant ironically but half-ironically. Sure, there is some residue of feeling that this is so. The poem is a rip-off of John Donne's great poem "Good Friday, 1613. Riding Westward." It was probably written on a day when I didn't go to the synagogue and spent the day at the beach, and probably has some residue of guilt in it because of that. But it was not meant to be didactic.

GP: You are a soldier-poet, a World War II hero.

HS: Not a hero. Come on!

GP: Holder of the Distinguished Flying Cross and Air Medal with three oak-leaf clusters. Do you recall the events that got you those medals?

HS: I flew thirty-five missions. I was part of an enormously powerful experience. How could it not be powerful? It was the experience I shared with my generation. We were all twenty years old. It's an experience I'm still working my way through. I'm sure it changed my life. In terms of public experiences, in terms of how outside events form you, that and the immigrant experience were the two great formative experiences for me. I went to Italy last summer and stayed with a friend and wrote a poem "Italy 1996," about being back in Italy and remembering that war. Outside of my long poem "Battle Report" there's no cluster of poems about the war, but there are poems in each of my books about it.

GP: War is a subtext to many of your poems. That is, it is as if the conflicts you describe within yourself and between yourself and others reflect war's battles. Have you ever thought about that?

HS: When I titled my book *Battle Report* in 1966, I was thinking about the war, but I was certainly thinking about middle-class life. That book was about middle-class life, about being married, having kids, trying to make a living, and living in the city. It was a battle report.

GP: Do you think that the mood and tone of dejection and despair, at least in some of the poems, might come from your war time experience? Do you think it had that kind of impact on you that might have exaggerated the battles of the domestic private life that you came back to?

HS: Possibly, possibly. I don't really know. That's a question I can't answer. Why do some of the poems show depression? Because I was somewhat fucked up in that period. But that has to do with family, childhood. You can't say war.

It has to do with who you are. It was a grinding life that I was leading. It has to do with insecurity. I was never quite sure how I was going to be able to support my family. It has to do with trying to do two things: hold down a job during the day and do my own work at night. That was part of the battle.

GP: In the poem "Battle Report," you speak of "the sex of guns and of cannon." Another quote from the poem: "Who knows that the unseen mime in his blood / will startle to terror, / Years later when love matters." It seems as if war's terror and pain reverberate in the love and sex life of the narrator.

HS: I would make a more generalized comment. I would say that there is a certain kind of freezing that goes on when you're placed in extreme situations. Each time you go out on a bombing raid there's a chance you're not going to come back. There's a certain kind of anesthetizing of the senses and the emotions that inevitably follows. After the war there was for those of us who participated in it a kind of thawing-out period, and I think that certainly some psychological problems grew out of that.

GP: In one of the poems, you describe the experience of being a gunner in a World War II B-17 bomber as "abstract as a drinker." Any thoughts about what it was like being up there, and does that phrase "abstract as a drinker" ring true?

HS: What I was probably bringing together in that are two parts of my life: my experience as a solitary drinker during part of my life and that experience of aerial warfare in a bombing plane. You were hooked up to the other members of the crew, but you were also, and certainly in my position in the plane, you were isolated. You didn't see any other members of the crew. You were hooked into a life-support system—oxygen mask; you were hooked into the body of the plane through your electrical heating cord; but you were by yourself. It was something like the experience of a solitary drinker.

GP: Many of your poems are filled with domestic strife, personal sadness, and pain. I'm thinking of poems such as "Saul's Progress," "Night-sounds," "The Gift of Remembering." Then there's another one called "From an Autobiography," in which you write about a mother who loses her beautiful daughter and rejects her infant boy: "Why did God / take away my beautiful child and give me / this ugly baby instead?" As I read the poem, the mother declares war against her own son, who becomes her victim. Did this happen to you? Do you see yourself in these poems as a confessional poet? You didn't mention identifying with the confessional poets, but that's obviously one of the big post–World War II schools of poetry.

HS: No, I never think of myself as a confessional poet, but as you say, that was one of the big movements in post–World War II American poetry, and it affected my work, as it affected the work of many other poets. That particular poem, "Autobiography," is confessional. It is about me and it is about what I thought was probably a key incident in my life. My mother, who married when she was very young, had a daughter, my sister Annette, who died before my birth and who was a very beautiful girl. It was a true story—the quote is hers— that she told me rather late in her life. When I was born, I was a very ugly baby. I was nursed and taken care of by my Aunt Gussie and my grandmother for the first months of my life, which I'm sure, according to current psychological thinking, was not too good for my character development. That's an unusually direct autobiographical poem. I'm not a confessional poet the way Anne Sexton is or the way Lowell was for part of his career. I don't think of myself programmatically as a confessional poet. On the other hand, I do think of myself as somebody who uses whatever comes to hand. I use whatever's around the house. I use my reading, I use my work experience, and I use my life in any way that feeds my poetry.

GP: The narrator in the poem "Experiences" says that he "was mugged / and kicked in the head / by three stalwart blacks" in a subway station. And in the same poem, you write, "Not having known any other life, / this is what one summons." Is the mind of the poet "locked in place" by relying on autobiographical subject matter? As part of that question, have you ever created personas, masks, or have you written fiction? That approach is different from the personal poetry that has been so prevalent in this century.

HS: Certainly in my earlier poetry what interested me was the escape from personality. Far from being a confessional poet, I saw the writing of poetry as a way of being someone else, as a way of escaping the limitations of self. Yeats's theory of masks was very important to me. The poem was not about you but a way of escaping yourself. That was one of my earliest impulses in poetry. As I said to you before in this interview, it was a period in my writing when a first-person pronoun was not something I could use. It simply would have broken the poem apart. I had to really change my writing when there were experiences I wanted to use that came directly out of my life. That's when a poet changes his rhetoric, when he has new subject matter.

In that particular poem I'm locked in place by my experience. I believed it when I wrote the poem. I believed it for that poem. It's not a tenet of my belief. I have more of a belief in the imagination than that. I'm a poet who does not believe that poetry is simply an extension of one's personal life, that the poem is simply part of one's own speech. I remember reading with a poet who had a lot of patter that went with his poetry, and it was very difficult for me to tell when the patter stopped and the poem began. He and I talked about that after the reading, and he said, That's the way I want my poems to sound. I want them to be just part of my speech, so that you can't tell when my speech ends and the poem begins. My feeling about poetry is quite different. I don't want to label it, but I believe that art draws a line around experience. There's a certain life-saving, safeguarding element in art that permits you to take language, which is after all a very ephemeral, evanescent thing, and draw a line around it and keep it fixed in place, so that it can last through centuries. What I want to do is what poets like Wyatt did, even put in their poems a woman's voice and have it speak to a reader four hundred years later. That seems to me a worthy objective for a poet and seems to me somewhat miraculous. That is not the poetry of plain speech and it is not the poetry which is an extension of one's own personality.

GP: How do you respond to modern Israel as a subject for poetry or as a place to live?

HS: I've written about Israel in several poems. In fact, I have a poem coming out in *Hanging Loose,* the next issue, which is about my trip to Israel about a year ago. I've gone there partly because I have a younger brother who settled there in 1955 and lives on a kibbutz, which is on the Sea of Galilee near the city of Tiberias. My brother is married and has several grandchildren. A large part of my family is there and so, for no other reason than that, the country would have some significance for me. Is it a place that I've thought of moving to? No. It's not an option of mine. I don't consider Israel my homeland. I feel like a lot of American Jews who go there, as alien there as I feel sometimes in America. On the other hand, there are resonances there that one can pick up in my poetry.

GP: How does one face death, and can poetry help?

HS: Gary, I can't answer either of those questions. "How does one face death?" is an existential question. You have to be there in the situation in order to formulate an answer. How did I face death when I was a twenty-year-old kid in the war? That was fifty years ago. With fear and apprehension. But when you're twenty years old, you're immortal. I can remember the moment when I realized—it was on my third mission that it happened—that you could get killed doing this. That came as a discovery for me, a real discovery. I did not believe that the shells, the flack, that was bursting around us could possibly hit me or the plane that I was in. Then that changed. I'm seventy-three years old now, so I've lived out my biblical span of three-score year and ten. Certainly I think about death, but I can't answer the question. How does poetry help? I don't know if poetry helps. I remember when I was in psychological trouble years back. I was reading Delmore Schwartz's stories, and I thought to myself: He knows so much and it's no help to him whatsoever. He was so fucked up and the stories are filled with such wisdom and even self-knowledge and yet that didn't seem to make any difference in his life. I don't know if poetry helps.

GP: What do you wish to still accomplish?

HS: I would take out the word "still" and say, "What would you like to accomplish?" I see there are poems and books that have accumulated, and I don't yet feel that I've accomplished anything in my writing. Yeah, it would be nice to die with a feeling of accomplishment, thinking that I have written what I was meant to write, if that makes sense. There's something a little insane about thinking that one was meant to do anything, but no, I don't think I've written the poem yet that I want to write. I don't think I've published the book yet that I want to publish. And I understand that the time is probably short.

GP: I want to try a couple of overwhelming questions. Do you have hope for the world or for America?

HS: Yes, I have hope for both the world and America. In a recent poem I quote this little saying of Rabbi Nachman, which I first heard in Israel. It was sung at a Passover meal, and it was the refrain to a song in which the rabbi says, "The world is a narrow bridge. The important thing is not to be afraid." Yeah, I have hope. We're going through a very difficult period of identity now of trying to figure out where we should be heading and of what this country's about. But I feel that we'll find ourselves again.

GP: If you could do it again, what would you do differently?

HS: I don't think about my life that way, because I never planned my life. I stumbled into my career as an editor. I don't know how I chose to write poetry or why I chose to write poetry. I never had a plan. If I had to do it all over again, I would like to be somebody completely different and lead a completely different life.

GP: What is the most amazing thing about life?

HS: The most amazing thing about the world is that it exists, as George Oppen says in his poems, that it is there. Every day of existence can be amazing to you if you're living. This just all sounds like New Age shit. But if indeed you're experiencing your life and you're there every day and every moment . . . On the subway going to work in the morning, I look at the people. It's amazing to me that this life goes on, that there is so much beauty in the world in spite of the carnage and in spite of the grime of the city. You can come out of the subway and see a face that just knocks you out with its absolute beauty. You see a conversation in which the body language of the people is so marvelous. It's a series of miracles.

GP: Finally, what is the most amazing thing about your life?

HS: The most amazing thing about my life is that I've managed to do as much as I've done. That I have two sons I'm very proud of. I have friends I'm very proud to call friends. And that I think I belong to a community of poets.

GERALD STERN

Born in Pittsburgh in 1925, Gerald Stern has published ten collections of poetry and received many awards and honors for his work, including a Lamont Poetry Prize, the Bess Hoskin Award for Poetry, the Paterson Poetry Prize, the Jerome J. Shestack Poetry Prize, the Melville Caine Award, and the Ruth Lilly Prize. He has taught at a number of schools, including Sarah Lawrence, Temple University, the University of Pittsburgh and the University of Iowa. *This Time: New and Selected Poems* was published in 1998 and won the National Book Award for Poetry.

Now in his seventies, Stern seems to gain momentum as he goes along, constantly charged with energy that is transformed into language in such a fluid stream that the poet's life can come to seem a continuous monologue, a long poem in process. When in Gerald Stern's presence, it is tempting to imagine that the poet is his poems. But when he is absent from the poems on the page, they still vibrate with the power of his rhapsodic voice and the force of his singular sensibility.

One of the engaging facts of Gerald Stern's career is his long apprenticeship in oblivion, his mysterious and silent past, during which he was barely known in national poetry circles. He was in his fifties when his career as a poet began to flourish. Stern's poetry has continued to develop from book to book. Even in his seventies, he creates new possibilities, such as the long poem "Hotdog," first published in *The American Poetry Review* and included in his recent book, *Odd Mercy*.

"Hotdog" is a poem about a homeless person, about someone abandoned, unwanted, unjustly treated by society. It is also a poem about the streets of New York. (Walking the streets of New York with Stern is a poem in itself.) So it is a love poem for a city as well as for a person who is homeless in that city. (The poet met Hotdog on one of his walks.) The more I think about Gerald Stern's poetry, the more it seems a poetry of praise and exaltation for the people, places, and things that he affirms. Like Whitman, he is mesmerized by the life around him and often writes in long catalogues. In our interview, he spoke of the most amazing thing in his life as "just being alive, being conscious in this beautiful blue planet."

The compassion that the poet feels for the disenfranchised, the dispossessed, may come from his Jewishness or it may be inextricably joined to it. The narrator of his poem "Behaving like a Jew" is tired of the cold, detached, philosophical WASP voice as represented by the anti-Semitic Charles Lindbergh. When he sees a dead opossum in the road, he refuses to be unmoved:

> —I am going to be unappeased at the opossum's death.
> I am going to behave like a Jew
> and touch his face, and stare into his eyes,
> and pull him off the road.

One of the ironies of the poem is that the Jew could well be both the person who cares deeply about the victim and the victim as well, the Jew recognizing the victim in himself and his people projected in another. The narrator implies that, according to Jewish teaching, behaving like a Jew means valuing and treating one life as if it is synonymous with all life.

Although he identifies with those who suffer, Stern has a comic side, filled with manic joy and energy and a strong sense of self-aggrandizement. Because of this and his ebullient long lines, catalogues, parallel structures, etc., Stern is often compared to Whitman, but in our interview he resisted that comparison and emphasized his love for the poetry of Emily Dickinson. "I guess the thing about her I love the most is her mystery, her elusiveness, and her metaphysics. I love how she presents every poem as a kind of problem to be solved. I do the same thing, in a way. Whitman doesn't do that."

It is a tribute to Gerald Stern that his poetry does indeed combine essential qualities of the two giants of nineteenth-century American poetry. Behind the powerful energy of the life force and the long, surging lines, there are depth and mystery. And he is just getting started. "I'm hopeful that I can move toward vision and clarity, and I feel more and more confident and happy that I took the route I took. I believe in language, in poetry, as a redemptive act, even a holy act."

▪

ON TUESDAY, December 5, 1995, I interviewed Gerald Stern in his temporary office at New York University, filled with boxes of Galway Kinnell's books and papers. Through the window one could see old office buildings in the Village. On the windowsill was a huge old *Webster's International Dictionary.* The plain white walls were decorated with Library of America posters of Ben Franklin, William Faulkner, and Mark Twain. During the interview a maintenance

worker knocked on the door, came in, opened the office window, climbed out
on the roof, and returned through the office. After the second trip by the
worker, the poet asked him not to return and pulled the already ripped Twain
poster off the wall. We took a break during the interview to buy some Jewish
pastries at a nearby bakery.

GP: You have written many poems about Jewishness. Do you consider yourself
a Jewish poet? And let's say, along with that, how would you define American
Jewish poetry, or should in fact we call it Jewish American poetry?

GS: The hardest question of all to answer. Of course I'm a Jewish poet. Some-
times I'm consciously a Jewish poet, though rarely. This morning when you
and I were walking to this office, I thought to pick some yellow, transparent
leaves from an old maple tree. That wasn't a Jewish act. At least fifty years ago
that would have been the case, to be so connected with nature. The poem itself,
though—I picked the leaf because of a poem I'm writing—and the poem itself
might be construed after a while as a species of Jewish poem, seen in context.

But quite frankly, writing that poem, I'm not thinking of my Jewishness
qua Jewishness. Now, I've written poems about the Holocaust; I've written
poems that turn into a Jewish subject. Different ethnic groups wear their eth-
nicity in different ways. I guess the more beleaguered they are, the more they
feel that ethnic entity. I myself sometimes feel beleaguered as a Jew. I also feel
beleaguered in various other ways: as an older person, as a man, as a poet, as a
lifetime subversive at universities.

But one of the subjects that's very important to me is my Jewishness, and
I'm interested in Judaism and have sentimental and loving as well as critical at-
titudes toward Jewishness. As far as that question about "should it be Jewish
American poetry or American Jewish poetry," that's a linguistic issue. I told
you yesterday that I'd written an article for an encyclopedia about Jewish
American poetry, and it's a complex subject. One can define it legally. Accord-
ing to the Talmud, one is a Jew if one is the offspring of a Jewish mother. One
can define it in terms of subject matter, in terms of association. In some re-
spects, poets who are not Jewish, living in a Jewish milieu, are often more Jew-
ish than Jewish poets who don't live in such a milieu. And there are many of
them. There is Jewish poetry, finally; however, it is not just Jewish poetry, obvi-
ously. But I think, from a distance, from a cosmic point of view, a slightly cos-
mic point of view, you could say, "Yes, he/she is a Jewish poet." Though I can
name you, if we're talking about it, many well-known American Jewish poets,
or American poets who are of Jewish birth, where the Jewish subject and taste
are very slight.

GP: Let's get a little bit more specific. As far as I'm concerned, two of your best poems, "Soap" and "Adler," concern the Holocaust, perhaps "Soap" more than "Adler." Can you comment about how these poems came to be written and the impact of the Holocaust and let's say Jewishness on these two in particular?

GS: They relate, in both cases, to my way of writing, my associative way of writing. How one thing leads to another. How I begin with an image or an idea or a concept or a group of words and just move along as the spirit, if you will, takes me. God knows what that spirit is. Call it the muse, call it unconsciousness, guilt, shame, love, hope, memory. I actually remember starting "Soap" in a little store in Iowa City that was selling soap, and horrified by the kind of graceless accumulation of soap for its own sake, and I may, I don't remember, I may have been thinking about something or remembering something or had read something or, in my gruesome, ironic way, had connected soap with the camps, and the poem came into being.

But as the poem came into being, as I got into that animal, that poem, it took over, my memory took over, and my horror and my anger and my pity and, most of all, my guilt as an American Jew of a certain age who, if I'd been in Europe, would probably have been dead but was not because I was American. A very common subject for American Jews in my generation. So in the poem itself, I talk about my other, my spirit, who would have been born in Europe—how I would have thrown gasoline bombs at German trucks. That's how that poem got started, that's how it works.

The other poem, "Adler," is about a famous Jewish actor, Jacob Adler, one of the great actors of the century. He starred in a play called *The Jewish King Lear*. I think it had a happy ending, if you can imagine such a thing, or not such a morbid ending as poor Shakespeare's. But that poem also worked its way through its own destiny, if I can put it that way. One of the critical issues in that poem was the issue of daughters. I was living with a woman at the time—Diane Freund, her name is. She had a daughter who was then fifteen years old, Heidi, whom I've written several poems about, who ran away from home eleven times. To Harlem, to Newark, to God-forsaken, horrible, threatening, overwhelming places. And my own daughter, who was six or seven years older, was going through an eating disorder. We were lying in bed on our backs, holding hands, our eyes open, staring at the light fixture, both of us.

So when I say "daughters, daughters" in that poem, I'm not just thinking of Lear's daughters. I'm not just thinking of Cordelia. I'm thinking also of Heidi and Rachael, my daughter. But of course it's structured in terms of the lucky people who could see, at the end of that poem, drama or melodrama, whatever, in terms of theater and could talk about it afterward, rather than those who had no exit from their horrible theater.

GP: The Bible is one of the two great sources of Western literature, along with the Greek myths. Has the Bible influenced your poetry? As you're writing in your unconscious, stream-of-consciousness way, has the Bible entered into your poetry that you can think of?

GS: I think there is an interesting rhythmic influence from the Hebrew prayers, which are memory to me, a manner of repetition, of modification that is the Hebrew way of organizing poetry, which I think is a big influence on me. I know that that's an influence on me. But that's in terms of music. In terms of content, in terms of reference, I think the Psalms are a large influence on me, but most of all the prophets, and particularly Ezekiel and Amos. Amos more than anybody, that angry, mad, unforgiving prophet, whom I take a slightly ironic view of. I don't identify with Amos. I'd be a little kinder than Amos. But it's a big influence on me, and I know it well. I read it, however, like many American Jews do, not so much for literature, but psychologically. Not for religion as such, depending on what we mean by religion; certainly for spiritual sustenance, but not for ritual practice. But I'm in love with the Bible and I read every translation that comes out, and certainly it's an influence on me.

GP: Should Jewish poets write out of the tradition of Jewish texts or are there other ways of expressing Jewishness in poetry? Harold Bloom takes the position that you have to do so; Robert Alter says the same thing. And because Jewish poets aren't always terribly knowledgeable in those texts, the critics argue that they're not genuine Jewish poets. Do you think that Jewish poets need to write out of that tradition or can they approach Jewishness, for example, through ethnicity?

GS: You know, we're talking about American Jewish poets. We're no longer in a ghetto. We are, what, enfranchised, liberated, humiliated, reduced in knowledge in various ways, blessed at the same time. There are different kinds of Jewish poets. Possibly in the evolution of Jewish poets, I don't know, there will be a give-and-take, there will be assimilation and then there will be a tightening up, then assimilation and that tightening up again. Some will strongly identify with certain texts, certain traditions; and Jewishness is not just religious texts. It has to do with a variety of other things and many languages. Even tales.

It's a very hard question, and it's a hard question to respond to. I think that, first of all, to talk about what a poet *should* do is beside the point. He will do what he does or wants to do. If Jewishness creeps in in the manner that I have been talking about, so be it. It will creep in or it will flood, either way. Or it will be ignored. As far as the issue of the need to be consciously aware of certain traditions in order to be officially defined as a Jewish poet, that's ridiculous. That's a ridiculous notion. It's a scholarly notion that has very little to do with the reality of writing poetry. John Hollander is a Jewish poet. Philip Levine is a Jewish poet. Allen Ginsberg is a Jewish poet. Adrienne Rich. Their subject matter is altogether different. Most of Adrienne Rich's poems are not Jewish poems, and yet one could make a thesis that her social consciousness and her anger, for example, derive partly out of her Jewishness, as well as her family tradition, which is partly Jewish.

It's a very difficult question to answer. I'm always shocked by the insistence on theoretical notions coming first, à la Harold Bloom, or Alter, and then defining in advance what the poem will or will not be. One more thing on this. When someone who is a "Jewish poet" writes his "Jewish" poem, it's sometimes his worst poem. There's a poet who lives near here who writes about dancing classes, Jewish dancing classes, and bar mitzvahs. When he does it, I cringe with embarrassment! They're so bad. But sometimes, when he writes about an uncle, say, or an experience he had as a child, when he's not thinking of himself as a Jew, voilà, there is a Jewish poem. "Voilà" is a Jewish word.

GP: Israel, the state of Israel, probably hasn't entered into American Jewish poetry all that much. Has it had an impact on your poetry? Just out of curiosity.

GS: Are you talking about Jewish literature or the concept, the state of Israel?

GP: No, no. Have you been to Israel?

GS: Okay. I've been to Israel one time. I spent a couple of weeks there. I wasn't intending to go there. I went there on the tail end of another visit. I was living in Greece. I was overwhelmed by Israel. I adored Tel Aviv, Jerusalem, the countryside. I have relatives there. I intended to come back, I intended to stay there, to teach and so on. Of course I haven't had a chance to do that yet because life takes over.

Many American Jews of my persuasion—East Coast Radical Leftist Cosmopolitan, eh?—have tended to be critical of Israel's foreign policy and that has affected our attitude to Israel. Many of us come from a Yiddish culture originally, that is, our parents or our grandparents did, and that runs counter to what was the prevailing mode of thinking in Israel. And finally, the language. We all studied Hebrew in cheder, we know it by rote, we know it phonetically. Many of us, those of us who didn't make a deliberate effort to learn Hebrew, know very little of it. We know Yiddish just as well, some of us. And that has been a problem. Obviously there are many younger Jews who've studied Hebrew, who've gone to Israel. As far as I'm concerned, though, I know cheder Hebrew, and I made two or three attempts to learn Hebrew again later in life. I read the Hebrew poets, whom I greatly admire, in translation. I have become—I've always been, however—more sympathetic than some of my rigidly puritanical radical friends, Jews and otherwise, for whom the criticism of Israel often cloaked a kind of latent anti-Semitism. I don't know if this is answering the question or not.

GP: Yeah, yeah! In "Self-Portrait," your poem in *Lucky Life,* you identify with Van Gogh's suffering and genius. Must artists suffer in order to create works of genius?

GS: Oh, dear. One of those big questions, but let me take it on. First of all, I haven't looked at that poem maybe in ten years. I'm a little sensitive to the subject. It was a pop subject at the time, Van Gogh. Which doesn't mean he is not a great and important artist. There are parts of the way the poem is constructed that I would do quite differently today.

As far as suffering, must poets suffer to be poets? Yes! They can't help it, though! They don't have to go looking for suffering. It hits everybody, poets and nonpoets. I suspect, at least in our age, that people who become artists have been dealt a certain blow at a certain time. I really believe that. The blow could be psychological, physical, God knows what, but a certain blow at a certain time. You talk to any poet. You know, it could be a blow that happens to his group, it could be a blow that happened to him personally, it could be a blow that he identified with imaginatively, it could be a blow that he denies.

In my case, as I think about it, I may or may not be right, I think the blow was my sister's death. Sylvia, my only sibling. She died when she was nine and I was eight. Not just the death but how that was handled, consciously and unconsciously, by my parents and extended family afterwards. My guilt about it, my feeling of helplessness and responsibility. That was a critical event for me. That was my blow. So much for suffering.

As far as the poem itself, that is, the poem "Self-Portrait," I think Van Gogh enters the poem in almost an accidental way. I was living in the country, I remember this, standing in the bathroom, six o'clock in the morning, looking out my back window, turned the window light on and I see out there a mountain of crooked limbs, and I say, "Like a huge Van Gogh."

And that is where Van Gogh enters the poem, as it were, in a metaphor. Then I go on to say, when I turned it off—that is, the light—the details change, the trunks appear, the ducks walk up the grass, and the candles begin to shine in the dark canal. Those are the lights reflected in the canal. And then the rest of the early part of that poem is a description of the river, the canal where I lived, and the countryside and myself as an artist living differently from the others. Not living in Paris, not walking up and down the boulevard, at least in this poem, wearing my country clothes, my graying hair, my old hat. And it's at that point that I think of Van Gogh also in a country setting, isolated, detached, exiled, wearing his country clothes, leading his isolated life.

I switched back and forth maybe a little melodramatically between myself and Van Gogh. The name of the town, by the way, that I lived in then was Raubsville. "And I will think of myself sitting in Raubsville, / the only Jew on the river, counting my poems / and—finally—counting my years; and I will think of / Van Gogh when he headed south," and "I will think of his depressions and exaltations." Finally the litany starts about him, but I return to the country in that poem constantly, as I return to other artists living in a romantic—and perhaps melodramatic—way, in exile.

But I extend it beyond artists to others. I talk about the Jews of Vilna, "the Armenians going back into their empty towns." I have a line, "the naked boys moving between the numbered tables." That's at the post office where they are being examined to go into the army. The slowly moving bodies under Lexington Avenue, that's in the subways. And then I go into a kind of generic or mystic place about horses laboring, wild wolves being trapped and such. I return almost to a kind of primitive imaginary state, and I end up with these words: "And in memory of the long life that stretches back now / almost a million years and in memory of the cold rain / that saved our lives and in memory of the leaves / that helped us breathe [which they do, you know] and in pleasant memory / of the grass that clung to our slippery arms and legs [as it were, when we came out of the water, in our evolutionary trek] / and in memory [that's not part of the poem, that's my critical comment] and in memory of the nourishing sand in which we lay like dead fishes [when we came out of the water] / slowly mastering the sky. In honor of Albert Einstein. / In honor of Eugene Debs. In honor of Emma Goldman."

Who are three figures I've picked out who may underlay, spiritually and psychologically, the poem itself. The poem is a little bit more complicated, on relooking at it after ten years, than I remembered it being. Parts of it. I like the language a lot. I find some reservations about the central theme, the way of constructing, the self-pity of the artist. But I hope this answers your question. But you see how my associations just automatically went to the Jews of Vilna, to the Armenians, to other creatures who were trapped, forlorn, abandoned, forsaken. That's where my thinking automatically went. And it's no accident it went to Eugene Debs or Albert Einstein or Emma Goldman.

GP: In another early poem from that same volume, "Behaving Like a Jew," you pit Lindbergh, talking about his "joy in death and philosophical understanding of carnage," against the Jewish speaker's physical empathy with a dead opossum. Is Lindbergh representative of WASP, non-Jewish culture, and I guess I could also ask, is the narrator who's so physically attached to, so compelled, by the dead opossum representative of Jewish culture? Are you stereotyping there?

117

GERALD STERN

GS: Yes, I'm stereotyping. But of course I have in mind a number of things. Lindbergh's political sentiments, the fact that he was a Nazi sympathizer— that's critical in the poem. And the history of writing that poem is relevant. Very briefly, I was in a waiting room in a hospital while my wife was having a "minor procedure" on her wrist, and I was reading a greasy *Reader's Digest,* and there was an essay, an article by Lindbergh, about death. I was, of course, full of cancer, heart disease, and such, and I was terrified. I had just passed, driving my wife to the hospital, a dead opossum on the road with a bullet hole in its head and had helped it off the road. Reading the article by Lindbergh, I thought of the opossum as a kind of Jew. Perfectly absurd. And I thought of Lindbergh's anti-Semitism, and I thought of the whole view of death that's expressed in that *Reader's Digest* article, almost a kind of mystic love of death, as being totally alien to Judaism.

I remember, at a reading in Philadelphia, where I read that poem shortly after I wrote it. It was a reading I was giving with Muriel Rukeyser, by the way. And there was a question period afterwards, and someone challenged me on the poem. He said, "I want to talk to you about your Jewish vision." I remember saying, in sotto voce, "I don't want to be mean," and Muriel saying, "Be mean, be mean." I tried to handle it with humor, as I often do, and I said, "You know, there's a Jewish view of death and there's a WASP view of death or a Lindberghian view of death." "No Jew," I remember saying, "in his right mind would cross the Atlantic Ocean all by himself." Which of course brought a laugh. "Excepting Israelis." And that partly answers the other question we had before. That's the history of that. There was a Jewish critic who objected to my identifying the Jew with the animal, which is very interesting. Because I don't know if Jewish critics are altogether sympathetic with my bizarre and nervous way of dealing with the Jewish issue.

GP: Well, you have a Jew as the one who empathizes with the victim, and now you're saying the Jew is the victim.

GS: "His little dancing feet, his round belly, his beard."

GP: The Jew as dog?

GS: That's an opossum, but it's certainly a Jew. He's both, you're right. Exactly.

GP: In the poem "Psalms," again from *Lucky Life,* you talk about the hills of Tennessee. You equate the hills of Tennessee with the Jewish rabbis. With

Orthodox Jewry, at least as I read it. What are some of your assumptions there? One thought that came to my mind was Wallace Stevens's little poem "Anecdote of a Jar."

GS: That's true.

GP: Where he talks about the hills of Tennessee.

GS: I remember writing that poem. I remember I was traveling with my wife and children, who were, you know, ten years old at the time, and we're driving through Tennessee. I think we were on our way to Florida. And the poem just happened. I think I gave it the title later, "Psalms." It wasn't a concept, it wasn't an idea, the images occurred first, "when I drove through the Little Bald Hills of Tennessee." I didn't know about the connection. It just occurred. I thought of the rabbis of Brooklyn bent over their psalms. So maybe the hills also looked like rabbis, imaginary, again, sentimental perhaps, bent over their psalms. I thought of the tufts of hair. Again the tufts of hair could be the trees or it could be their hair, and the bones and ridges and the small cows eating peacefully out in the open slope or in the shadows, while the forehead wrinkled. And suddenly the hill becomes a gigantic forehead. It also becomes the forehead of a kind of superrabbi, if you will. "While the forehead wrinkled and the gigantic lips moved through the five books." Of course that's the Torah. "Of ecstasy, grief and anger." I name three of them there. I make them up, you know? "Through the five books of ecstasy, grief and anger." And I think the language just occurred to me.

I think I wrote this poem in—this is one of the poems you can write in two seconds, if you could write fast enough. No changes, no labor. The labor was done fifty years earlier. I just wrote the poem, and then I "examined" it later; I gave it the title later, "Psalms." And all I had to do was see things strangely. I often see things strangely. That's a critical issue in poetry, seeing things strangely, that the critics don't pay enough attention to—and making absurd comparisons. In this case, between . . . creating metaphors, showing connections, showing connections that never before existed. A hill of Tennessee and a rabbi bent over a book. And that's what happened in the poem.

Well, is it a Jewish poem? There's a nervousness about the countryside. The Jew is considered in America and Europe to be urban, alien from the countryside. I don't know if you were going to ask me this question, but it's a question you should ask me, and we should deal with it, my attitude to the countryside, to country matters. Of course Shakespeare talks about country matters and he means something else. But my family were, my father's side of my family were, farmers in the Ukraine. They couldn't own land because they were Jews, but the land was owned for them by ethnic Germans, Volga

Germans who had lived there for hundreds of years. And there have been farmers in my family on both sides of the family, in many cases. And I love the countryside, and I feel at home in the country, and I need that touch. There's possibly some root connection here—country-city, you see? Tennessee and Brooklyn—that I'm just noticing now for the first time. A foot in both places. I have a poem, an early poem, I think it's in this book, called "One Foot in the River," where I'm halfway into one world and halfway into another. We're all in two worlds, and they redefine themselves in different ways. But one of the two, one of the polarities that I experience, is city-country.

GP: The person who introduced you at your reading at Barnes & Noble yesterday said you're often compared to Whitman, that you're a reincarnation of Whitman, which is not terribly accurate. But he's influenced most of the American poets who followed him. And in your poem "Lucky Life," again from that earlier volume, I see a lot of Whitman there. And of course in a lot of the other poems: the use of catalogues and parallel structure. Of course, one could argue that you got that from the Hebrew prophets. And your affirmation of self, your kind of manic joy and energy remind me of Whitman. And then even the very title, "Lucky Life." Any thoughts about Whitman?

GS: I love Whitman, and in the long poem "Hot Dog," which is in *Odd Mercy*, one of the two principal figures, characters, personalities, voices, in that poem is Whitman. The other is Augustine. I present them as kind of polar opposites, for good or ill, correctly or incorrectly. And Whitman even as a literal figure in the poem. There's a section of that poem where he is dying; he's dead. When I wrote that, and in the poem itself, I'm lying on my back in his little bed in the last house he lived in in Camden, New Jersey. I actually was there and I was doing that.

I love Whitman. I don't love all of Whitman. There's a lot of Whitman that is repetitive, flat, excessive. But when he's on, there's no one like him. In "Song of Myself," he's elusive, he's a genius, he's brilliant, and he's smart. And I love that Whitman. I don't know how it happened that there are so many connections between him and me. There are with Whitman and many contemporary poets. One could say the same thing of Galway Kinnell, one could say the same thing of Allen Ginsberg, to a degree Philip Levine, to a degree Robert Bly. Maybe me more than the others or maybe a little less than some of the others. Certainly less than Ginsberg; I think even less than Kinnell.

I find myself getting a little angry and resisting it. But resisting it has nothing to do with Whitman as a poet. It's got to do with what seems to me too easy an identification. Resisting the connection. Maybe I want to be more "original" and not be derivative; maybe that's an element. As far as the two grand masters, Dickinson and Whitman, I find that Dickinson is the one that continues to interest me more. She is the one I read more. The last time I went to Europe, I took two books with me: Dickinson's letters and Dickinson's poems. I didn't take "Song of Myself."

What that means, I don't know. Psychologists, Jungians, tell us about the opposites. I don't know what I can say about Whitman that is not obvious: his expansiveness, his openness, his liberal view of the world, his sense of an open future, his belief in redemption through unforeseen ways, his use of ideology and various ideologies metaphorically rather than literally. So that at the end, for example, of "Song of Myself" where he's almost a Christ figure, and I think possibly that was deliberately in his mind when he wrote that poem, he says, "Look for me somewhere else." He says, "It's time to explain myself. Let us stand up." I love that Whitman—that humorous, serious Whitman.

It's interesting about Whitman. He speaks very little about the Jews. I'm sure he loved the Jews. I'm sure he had a good nineteenth-century liberal vision of Judaism, if he thought about it. I don't think he thought about it a lot. Certainly he's an important element in Yiddish and Hebrew thinking. There are many, many early translations of Whitman into Yiddish and into Hebrew. But Whitman does not have a Jewish taste. There is humor in Whitman but it's a different kind of humor. I think that quality in me that is nervous, ironic, mean, even nasty, elusive in my way, derives from another place than Whitman. I think there are other connections. One doesn't always know the connections. Certainly Yeats is a connection, certainly Marlowe, Shakespeare, Christopher Smart, Eliot and Pound, Stevens in different ways, Williams, Coleridge. Coleridge very, very much so. But I don't reject it, I'm just trying to elaborate on this. I'm not speaking against Whitman. God love Whitman.

GP: What about Dickinson, though? I mean, I was surprised when you said—

GS: I know. I saw the look of surprise on your face. I don't know what I can say about it. I love her metaphors. I guess the thing about her I love the most is her mystery, her elusiveness, and her metaphysics. I love how she presents every poem as a kind of problem to be solved. I do the same thing, in a way. Whitman doesn't do that. I love, of course, her music. I love her bizarre imagination. I love her grotesqueries. I don't like the mechanical rhymes and the woodenness.

GP: You have a poem about Auden.

GS: Yes.

GP: In *Paradise Poems,* "In Memory of W. H. Auden."

GS: Which is of course a paraphrase of his "In Memory of W. B. Yeats."

GP: Ah, that great elegy.

GS: "Earth receive an honored guest; / William Yeats is laid to rest."

GP: Did you meet him? In the poem you make it seem like you met him.

GS: I met him, yes. Several times.

GP: What kind of personal impact did he have on you and, of course, what kind of impact did he have on you as a poet through his poetry?

GS: Well, it's interesting that, when I first started to think about poetry, memorize poetry, read poetry, and even write poetry in my early, early twenties, one of the poets I read intensely was Auden. I loved Auden, and I thought that Auden was my maître, my master. The interesting thing was that in many ways we were absolute opposites. He was ironic, intellectual, academic (maybe not academic), formal, coming from quite a different tradition with a different view of things, a different use of language. Yet I loved him, I loved his songs and sonnets, I loved his elegies, I loved his biographical poems (about Forster, about Freud, about Yeats, and so on).

GP: Your poem called "Near Perigord" in *Paradise Poems* has the same title as one of Pound's poems.

GS: Right.

GP: Pound was an influence, as you said, on yourself and so many other people. He's emerged as the most important poetry person of the twentieth century. Can you forgive him for his hatred of Jews and his pro-Fascist and pro-Nazi stance during the Second World War? And along with that, how can such a person influence Jewish poets?

GS: You know, Pound often would defend himself and his relation to Jews and the libel, as he saw it, by saying that so many of his friends were Jewish, and they were. "Some of my best friends." As far as Pound's influence on me, I was obsessed with Pound and fascinated with him and his work, including "Personae" and *The ABC of Reading* as well as *The Cantos*. I admired so many things about him, even his rigidity and his formality and his assumption of being a guru. The teacher, the only teacher. We were looking for such a man. I think he has written some extraordinary poems. But I think *The Cantos* is a flawed poem. I think it's flawed because he was flawed. I think it's unfinished, undeveloped. It is not a great poem. I think there are parts of it that are extraordinary. The parts that are extraordinary are really lyric outbursts. The poem doesn't have a superstructure. Maybe a long poem can't have such a superstructure in our time, connected with a core belief. Clearly I love those parts of that poem, for example, the part which he wrote in 1945 when he was in prison.

GP: *The Pisan Cantos.*

GS: *The Pisan Cantos.* One loves those poems. But I find them flawed, too. I mean, there's a lot of self-pity and a lot of self-congratulation and self-forgiveness in those poems which now I find objectionable and even abhorrent. His influence on me has been in an overwhelming sensitivity to language and to the urgency and importance of the poem, and that's his influence on all the poets. Merwin and Kinnell and so on. Levine. Rich. He's taught me to be precise, to try to be precise about language, to make the words be authentic, to reject Victorianism, as he understood it as a young man. It's language where he's the major influence. And the importance of literature, where literature had become like almost a, well, I hate to say it, a kind of religion to us.

As far as his philosophy, as far as his Jew baiting: disgusting, vile, abhorrent, unforgivable. As far as Ginsberg's forgiving him in the famous incident that's recorded in the *Paris Review* interview, Pound embracing Ginsberg, Ginsberg embracing Pound, Pound saying it was a suburban prejudice, whatever the hell that means, Ginsberg kissing him and forgiving him, I find that to be sheer bullshit. I can't forgive Ginsberg for that stupidity. Ginsberg has no right to forgive Pound. For whom? For the Jews slaughtered? Of course Pound didn't slaughter Jews. Pound possibly didn't even know about the camps. Possibly. We're talking about words here, we're not talking about actions. That's another complicated subject. I don't forgive that in Pound. I found Pound never asked for forgiveness. I find that part of Pound is unforgivable. The sad thing about it is his defenders, his critics, never truly accounted for that aspect of Pound, Pound as Fascist, as Jew baiter, as racist.

That aspect of Pound I can't forgive. But most of all, seen from a literary point of view, it was the central flaw in his writing, and in his soul, that prevented *The Cantos* from being a great poem. My dear friend, Jack Gilbert, whom I grew up with in Pittsburgh and who adores Pound, tries to separate the fascistic poems from the others. I think that's a mistake. I think that you can't ignore Pound's Fascism. It's a critical part of his thinking, or it became so at a certain point in his life. Was he crazy? Was Hitler crazy? Of course he was crazy. So nu, what does that mean? Does that answer the question?

GP: Let's start talking about what's going on with you now. Can you tell us about your long poem "Hot Dog"—just published in your new book—an extremely long poem? How did you come to write it, for starters?

GS: Well, it is the longest poem I've ever written, and it's as if I have been preparing to write that poem all my life. I've had a number of long failures or partial successes. I wrote a long poem, which is the central poem of my last book, *Bread without Sugar*, a biographical poem about my father and his death. Hot Dog is a person, a street person living in the East Village in New York City. She hangs out in front of a Ukrainian restaurant called the Odessa, across from Tompkins Square Park on Avenue A.

I became obsessed with that young woman. She's a black woman, probably in her early thirties, short, very beautiful. She probably belongs in an institution. She was a little more distraught and strange each time I saw her. Part of the poem is about her, her suffering. She's a homeless young woman who is just abandoned by New York City, New York State, America.

The poem has an overall structure. This structure was not, so to speak, to an extreme degree planned in advance, but it grew out of the dynamics of the drama of the poem. Essentially it's concerned with two alternate visions of life—I alluded to this before—one represented by Augustine and the other represented by Whitman. It's biographical. There are characters in the poem, and it's comical. The characters besides Hot Dog are Augustine, myself, Whitman, Noah, my uncle George, and to break the Aristotelian unities, a black preacher from Iowa City, Reverend Penny, whose little church (he died last year) I used to visit periodically, and I describe that in one of the sections.

I was able, finally, to include in this poem everything I wanted to talk about all my life. I'm happy with it. It's a hard poem to read. It's fifty to sixty pages long. It's the longest poem ever published in *The American Poetry Review*. It will take time, maybe, for it to be assimilated and understood. I think it's successful. We'll see what happens. I've gotten a lot of letters from friends, some strangers—I'm waiting for a serious critical response to it.

On one level, it's very, very available as far as the language, and critics resist poems that are available. I'm waiting for an intelligent critic to take it up. It does have a shape, it has a structure, don't make me talk about that now. Is each section a canto? Each section has a focus, a center of interest, much as *The Cantos* themselves did. The poem takes a journey, though. It's a single large dramatic event. There's a beginning, a middle, an end. I think it's a finished work. See, I'm speaking in praise of it. I really feel good about the poem.

GP: Now that you're no longer thirty-nine . . .

GS: Could I say one more thing, though? One of the critical issues of the poem is homelessness. And I write at length about the homeless who live on Avenue A across from Tompkins Square, moving into the park across the street, which they occupied once and even set up as a kind of community. They had a whole city before the former mayor closed the park for "repairs" for a couple of years. The park, in the poem, became a kind of symbol of heaven, as it was at the same time literally a park. And I have another poem that anticipates this that I would like to call your attention to. It's called "Aspiring to Music." I wrote it on one of those little dirt islands on Houston Street, while the trucks were passing by me; it was written a week after Mayor Koch was voted out of office, and it was a poem for the homeless.

Even in that poem, though I did not have Hot Dog in mind yet, I talk about St. Mark's Place and Avenue A; I'll just read a few lines. "It takes 27 minutes to walk / from Tompkins and Houston to St. / Mark's Place and Avenue A, / the left side of Tompkins, the center / of Bombay, the absolute horror / of the known world. One time I was stuck there / with the other pieces of paper. / I didn't know how to get out, / I couldn't find the gate, / I finally walked through the playground / and ended up going west / instead of east" and so on. I'm interested in the abandoned and the unacknowledged, which maybe is a subject for us all. I think it's Levine's subject, and I think it's James Wright's subject, and I think it's Kinnell's. Maybe it's natural that I would have ended up doing "Hot Dog." Now go ahead. You were going to ask me about being thirty-nine. I'm older than thirty-nine; I'm forty-one.

GP: You're forty-one. Does that kind of maturity give you a new, fresh perspective or vision? Let's put it this way: has your vision changed, do you think, since you've become mature?

GS: Of course it has, but not just the vision. You know, one changes physically, psychologically, spiritually, as one gets older. One can't resist it, one can't help it. There's new joy and there's new sadness. There are sadnesses you absolutely forgot about, they seem so unimportant, and new sadnesses that enter. Obvious ones. Closeness to death, for example. There's also new joys, surprisingly enough. I'm more joyful now than I've ever been in my life. I have periods of absolute elation. To some degree it's connected with the satisfaction that I did what I wanted to do in this life, quite frankly. To the degree that I didn't do exactly what I wanted to do, there's sadness, or if I didn't achieve what I wanted to achieve in my way, you know? The language changes in the poems, the subject matter changes. On one level, I'm writing longer poems in order to work out the matter. On another level I've also started to write shorter lyrics again.

A friend of mind said recently to me, "You know, the poems of yours I really like," and I took this as a kind of criticism, "are your shorter lyrics that you were writing in *Rejoicings* and *Lucky Life*. Later the longer poems are interesting, but they don't have the intensity of the shorter lyrics." I don't agree, but I listened to what she said. I'm trying almost deliberately to know what's happening by itself; also, to return to the shorter lyric. I think I'll be doing that. The language changes, the focusing changes, the point of view changes. It's hard to talk about it without being just banal: talking about the wise old man, or the gray beard, or wisdom or knowledge. I prefer to talk about knowledge rather than wisdom. It's knowledge I seek, and knowledge does not mean information, and it does not mean scholarship. Knowledge is, for me, a deeply emotional, intensive, energetic, mystical quality.

GP: Well, as a continuation of that, it may be an impossible question, but how do you face death? And as a corollary, can poetry help? You referred to poetry earlier, I guess with a little question, but you referred to it as possibly a religion, a form of religion, which it probably is for a lot of us. Can poetry help one face death?

GS: I prefer to restructure the issue this way: Labor can help one face death. Poetry finally is my labor. My labor is writing poetry and thinking about poetry. And in a sense, when I'm involved in a poem, deeply involved, and think that the poem might be a success, for two out of three are not and I throw them away, then I feel very much alive, and I feel, even if I talk about death, somewhat indifferent to it or distant from it. When I'm not writing, and maybe it's a crutch, then I feel more vulnerable and more helpless. But it's labor. It's labor that counts, it's work. And this is my work now, and when I'm working I feel alive. When I'm working I am alive.

Can poetry, in terms of its subject, in terms of its spirit, help us allay the horror of death? Probably not. I don't think poets face death easier than other people. Possibly you can draw a thesis that poets as a species are those people who are even more horrified about death than other people. I don't know if that's true or not. Or artists in general. Possibly that's the case. Maybe left-handed boxers, or single-wing right halfbacks. I was one once.

I'm amazingly cool about personal encounters with the horror. I mean, I had two encounters over the last ten years that were very, very critical, and I faced them with, quite frankly, equanimity and calmness, almost with humor. I'm reminded that former heavyweight champion Max Baer died in a hotel on Forty-second Street. He was having a heart attack and called up the switchboard, and said, "I'm having a heart attack. Can you send up a doctor?" And they said, "Do you want a house doctor?" And he said, "No, send me up a person doctor." And then he was dead when they arrived. I was shot about seven, eight years ago and almost bled to death in Newark, New Jersey. That bullet is still in my neck. And when it happened, it missed the aorta by a sixteenth of an inch or I'd have been dead in two minutes. And I survived and I'm fine. When it happened, I was very calm and very shrewd, very cunning. Through a series of events, which I'm not going to retell now, I saved my own life, got to a hospital, directed the doctors what to do, took control of the situation.

On another occasion, three or four years ago, in Iowa City, I had a heart attack. I was suffering pressure under my chest for a week, and I didn't go to a hospital, and finally one night I had what finally was diagnosed as a heart attack. I thought it was coming, and I calmly left my house, drove myself to a nearby hospital, walked in, and said, "You know, I either have indigestion or a heart attack." And they said, "Get on that table!" I was very, very calm about it. Maybe something happens to the body, maybe the body exudes certain enzymes, or God knows what they're called—juices? metaphors?—to help us in that hour of need. You know? But I was extremely relaxed and calm about it.

GP: Did you think about where you were going next?

GS: No.

GP: You're obviously not . . .

GS: I was totally involved in the present. I wasn't thinking of where I was going. In both cases, I was completely, animalistically, involved in my crisis. That's as far as I went. And I was very peaceful about it. I'm absolutely sure that some biologist or doctor could describe what was happening to me physically. But, you know, one person doesn't behave like another. When I was shot, I was with a person who got hysterical, went into shock, and fell apart. She was not shot, but I was. I had to control the scene for us both.

GP: Any thoughts about the latest movements in poetry? The Language poets have gotten a lot of play, especially in academia. Obviously, as you said earlier, your language is mostly accessible. Theirs seems to be, in many ways, inaccessible. What do you think about them and other movements in poetry?

GS: Well, what's happening in American poetry in the last ten, twelve, fifteen years is that there is no central pantheon. There are no given masters the way there were, say, a generation or half a generation earlier. Eliot, Pound, Stevens, Williams were the focus. Later Lowell, Roethke, Berryman, Bishop. Perhaps there always were a lot of schools going on simultaneously, but it seems not just in poetry but in painting, drama, sculpture, dance, music. It's truly up for grabs.

Two things are happening. One is that there is a series of things going on simultaneously. Often they are in contradistinction to each other, and tied in with that and connected with that and maybe the cause of that, there are no central masters. If we could name important, major senior poets, say, in America now, we would name, probably, people in their sixties and seventies, aside from Stanley Kunitz, the grand master, who was just ninety and belongs to an earlier generation. Aside from Kunitz, I would say we would probably talk about Ashbery, Rich, Kinnell and Levine and Levertov, and Creeley, and Merwin, and Ginsberg.

But although Ashbery is a much written about and critical and central figure, I don't think that he's achieved the kind of status that Pound or Eliot did. It may be that the more democratic way of looking at things doesn't allow us to have that hieratic view. That's one of the elements at issue here, which doesn't mean that he's less of a poet, or that Kinnell's less of a poet, than Pound or Eliot. I'm not suggesting that. But I'm talking about the masters, such a figure as Auden. Maybe one is always indebted to his teachers and elders and never sees himself and his peers appropriately.

There's a whole series of things going on simultaneously and all seem to be equal. Feminism. Various kinds of ethnicity. African American literature, Puerto Rican American literature. Gay literature. And we've developed into groups of specialists who only read our own kind.

I was at a reading a year or so ago where two people were reading: Susan Mitchell and Susan Howe. Susan Mitchell is a wonderful poet from Florida and Connecticut who's written a marvelous book called *Rapture*. She was reading from this book. I don't have to define her in terms of these groups. She occupies the center, she's a little to the left, she's a little up, she's a little down. She was reading with another poet named Susan, Susan Howe, who is clearly a kind of half Projectivist, half Language poet, half critical theorist, at the same time as she's other things. And there was a group of Howe's followers at that reading, who knew her work and studied it as if it were the Bible, had her texts (that's one of their favorite words) with them, and walked out when Susan Mitchell read. Paid no attention to her, as if she didn't exist. This is one of the things that's going on today. And I think it's sad, horrible. It's as if people are in love with other things than beauty, than literature, than poetry. It's ideological; it's concerned with ideas, with theory, with the dominance of theory in the universities. It's connected with the place of literature itself, poetry itself, in the universities and their role vis-à-vis the Workshop and the workshops. That is to say, poetry has come into being and exists to a significant degree in recent years through, by, connected with, English departments, the mind, intellectuality, critical tradition, theory.

As far as Language poetry, I've read as much as I could about it in various magazines. I admire Perelman's work. I admire Michael Palmer's work. There are other poets, like Charles Bernstein, who's a friend and an interesting critic, whose poetry I don't admire much. So it's hard to lump them all together. I mean, here is Michael Palmer, a wonderful poet. Here's Bernstein, not a wonderful poet. What is their connection with each other? Are they both Language poets? What does it mean? I suppose they would resist what I say, and would talk about their politics, their construction of language, their rejection of certain realities.

I tend to be fairly catholic and fairly embracing and accepting. But there are things that I believe in in poetry. I love simplicity. I'm not always guilty of it. I love the grace of simplicity, almost transparency. My dream is to write, is to be so moved that I can write, that I am enabled to write, poems that are available. That isn't always the case. Sometimes things are more difficult than I want . . . but I don't move towards incoherency. Many of my students at Iowa moved deliberately towards incoherency. It may be that they felt they had to go in a certain direction of incoherency (I'm calling it incoherency) for the sake of finding their own demon. Maybe that's the case. Maybe they're right. I remember once sitting in a room with a young graduate student at Iowa, and I was trying desperately to say that I couldn't understand her poem, that it didn't make sense, that it didn't work. And she said, "What are you telling me, that I can't write?" And I said, "Yes. You can't write." Things have changed, standards have changed. There is—well, let me let that one go. There are the narrative poets, there are the neoformalists. It's the same thing in painting. We have decorative eighteenth-century painting, revived German Expressionism. We have illusionism of various kinds, non-Objectivism, cool and hot painting, and so on. The same thing is happening in poetry. Where do I see my place in all of this? I'm hopeful that I can move toward vision and clarity, and I feel more and more confident and happy that I took the route I took. I believe in language, in poetry, as a redemptive act, even a holy act. I don't know what else to say on that.

GP: I already have an answer to my question about what is the most amazing thing about your life, because you've already suggested that you're still alive with a bullet in you after having been shot in a horrifying incident. But why don't you tell us what you think the most amazing thing about your life is?

GS: Well, I don't think that's the most amazing thing about my life. I think it's being the son of immigrants, growing up in a house, and I say this with respect, where there wasn't one book and taking the turn I did. I may have mentioned this earlier to you, having breakfast, when you asked me where I went to college. I went to the University of Pittsburgh, but I didn't even know as a boy where the university was. I discovered it literally by accident. I saw some people lined up on the lawn outside the university registering for courses, and it was the war, and anybody could get into college. And I decided, "Hey, I'll take classes!" And I became a college student. No one ever advised me. No one at home ever talked to me about college.

The most amazing thing about my life is that I could go from there to being a fairly well known American poet. Like my friend Gilbert, also from Pittsburgh. In a poem, I talk about Jack as the grandson of a tenant farmer from North Carolina and myself as the grandson of an Orthodox rabbi from Poland. Both of us are consciously aware of this enormous move from darkness into light, *if* that's what it is. Maybe it's light into darkness or darkness into darkness. Maybe it's light into light. But the move away, over the Allegheny Mountains into Europe, into New York, was such a move.

I remember returning to the University of Pittsburgh in the late seventies and teaching there, a graduate class, and I was telling the students what it was like when I grew up in Pittsburgh. I was congratulating them that they had opportunities to get money, to go on trips, to get published; the magazines were lying on the table, there were scholarships, fellowships, competitions, readings—how lucky they were. There were no poets, there were no programs, there were no readers when I was a student there. I didn't know what a live poet looked like. The next week when we met, before we started, they said, "Tell us again about the darkness." They had romanticized my darkness.

For me the most amazing thing was moving out of that darkness. But also the most amazing thing is just being alive, being conscious in this beautiful blue planet, you know, for a few years. Just absolutely amazing. I constantly think of that, and I think about that more now than I ever did before.

GP: Well, if you could top that, what do you wish to still accomplish? And I guess I mean as a poet, but also as a person.

GS: Well, I want to be a grandfather. I would hope one of my dear children, my Rachael, my David, would do the trick, but that's their business, I guess. I'd like to write some good poems. I'd like to write some great poems. I'd like to finally do what I've always wanted to do, to write perfect poems. Okay, there are no perfect poems. Wonderful imperfect poems. I remember at one point I said, "I want to write a hundred poems, a hundred fine poems." You know, thirty years ago. That'll be enough for this lifetime. I guess I've written a hundred decent or good poems. Now I want to write ten poems that will last. I think that's what I want to do. I would like to fall in love again. I would like to visit places that I haven't been: Asia and Africa. I'd like to retrace my steps in certain places that I have been, now that I have the leisure, and indeed the money, to do that. Like Italy. What else do I want to do? Read some novels, reread some novels. I'm even going to reread *War and Peace* and *Anna Karenina.* Can you believe it? Dostoyevsky I want to reread. I want to learn more Yiddish. I don't know it well enough. I want to really learn it. There's a lot of things I want to do. I'm just getting started. Really, it's true.

ALLEN GINSBERG

ALLEN GINSBERG was born on June 3, 1926, in Newark, New Jersey, the son of Naomi, a Russian immigrant, and Louis, a high school English teacher and published poet. As a youth, he met William Carlos Williams, who encouraged him to trust his own extreme instincts as a poet and later wrote introductions for Ginsberg's *Empty Mirror* and *Howl*.

While attending Columbia University, Ginsberg met the writers with whom he was to inaugurate the Beat Generation: Jack Kerouac, William Burroughs, and Gregory Corso. *Howl*, published in 1956, became the target of a famous censorship trial at Berkeley, which helped to make Ginsberg and the Beats the objects of international attention.

From 1956 through 1982, Ginsberg's little paperbacks with black-and-white covers were published by Lawrence Ferlinghetti's City Lights Books. It was only with the publication by Harper and Row of his *Collected Poems, 1947–1980* (1984) that his poems became available in a hardbound edition. Harper & Row and HarperCollins subsequently published two more collections, *White Shroud* (1986) and *Cosmopolitan Greetings* (1994), as well as a new *Selected Poems* volume. There are also several collections of the poet's letters and journals as well as the original draft facsimile of "Howl," edited by Barry Miles. Besides his poetry and prose, there are collections of Ginsberg's photographs, plus tapes, CDs, and records of his readings and musical performances and collaborations. Posthumous publications include *Deliberate Prose* and *Death and Fame: Poems, 1993–1997*. Allen Ginsberg died on April 6, 1997.

ALTHOUGH IT may be argued that Allen Ginsberg's status as a Beat antihero during the fifties and later as a counterculture guru was the primary reason for his fame, he always saw himself as a practicing poet, expressing, as Blake did, the genius of his poetic imagination as spontaneously and uncompromisingly as he could. Certainly Ginsberg's long poem "Howl" established his reputation as the seminal poet of the Beat Generation, and "Kaddish," his elegy for his mother, Naomi, is one of the great original poems of the century. No less an authority than Harvard critic-scholar Helen Vendler believes that Ginsberg's "powerful mixture of Blake, Whitman, Pound, and Williams, to which he added his own volatile, grotesque, and tender humor, has assured him a memorable place in modern poetry" (quotation on back of Ginsberg's *Collected Poems.* Also, see longer discussion in Vendler's *The Music of What Happens: Poems, Poetics, Critics* [Cambridge: Harvard University Press, 1988], pp. 216–71).

Hundreds of years after Ezekiel and Jeremiah, Allen Ginsberg became a poet-prophet, enlightened by "a common key" to the universe, a key that his mother shares with him in "Kaddish." It was his memory of his mother's leftist politics, her fears of Hitler, fascism, and capitalism, her sense of exile from both her native Russia and most of American society, her subsequent breakdowns, and her visions that prompted the poet to perceive himself as an exiled poet-prophet, willing to risk madness and even death to sanctify his mother's suffering and to vindicate all personal consciousness as opposed to the impersonal machinery of modern industrial technology. His mission was twofold: to condemn capitalist America for destroying his mother and a whole generation of geniuses and to affirm the mystical knowledge that she and now he claimed to have and that he recognized in the saints of the Beat Generation.

While embodying an image of gentleness and kindness, Ginsberg also showed remarkable courage in writing openly and freely about his radical politics, his gay sexuality, and his wild, mad, profane thoughts and visions during the bleakly conservative Eisenhower fifties. His courage was based on faith in personal honesty and the poetic imagination. "But the whole point of poetry is not to be afraid of worst-case neurosis, but to reveal it, go right into the wind rather than being afraid of admitting it."

In living out this spirit of freedom and liberation, Ginsberg turned on thousands of counterculture people and taught everyone who paid attention to be less afraid of society's prohibitions. He was speaking accurately when he told me, "So I'd like to be remembered as someone who advanced, actually advanced the notion of compassion in open-heart, open-form poetry, continuing the tradition of Whitman and Williams. And part of the honorific aspect of the whole Beat Generation."

Up to the last moments of his earthly life, Ginsberg experienced all that he possibly could: conversing with friends, writing poems, maintaining his intelligence, candor, and humor to the end. Upon the poet's death, there was a huge outpouring of testimonials from admirers around the world. The extent of his influence became apparent as poets, novelists, rock stars, political figures, and others spoke of the poet's mark upon their life and work.

I FIRST MET Allen Ginsberg before his reading at the University of Dayton in the early seventies. Before the reading, with my wife and young daughter at my side, I saw the poet in the school's cafeteria in the basement of the Kennedy Union. When I approached Ginsberg, he was wearing an old gray tweed sport coat and was clutching that day's *New York Times*.

"Allen, what is a breath unit?" I asked.

He said he would show me, and he did, chopping the air with his extended hand as I spoke to indicate my pauses. Later with hundreds of people in the audience, the gentle Jewish intellectual transformed himself into a wild Buddhist bard and exhibitionist. When he read his "Please, Master," I thought the Catholic clergy in attendance might not last through the performance.

In 1993 I encountered Ginsberg at a poetry conference sponsored by the National Poetry Foundation at the University of Maine, Orono. For four days the poet attended sessions; he also gave a reading with Carl Rakosi and spoke on poetics. While he seemed wary of me at first, the poet tried to answer my questions when I encountered him.

Shortly before Ginsberg's death, I visited his spacious loft on the Lower East Side and spoke with his personal secretary, Bob Rosenthal, but the poet was too sick to meet visitors. Stanford University had recently paid one millions dollars for Ginsberg's papers.

■

ON SATURDAY, February 10, 1996, I interviewed Allen Ginsberg by phone using an answering machine with a tape recorder. My colleague Martin Maner had lent me a telephone device with a built-in tape recorder, which I had never used before. When I called Ginsberg and couldn't get the tape recorder to work, he said he was going to hang up and to call him back if I got the device to work. It was probably sheer luck that turned the recorder on and enabled me to call Ginsberg back and record our interview.

GP: The tape is on now; this is the beginning.

AG: "This is the forest primeval. The murmuring pines and the hemlocks / Bearded with moss."

GP: Allen, what have you found the hardest thing about being a poet?

AG: Nothing particular. I mean—nothing particular. No hard part.

GP: Okay.

AG: Making a living at it. Making a living.

GP: Well, what about inspiration? Has it always been easy?

AG: Inspiration comes from the word *spiritus. Spiritus* means breathing. *Inspiration* means taking in breath. *Expiration* means leaving breath go out. So inspiration is just a feeling of heightened breath or slightly exalted breath, when the body feels like a hollow reed in the wind of breath. Physical breath comes easily and thoughts come with it. Now that's a state of physical and mental heightening, but it's not absolutely necessary for great poetry. Though you find it's a kind of inspiration, a kind of breathing in Shelley's "Ode to the West Wind" or "Adonais" or Hart Crane's "Atlantis" or perhaps the Moloch section of "Howl." But for subject matter, which is what you mean, for ideas, ordinary mind and the thoughts that occur every day are sufficient. It's a question of the quality of your attention to your own mind and your own thoughts.

GP: Where does this breath come from that you find in the second part of "Howl," for example?

AG: Well, it's a more excited breathing, longer breath, that you find in the examples that I cited which build sequentially as a series of breaths until finally there's a kind of conclusive utterance. "Moloch whose name is the Mind."

GP: You talk in the *Paris Review* interview and other places about being inspired by Blake's reciting "Sunflower."

AG: An auditory hallucination, hearing it, but that's a different kind of a breath, completely. That's a quieter breath from the heart area. Like my voice now rather than the stentorian breath of "Atlantis" or "Howl."

GP: So you're not talking about what we usually talk about in terms of prophesy, in terms of some divine voice.

AG: Now wait a minute. You're switching your words now. We were using the words *inspiration* and *voice.* Now what are you talking about? What's your question, really?

GP: What is a breath unit?

AG: A breath unit as a measure of the verse line? Why, a breath unit as a measure of the verse line is one breath. Why "a" is another breath, and then continuing with the sentence is another breath. Or saying "or" is another breath, and then you take another breath and continue. So you arrange the verse line on the page according to where you have your breath stop, and the number of words within one breath, whether it's long or short, as this long breath has just become.

GP: Okay now, you're talking about great poetry—

AG: No, no, I'm talking about how you arrange the verse lines on the page by the breath.

GP: No, I understand, but when we were talking about inspiration you used the word *breath* again.

AG: Because the word *inspiration* comes from the Latin word *spiritus,* which means breathing. So I was trying to nail down what the word *inspiration* means rather than have a vague term that we didn't know what we were talking about.

GP: But to me, and obviously I could be totally off, it sounds like you're talking about poetry as a kind of series of breathing exercises.

AG: Well, it is, in a way, or the vocal part, the oral part, is related to the breath, yes.

GP: What inspires the breath?

AG: The breath is inspiration itself. Breath is itself, breath is breath. Where there is life, there is breath, remember? Breath is spirit, spiritus.

GP: So every once in a while this spirit breath visits you and other poets?

AG: No, you're breathing all the time, it's just that you become aware of your breath. Every once in a while you become aware that you're alive. Every once in a while you become aware of your breathing. Or of the whole process of being alive, breathing in the universe, being awake, and so you could say that that's the inspiration or the key, that you become aware of what's already going on.

GP: You probably didn't know this when you were sixteen, eighteen, twenty years old and first writing poetry.

AG: Oh, well, pretty soon. A sort of latent understanding, yeah. That notion of awareness, conscious awareness.

AG: Pound and Williams specialized in this. They broke the ground for this kind of thinking: Williams trying to write in vernacular speech and dividing it up into pieces, and dividing the verse line into pieces of vernacular speech, sometimes by counting syllables, sometimes by the breath stop, sometimes by running counter to the breath stop. Do you know what I mean by the breath stop?

GP: You were in Dayton years ago and I was there with my wife and child, and I said to you, "What is a breath unit?," and you were sort of showing me with your hand as I spoke. Charles Olson talks about it. But Pound and Williams don't talk about breath, do they?

AG: Well, it's implicit in what they were doing, because they were talking about actual talk.

GP: I understand.

AG: And measuring the measure—what Williams talks about was an American measure, a measure of actual speech.

GP: Right.

AG: And his disciples like Olson and Creeley drew from that the notion of projective verse or verse by breath or measuring the verse line by where the breath stops.

GP: But we both know that your breaths in "Kaddish" and "Howl" and your other inspired poems are—

AG: Different from somebody else?

GP: Not only different, but so long.

AG: Everybody's is different. Everybody's breath is different. Everybody, like Creeley's is short and minimal, in a way.

GP: Well, it's beyond short and minimal. It's like one one-hundredth of what yours is in some of your longer lines.

AG: Well, sometimes. But on the other hand there are the poems that are like those, too, like Williams's or Pound's.

GP: Does that mean, since your line is the longest, that you're the most inspired?

AG: Well, the deepest inspiration, probably, yes, the deepest breath.

GP: So you are, you're literally equating poetic inspiration with breath.

AG: That aspect of it. There're two kinds, I said. There is the deep breath, but there's also, in the more common use of the word *inspiration*—i.e., where do you get your ideas—is also just ordinary mind and ordinary breath, and short breath, too. Ordinary mind means what passes through your mind while you're sitting on the toilet.

GP: But in your poem "Kaddish" you're doing more than that.

AG: But I'm saying there are different kinds of poetry. In "Kaddish" what I'm doing is a longer breath, yes. Then in other poems, like in *White Shroud* the poem to William Carlos Williams, "Written in my Dream by William Carlos Williams," it's a short breath.

GP: Let's switch it a little bit, then maybe we can come back to that. In "Howl" you affirm the Beat lifestyle.

AG: You know, one thing is, you're fixated on poems of thirty, forty years ago. I don't mind talking about them, but in context of a whole curve of poetry up to the present. But go on.

GP: Okay, fine. You affirm the Beat lifestyle that often leads to madness and/or death.

AG: I didn't use the word "lifestyle." That's a later sort of media term and I don't like you to use it. I think it's bullshit.

GP: You said, "Mad generation! down on the rocks of Time!" A lot of the people, most of the people, have died.

AG: Not so. Just the opposite, sir. Just the opposite. You've got it all wrong, inside out. Burroughs is alive at the age of eighty three and just had a birthday. Huncke just had his birthday in February also, and he's eighty-one. Gary

Snyder is in very good health in California and is a world-renowned influence in poetry. Philip Whalen is a Zen master now. I'm doing quite well at Naropa and Brooklyn College and writing poems. Michael McClure is touring with Ray Manzarek. So Kerouac died, Neal Cassady died, and Lou Welsh died. But on the other hand Gregory Corso is living across town. We're all in touch with each other. Ann Waldman has founded the Kerouac School of Poetics at Naropa and John Ashbery and everybody go there, and I go there between terms. So we have a better actuarial span than most insurance people. But you've got the stereotype I'm trying to get away from.

GP: Let's go to "Howl" itself.

AG: As I keep saying, you're fixated on images of that. Anyway, go on.

GP: Well, those people are very unhappy, the people you portray in the poem.

AG: Yes. They were young.

GP: Okay. Let's just say you have survived.

AG: And so have most of my friends.

GP: Where do you draw your strength?

AG: Oh, inspiration. I keep breathing. Also I never drank.

GP: You never drank?

AG: No. I never drank. And I was very moderate in my use of drugs. I was more interested in the politics than the drugs themselves.

GP: But you have all those poems that are titled after drugs.

AG: If you'll notice, it's about one percent of my poetry.

GP: Okay. I'll go back and take a look.

AG: You'll find a poem called "Nitrous Oxide" and another called "Ether" and another called "LSD," another called "Marijuana Notation," another called "Mescaline." And that's about it. And you have Peyote for the central section of "Howl"—

GP: The religious visions.

AG: And a couple other things, then you have some stuff from the "Yage" and that's it. Out of about eight hundred pages, you've got about fifty pages of drugs.

GP: All right, that takes care of that.

AG: You have the media stereotypes you're dealing with.

GP: Well, I don't know you.

AG: Well, you don't have to. Just look at the texts. I've named all the texts that are on drugs.

GP: In "Kaddish" were you responding to the Hebrew prayer in any particular way, or were you responding in a more general way to your grief over Naomi's death?

AG: Both. You know, I had never heard the formal rhythms of the Kaddish before, pronounced aloud, or never consciously heard them. They sounded familiar. But all of a sudden I realized it was some kind of an interesting, moving, powerful cadence.

GP: You must have been to a service.

AG: Yes. But I just never noticed or heard or consciously heard it, as I said.

GP: But you have said it, though.

AG: No, I've never said it. I don't read Hebrew. I wasn't bar mitzvahed. And I was kicked out of Hebrew school for asking questions. I don't know.

GP: Were you being sentimental when you named it "Kaddish"?

AG: No, 'cause I used the basic rhythm of the Kaddish, and I quoted the Kaddish.

GP: But you said you didn't know it.

AG: I heard it that morning. Someone read it to me that morning.

GP: The morning you wrote the poem?

AG: Yeah, when I started writing it, or that evening. About 3 A.M. And I was impressed by the cadence and the rhythm and the depth of the sound, as it says in the very opening line, "Reading the Kaddish aloud," "the rhythm the rhythm—and your memory in my head three years after." It says exactly what it was. Mixed with "Ray Charles blues shout blind on the phonograph." With a similar rhythm, by the way. "I got a woman, yes indeed."

GP: So—

AG: A sort of repeated cadence that was right, like Ray Charles or like the Kaddish.

GP: So you're inspired by that prayer, you're inspired by music, by the rhythm of the music. What about the image, though?

AG: What's the image? Which one?

GP: Williams and emphasis on—

AG: Minute particular details. Now the phrase that I am thinking of is "minute particulars." Do you know that phrase? Do you know where that's from?

GP: "Minute particulars."

AG: Yes. "Labor well the minute particulars. Take care of the little ones." That's from William Blake's "Jerusalem." Little ones, the little details. And Kerouac says, "Details are the life of prose." And Pound says, "The natural object is the adequate symbol." And Trungpa says, "Things are symbols of themselves."

GP: Well, let me ask you this—

AG: So the image comes from, or the image is related to, the following idea. If you want to give a mirror of your consciousness and you become aware of your consciousness, conscious awareness manifests itself sacramentally in the quality of attention to clear-seeing focus on chance, minute, particular details that present themselves with charismatic vividness to author and to reader.

GP: You do both that and you hear music also? Simultaneously?

AG: No. You have a picture in your mind, as Pound points out, in "Chinese Written Language as a Medium for Poetry," published by City Lights now. The Chinese is interesting as a poetic language because it consists in little pictographs. So you can't be vague and talk about beauty. You have to talk about something concrete and process. At the same time, the language has got a sonorous aspect or sound or vocal sound, so you hear it in your head sometimes. Sometimes you make the language up out of the picture. Sometimes the language itself has its own melodic part that comes up by itself. Like the other day I got up off the toilet, and I said, "That was good, that was great, that was important!" And stood up to pull the chain. And I heard myself saying that, and I noticed I had said that, and I said, that's fairly interesting, that's like a haiku. How many syllables was that? "That was good, that was great, that was important!" That's eleven syllables.

GP: Maybe twelve.

AG: Ending on the twelfth. "That was good, that was great, that was important!" No, that's eleven. "Standing up to pull the chain." Yeah. "Standing to pull the chain" adds another six, so that's seventeen all together. So, okay, I noticed the situation, there was the visual element, standing to pull the chain, the picture there, and there was what ran in my mind, so the picture gave the context for the interior utterance.

GP: Okay, so the picture can sometimes inspire the music.

AG: Not inspire! No, no, no! I hear you using that word over and over again, abusing it, using it out of its meaning. You're making it into oatmeal.

GP: How would you say it? The picture induces?

AG: The picture originates the poem or the origin or the flash. You flash on a picture, and you write it down. Or you flash on something you say to yourself, and you write it down.

GP: And sometimes that can have music.

AG: You can hear a tune. But the words "That was good, that was great, that was important!" have a rhythm. (*Demonstration of rhythm.*) That has its own cadence; you know what it's saying and the rhythm of the sounds are both the same.

GP: It's not metrical, obviously.

AG: It is metrical. (*Demonstration of rhythm.*) That's a meter. That's an old classic Greek meter.

GP: Anapest? Short, short, long?

AG: It's an anapest. Ta ta ta ta-ta. One, two, three, four-five. There's a Greek rhythm that is a four-beat rhythm or a four-syllable rhythm. I don't know what it's called, maybe dithyrambic or something.

GP: Do you know Greek?

AG: No, but I know some of the Greek rhythms.

GP: You're the prototype, I guess it's a stereotype, of the free-verse poet, but you're saying you hear meters.

AG: Yes, sure I hear meters. My father was a poet, it's a family business, and I grew up with a facility for rhyme and stanza from when I was very young, without even trying. I know yards and yards of poetry, like Edgar Allen Poe's "Bells" or Vachel Lindsay's "Congo," poems by Edna St. Vincent Millay and Elinor Wylie.

GP: But didn't you—I mean, you've said many times you had to go beyond that in order to write "Howl" and "Kaddish."

AG: Well, naturally, you know, but the point is those forms are appropriate, they're called lyric poetry, or the shorter forms, which have short stanzas, they're called lyric poetry. Now, what is the root of the word *lyric*?

GP: Song, isn't it?

AG: No, no. Think. What is the root, literally, of the word *lyric*? What instrument?

GP: Lyre.

AG: Right, right! And what was a lyre? It was a stringed instrument played by Homer or Sappho or the early poets, the Muse's lyre. So it's just like to Bob Dylan or something, a stringed instrument, where you sing to stanza with rhyme and you have a melody that revolves around itself and has a recurrence, right? So because the melody has a recurrence, you therefore have a recurrence, a cadence for the stanza, and you use rhyme. When you stop using the stringed instrument and just write the form without the music, then it begins to degenerate and lose its muscularity and its variety and its syncopation. So when I came in in 1950, people were trying to write those lyric stanzas, but without music. And that was the complaint that Pound and Williams had. And so historically—and also Whitman—so they moved away from a fake lyric, that is to say a half-assed lyric that did not have the musical accompaniment, but just spoken language, but arranged as if it were a song. They moved away to the use of living language rather than a dead form and began rewriting the idea of rhythm and measure. And so Williams had the idea of an American measure rather than the old English lyric, which was being imitated in the twenties by Edwin Arlington Robinson and Elinor Wylie and Sara Teasdale and Edna St. Vincent Millay and all the minor poets of that time. He moved out into trying to isolate the rhythms of actual speaking and that led to my own generation of projective verse, writing in the living speech rather than in an imitation of an older English cadence. It didn't mean that there wasn't rhythm, it meant that the rhythms were the rhythms that you heard in speech, like "da dada da da dada dada." It didn't mean that there wasn't rhythm. That's a rhythm.

GP: Frost supposedly hears a meter. There's meter in Frost as well as the rhythm. "Something there is that doesn't love a wall."

AG: Okay, that's a metronomic meter, where it's recurrent. But you know, the classic meters of Greece were much more varied than the four or five, four usually, used in English. We have iamb, trochee, dactyl, and anapest.

GP: Spondee.

AG: And that's usually the range. Spondees are used less, but they come in. So now there are the two-syllable and three-syllable meters. We have mostly the iamb and trochee, but then there's also molossos, the three-syllable meters. "Oh, good God!" Da da da. Or there is the bacchius meter, "Is God love? Believe me." Dada da, dada da. Then there are four-syllable meters, like, oh, "insistently." Dadadada dadadada dadadada dadadada. "Insistently, insistently, insistently." Or the ionic A minor, which is "in the twilight," dadadada dadadada dadadada. Or "delightfully, delightfully, delightfully." That's the second ionic. Or the epitritus primus, "your sweet blue eyes," "I hate your guts." So then there's the epitritus secundus, "Bite the big nut," dadadada, or "Give her a dime," dadadada. And then there's the five-syllable ones: "I bit off his nose," da da da dada. Or the dulcimaic, which Hart Crane used, "Lo, lord, thou ridest!" Bom bom dadada. "Fall fruits and flowers." That's Ben Jonson. Dom

dom dadada. Those were the ones we used at the climax of Greek plays, with the revelation of the moment. Bom bom dadada.

GP: So there's a lot more, you're saying, than the simple two-syllable foot.

AG: So and they could use these different feet like a Leggo set and could build very various musicality, complex musical things, like Sappho? You know the Sapphic stanza?

GP: No, I don't know much about it.

AG: You know the rhythm of it.

GP: No.

AG: Trochee, trochee, dactyl, trochee, trochee. Trochee, trochee, dactyl, trochee, trochee. Trochee, trochee, dactyl, trochee, trochee. Dactyl, trochee. (*Demonstration of rhythm.*)

GP: So the first line of "Howl"—

AG: No, I wasn't thinking of that, but I was so trained and I had all those in my bones. But the one that pointed out to me, many years later, that the Moloch section (*demonstration of rhythm*), "Moloch whose eyes are a thousand blind windows," was Ed Sanders, who's trained in classical prosody and versification. Then I got interested in what the names of these were.

GP: Let me ask you something else.

AG: Yes, well that's what you're doing.

GP: Have you ever considered yourself a Jewish poet?

AG: Yeah, I am a Jewish poet. I'm Jewish.

GP: You are? You surprise me.

AG: I'm Jewish. My name is Ginsboig. I wrote a book called *Kaddish*.

GP: No, that's great!

AG: My last book has a long poem called "Why I'm Jewish."

GP: I'll have a take a look. I've got it.

AG: It's called "Yiddishe Kopf."

GP: *Cosmopolitan Greetings?*

AG: Yeah. "Yiddishe Kopf."

GP: I'll have to look it up. So you're a Jewish poet.

AG: I'm also a gay poet.

GP: I know that.

AG: I'm also a New Jersey poet.

GP: You're a Buddhist poet.

AG: And I'm a Buddhist poet. And also I'm an academic poet, and also I'm a beatnik poet, I'm an international poet—

GP: What was the Jewish influence? Your mother, essentially?

AG: No. My mother, my father, my grandparents were all Jewish. My whole family is Jewish and that's just the whole thing in my bones.

GP: What about the Bible? Did that influence you?

AG: Yeah, I read a lot of the Bible, sure. I read it all through, a number of times. But you know, like I know the wherever the golden bowl be broken and the silver cord be loosed wheel be broken at the cistern and so forth.

GP: Is there a cadence—

AG: The cadences of Ecclesiastes and the Psalms. The Song of Songs.

GP: And you probably got some inspiration from the parallelism of the Hebrew prophets.

AG: Oh, of course. But also, you know, indirectly. One of my great models as a poet, or for me a great model, is Christopher Smart.

GP: Right. "Jubilate Agno."

AG: Right. And he was a fantastic translator of the Bible, of Hebrew.

GP: Of psalms?

AG: Of psalms and everything like that. And his "Jubilate Agno"—I don't know if you've seen my annotated "Howl"?

GP: I have, yeah.

AG: Well, at the end you'll find a selection from Smart.

GP: That's right. I remember that.

AG: If you'll notice, it's done in the parallelisms of the Bible. And my own verse line in "Howl" and elsewhere is drawn from that. The Bible via Smart, as well as the Bible itself that I'm familiar with. You know, my father was a poet and so all this stuff, the Song of Songs, was part of the family heritage.

GP: Are being Jewish and being gay connected in any way? I mean, being oppressed?

AG: I've known gay Jews. Who was it, David and Jonathan? I mean, that's an old business. What is it, Jesus and young John?

GP: Here's a chance to talk about the present. Because I started out interviewing Stanley Kunitz and Carl Rakosi, who are in their nineties.

AG: Yeah, marvelous people. Rakosi I love. I love Rakosi.

GP: Well, I was in Maine and I talked to him a lot. I was in Maine when he did that reading with you.

AG: And I saw him last summer at Naropa.

GP: And I interviewed him in December in San Francisco, and he's great.

AG: I think he is our greatest poet, Jewish or non-Jewish.

GP: He told me you like Reznikoff even more.

AG: No, I like both.

GP: It's good that you like him.

AG: I think Rakosi—you know, his *Collected Poems* is a great volume.

GP: Yeah, I have that. I got it in Maine. I really fell in love with it.

AG: Did you think I liked Reznikoff more?

GP: Well, Rakosi said that. He said that when I saw him in San Francisco.

AG: I discovered him earlier.

GP: But he hasn't gotten enough attention.

AG: He got a lot from me.

GP: Most of the attention has gone to the other Objectivists: Zukofsky and Oppen.

AG: Well, fortunately we pay a lot of attention to him at Naropa.

GP: That's great.

AG: And in Maine.

GP: Are you going to go to Maine again?

AG: I won't be able to this summer. It's there when I'm in Naropa.

GP: I was there, I talked to you a lot. I'm going to England this time. Well, let me ask you another line of questions. Let's go on. Does maturity give you any kind of new, fresh perspective?

AG: Look at my new poems. *Cosmopolitan Greetings* is all about that. There's one particular poem, but you know there are lots of poems about being a senior citizen in there.

GP: Yeah. That's right.

AG: But there's one particular poem that begins, "At 66 just learning how to take care of my body." Do you know that?

GP: I've got it right in front of me. I'll look at it.

AG: Hold on. I'll get it.

GP: The one I really like is the one where you've got the photograph?

AG: "May Days."

GP: And then you've got all that detail about the apartment. There's great concentration of imagery, the minute particulars.

AG: Yeah, that's a good one. That was translated, incidentally, into Hebrew by Natan Zach, a Hebrew poet.

GP: Did you take the picture? May Days 1988 with the *New York Times* on the windowsill.

AG: The new book has similar stuff, a thing called "Charnel Ground," which is going out the window and looking around at the neighborhood. Anyway, there's a poem called "Autumn Leaves."

GP: It's also in *Cosmopolitan Greetings*?

AG: "Autumn Leaves."

GP: All right. How does one face death? You've written poems about death.

AG: Every poet does. Shelley did when he was twenty-seven. Keats did when he was twenty-four.

GP: Does poetry help?

AG: Yes. I think poetry helps because you imagine your death, and you begin to blueprint and plan and realize mortality and then after a while you become consciously aware of the fact that mortality is limited and then you begin to appreciate living more. As well as appreciate the great adventure of dying and then realize that it is part of the vast process and an occasion for lamentation and rejoicing and everything. The whole thing comes together. It's the great subject. Because, you know, without death there's no life. Without life there's no death.

GP: So, sort of like death is the mother of beauty.

AG: I think in "Kaddish" I said death is the mother of the universe.

GP: What about love?

AG: Well, what about it?

GP: That's not as big? Okay.

AG: I think above death and above love, I would say, in a poem I did say, awareness encompasses love, death, and everything.

GP: Awareness of mortality?

AG: No. Awareness itself. Conscious awareness. It leads to, encompasses compassion, love, and awareness of death.

GP: What has poetry taught you about language, words?

AG: I don't know. What have words taught me about poetry? You could say that's the same thing.

GP: Well, how about it?

AG: It taught me not to bullshit. It taught me not to indulge in abstract language which is undefined, but to try and nail down any generalization with a "for instance." You know, like "give me a for instance." So it taught me that. "No ideas but in things," as Williams says. Or "The natural object is always the adequate symbol," says Pound. And again, I'll repeat, as Trungpa said, "Things are symbols of themselves."

GP: Okay. I like that.

AG: That's a great one.

GP: I believe in all that. It's just that it's all being challenged today.

AG: By whom?

GP: The Language poets.

AG: Well, they're saying that language is language. A word is a word.

GP: But it doesn't symbolize anything. It's just a nonsense sound.

AG: No, they're saying that it actually—there are conditions. Their angle on symbolization is something different, that the conditioning, the social conditioning is built into the use of the word. That the social conditioning outweighs the visual or the auditory meaning.

GP: Well, they deconstruct or break down all the syntax and the meaning and you end up with nothing but sound.

AG: But the purpose of the deconstruction was to break down the social conditioning associated with the sounds.

GP: Right. And then you end up breaking down poetry, I think, as well.

AG: Ah, I wouldn't worry about poetry. Poetry can take it. And sometimes it's interesting, like Burroughs's cut-up aspect was very interesting. A deconditioning to conditioned language. A whole way of inventing new, interesting phrases like "wind hand caught in the door" which is a by-product of Burroughs's cut-ups. "Wind hand caught in the door."

GP: Your poetry always makes sense to me. I mean you don't seem to try to distort—

AG: Well, I try, and you know, I'm out of Williams. I come from the Williams lineage and Kerouac. Kerouac wrote spontaneously and wrote nonsense, but there was always this basic theme. Burroughs cut up his stuff, but there was always this basic theme. No matter how you cut it up, it's still Burroughs talking about authoritarian hypnosis from the state.

GP: And you can always see that.

AG: Yeah. It comes through no matter how you cut up his works.

GP: Because when I read these Language poets, it's more like Gertrude Stein. I don't know what they're talking about.

AG: Stein is interesting in her own way, you know what I mean? Have you ever heard her record?

GP: No.

AG: There's a Caedmon record of Stein and if you hear her once you really get the idea what she was after. Williams told me that she had one specific simple thing and it was really great and you know, if you get that then you get something. An inimitable voice. Speaking voice. A Yiddish voice, too.

GP: A Yiddish voice. Not Stein! What place do you most identify with, in other words, what physical location, like Jersey or—

AG: Living Lower East Side, probably.

GP: Have you lived there much of your life, even though you've traveled all over the world?

AG: Well, I've had this one apartment where I am now for twenty-one years.

GP: I didn't know that.

AG: And then before that I had—see, my mother, when she came to America, moved to about a mile from here on Orchard and Rivington. That was her first place of residence. Then they moved to Newark. So Orchard-Rivington is about a mile from where I am now.

GP: So it's really your roots.

AG: So I'm really back where my mother's family—my father's family came to New York and then Newark. But before I lived here, I moved here in '75, I lived for five years or so on East Tenth Street, a couple blocks away. And before that on East Second Street in the sixties. And in the fifties, where I took all those photographs, early photographs of Burroughs and Kerouac, that's East Seventh Street.

GP: You wrote a powerful poem about being mugged. It must have been down in one of those neighborhoods.

AG: That was in 1972 on Tenth Street, when I was living there. Two blocks from here.

GP: And where are you now?

AG: East Twelfth Street.

GP: In the Village?

AG: East Village. Lower East Side.

GP: If you could do it again, what would you do differently, if anything?

AG: There's a certain guy I was in love with when I was young who invited me to bed and I was too shy, because I was in the closet. And I've always regretted it. And I wrote a poem about it. I wrote about it in Sapphic verse. In *Mindbreaths,* something like that. One of the books. It's in my *Collected Poems*— 1978 or so.

GP: Helen Vendler, sort of surprisingly to me, wrote very warmly of you, I think, in her anthology.

AG: Yeah, I was surprised.

GP: Right, I was surprised.

AG: She likes me and Snyder and she has no reaction at all to Creeley or Corso or Kerouac's poetry or anyone else.

GP: Maybe it was another critic I was reading, and she talks about what must have been the great difficulty for you, especially as a young Jewish man being gay. I thought that was a sensitive remark.

AG: I didn't think it was that difficult, you know? I was in the closet until I was about seventeen. But then I had such nice company, with Kerouac and Burroughs, who were themselves so far out, and Burroughs was gay. Kerouac was very straight, but none the less—

GP: He wasn't gay or bisexual?

AG: I wouldn't say so.

GP: What about Neal Cassady, whom you're always writing about?

AG: Cassady was a lady's man, but he was sort of pansexual. I made out with him, but I was one of the few people he made out with. Maybe he hustled as a younger kid, as a young orphan.

GP: In a sense, you always had a family.

AG: Yeah. I had my regular family. I was pretty close. And also an alternative family.

GP: What is the most amazing thing about life?

AG: Oh, the fact that it's here at all, and that it disappears.

GP: What's the most amazing thing about your life?

AG: I'm pretty dumb, quite stupid, in a way. Even backward. I don't know how I got where I am now, to be like a kind of great poet of some kind. And I don't understand how it happened.

GP: Well, from what you told me at the beginning, it had to do with breath.

AG: Breath, but also the other quality was because I ran into Kerouac and Burroughs when I was sixteen and seventeen. I suddenly realized how provincial and dumb I was, and I resolved, rather than asserting myself constantly and arguing and being argumentative, which would have been my normal nature, I should shut up and listen and learn something. So I always took a kind of back seat and listened to my elders. I always had teachers and gurus, you know, from the very beginning. So actually I learned a lot from other people and had the quality of attention, to listen to Burroughs and serve him, in a way. You know, like work with him and be his amanuensis or his agent or work with him and encourage him and listen to him and do what I could to make his life workable, and I learned a lot that way. And I have relations, had relations like that with Chogyam Trungpa, the Tibetan lama, and with Gelek Rinpoche right now, since Trungpa died, a Tibetan lama. And so I've always had teachers and I've always listened to them. And I think that's really delivered me to some kind of workable, practical self-confidence.

GP: But you wrote "Howl," no one else did. I think that's what made you famous.

AG: Yeah, but you know, I was trying to imitate Kerouac.

GP: That's interesting.

AG: I was a student of Kerouac's, Kerouac broke ground, and I moved in on that territory. And he said, "You guys," me and Gary Snyder, "you guys call yourself poets. I'm a poet, too, except that my verse line is longer than yours. I write verses that are two pages long!" Like the opening sentences in *The Subterraneans*. Which are beautiful, poetic sentences, you know.

GP: He was the key influence, then.

AG: Yeah. I would say him and Burroughs. He was the key vocal influence, or verbal, and Burroughs the key intellectual.

GP: And then, of course, as everyone's written about, also Blake and Pound and Whitman and Williams.

AG: Well, I had a good education, I had a regular Columbia education, but I also had the advantage of an education through Kerouac and Burroughs and the books they suggested, but also through my father, who was very well cultivated in poetry.

GP: And wrote in a very, very traditional lyric style.

AG: Yeah, well, you know, he would stomp around the house, not stomp, walk around the house reciting Milton and Shakespeare and Poe, "The Bells," "The Raven," "Annabel Lee." I memorized those when I was a kid. When I was eight years old I could recite a lot of "The Bells."

GP: Your parents are in the poem "Kaddish," which to me is probably the most powerful one. Did Naomi actually speak about the key in the window?

AG: Yes, she did speak. No. After she died, a day or so after I got a telegram saying she was dead, I got a letter from her that had been posted just before she died of a stroke. And I'm quoting that letter, yeah.

GP: And then that wonderful talk in there, that Yiddish talk, where she's talking about soup. That's pretty much what she sounded like?

AG: She likes lentil soup. That's literal. Now that I look back, I said, how come she said that? How come I didn't ask her what she meant? That I wasn't more persistent. It was so vivid but I was a little shy of pursuing the subject. For fear that she was completely nuts rather than discovering that she had a good sense of humor.

GP: You put more of the personal into that poem than just about anyone I can think of. I mean of that kind of material. And your father comes off, to me, as a very sad man.

AG: In that poem.

GP: But he wasn't that sad?

AG: Then, but a little later on he and I read a lot together and we got closer and closer. We went to Europe together, and he blessed me on his deathbed and I blessed him.

GP: He remarried, I gather, at some point.

AG: He remarried a very nice woman who was a very good influence on him, and brought us together quite well, and just had her ninetieth birthday this week.

GP: A Jewish woman?

AG: Yeah, yeah, Edith Ginsberg. She just survived, at the age of eighty-nine, two valve transplants. A pig valve and a sheep valve, so she says, joking, she's no longer kosher.

GP: Let me ask you one—

AG: I don't know if you know this, about a little film, *The Life and Times of Allen Ginsberg*?

GP: I saw it.

AG: She's in there. Very nice.

GP: I'd have to see it again. I saw it in Yellow Springs, Ohio. Have you ever been to Yellow Springs, Antioch College?

AG: Yeah, sure. Long ago, though.

GP: I saw it there. It was too short, almost.

AG: Well, enough for me. But mainly family-oriented, in a way.

GP: How do you see your place in American poetry?

AG: Well, I have a poem called "Ego Confessions," which is sort of like a grandiose vision. Take a look at that. Because I want to be known as the most intelligent man in America. Worst-case scenario of megalomania. But the whole point of poetry is not to be afraid of worst-case neurosis, but to reveal it, go right into the wind rather than being afraid of admitting it.

GP: Well, you certainly showed us that.

AG: So I'd like to be remembered as someone who advanced, actually advanced the notion of compassion in open-heart, open-form poetry, continuing the tradition of Whitman and Williams. And part of the honorific aspect of the whole Beat Generation.

GP: You seem to have accomplished a lot of that.

AG: Well, not really, because you know my major poems that we're talking about are banned from the air, from radio and television now, with a law suggested by Jesse Helms. He directed the FCC to ban all so-called indecent language off the air, I think it's between 6 A.M. and 10 P.M. And the Supreme Court just affirmed that by refusing to hear our appeal. And that's just been extended to Internet. So it may be that the text of "Howl" or "Please Master" or "Kaddish" or "Sunflower Sutra" will be soon inadmissible on Internet because of foul language that might offend the ears of minors. So the right wing is reimposing the same kind of censorship on the electronic media that we overthrew in the written, printed media, '58 to '62.

GP: That was the famous Berkeley trial?

AG: Yeah. Well, that, and also the trials of Henry Miller, D. H. Lawrence, Jean Genet, up to *Naked Lunch* in 1962, which liberated literature.

GP: So we're back there.

AG: No, on a more grand, international scale, we're back with censorship in the electronic world, but not in the written book world.

GP: Are we at the end of the long journey of poetry, then?

AG: What do you mean?

GP: I mean—let's put it this way. What can a late-twentieth-century poet, given what you've just told me about Jesse Helms and all that, what can a late-twentieth-century poet hope to accomplish?

AG: Oh, the poetry doesn't depend on electronic media. You could pull all those plugs and it wouldn't affect poetry. Or plug them all in. Poetry is an individual thing that gets around by word of mouth. It's an oral tradition, as well as a written, printed tradition, as well as a spoken tradition. So it'll get around. Anything really good will get around.

GP: You have that faith.

AG: Well, it's experience. I mean, when "Howl" was on trial, I didn't care one way or the other. Well, I mean, I cared, but I realized if I lose the trial, I'll be a big hero and everybody will want to read my book. If I win, I'll be a big hero and everybody will want to read my book. All the police did was do me a big favor by publicizing my poetry. They always do that. They're so dumb. Like, do you think Mapplethorpe would be so famous if it weren't for Jesse Helms trying to quash him or something? It's amazing!

GP: Well, they made you famous.

AG: They made Mapplethorpe famous. They're going to make Michelangelo famous when they start censoring his statues of Bacchus or the Slaves. They're already censoring his *David.*

GP: Oh, you're kidding me.

AG: Yeah, you can't put that on the Internet, because it's got a big dick that minors might see. Frontal nudity. (*Laughter.*) So they just make people more conscious of the censorship and of the restrictions and of the mentality and mindset and then they'll cause a counterreaction.

GP: One base we haven't touched: How has Buddhism helped you?

AG: Oh, it's made me more aware of the fact that everything can be done 'twixt earnest and joke. Things are completely real and simultaneously and without any contradiction, they are also completely empty and unreal. Just like a dream.

GP: Both?

AG: Both at once. Without contradiction, i.e., a dream is real while you're dreaming but then when you wake up it vanishes. There's no inherent permanence. Life is real while you're alive, but then when you die, it vanishes. It has no inherent permanence. So it's like—so it's real, but it also simultaneously has that aspect. One aspect is the reality, the other aspect is the transitoriness or mutability, as Shelley said.

GP: And you see both?

AG: Well, everybody sees both. So it's the ability to see both simultaneously that gives life it's sort of charisma and glamour and workability. You're never stuck. There's no permanent hell. There's no permanent heaven.

GP: So that liberates you.

AG: Sure! It liberates you from the nightmare of thinking, "Oh, god, I'm stuck, I'm gonna die, blah, blah, blah."

GP: You're not afraid.

AG: What's there to be afraid of? It's like being in a dream and realizing it's a dream, so then you're not afraid anymore.

GP: And where do you end up? In the dream, just an extension of the dream?

AG: Well, you end up waking up somewhere else. I guess. Or maybe you don't wake up. Maybe you just go to sleep and that's the end of it.

GP: Maybe that wouldn't be so bad.

AG: Well, have you ever been in a dentist's chair with nitrous oxide?

GP: Yeah.

AG: Have you ever been put out? Okay, so what's the last thing you hear? Or what's the last sense that disappears? To me, it was sound. The music, the Muzak. So what if the last thing to go is the end of the symphony? Like, the pain is gone, physical feeling is gone, sight is gone, taste is gone, smell is gone, the only thing left is sound. The sound is the music, then you hear the last note of the symphony and—

GP: Well, that's a nice one. But then there's all the folks during the Holocaust who were butchered every second by the Nazis.

AG: Yeah, but on the other hand, the last thing they heard was the sound of a scream and then the scream ended. And then there was nice, peaceful—

GP: Let's hope.

AG: Well, unless they were reborn. Do you think they went to hell or something?

GP: I don't believe that.

AG: They wouldn't have gone to hell. Do you think they went to heaven?

GP: I don't think so.

AG: I don't think there's a heaven. So therefore where did they go? They certainly went to a peaceful place.

GP: I hope so.

AG: Well, where else?

GP: I think you're right!

AG: Can you imagine anywhere else? Can you even imagine someplace that wasn't peaceful?

GP: I'm Jewish. I'll have to go with that.

AG: The Sheol, or maybe Sheol.

GP: Sheol. Okay.

AG: The Buddhists might give the worst case, that they get reborn to go through it all over again. Reborn as Nazis. Reborn in Israel and persecuting the Palestinians.

GP: That would be hell.

AG: Okay. I gotta stop.

PHILIP LEVINE

PHILIP LEVINE was born in 1928 in Detroit and was edu-
cated at public schools and at Wayne State University. After
working at many industrial jobs, he left the city and lived in
various places before settling in Fresno, California, where he
taught at the Fresno State University until his recent retirement.
He has received many awards for his books of poems, most re-
cently the National Book Award in 1991, for *What Work Is,* and
the 1995 Pulitzer Prize for *The Simple Truth. The Mercy* is
Levine's seventeenth volume of poetry. He was recently inaugu-
rated into the American Academy of Arts and Letters. Besides
his *Selected Poems* (1984) and *New Selected Poems* (1991), he has
also published a book of essays, *The Bread of Time* (1994), and a
book of interviews, *Don't Ask* (1981).

PHILIP LEVINE writes about his world with visionary intensity. In his most
memorable poems, he transforms realistic details into imaginative visions.

Born and raised in Detroit, Levine uses this grimy, seething, racially trou-
bled industrial city as the setting for many of his poems. While in Detroit, he
worked in factories, and he has never forgotten the workers: "These were the
men and women I met as an industrial worker and bum in America; they were
mainly Southerners . . . and they were closer, I believe, to some great truths
about people, to the truth that we are the children of God, and that we were
meant to come into this world and live as best we could with the beasts and the
trees and plants and to leave the place with our love and respect for it intact"
(quoted in *Contemporary Poets,* ed. James Vinson, 3d ed. [New York: St. Mar-
tin's Press, 1980], p. 910).

Although Levine is from the city and writes extensively of urban life, he is
also attracted to nature and to rural people. In both city and country, he finds
suffering and oppression but also grounds for belief in the courage and en-
durance of the human spirit. "They Feed They Lion," one of Levine's most
powerful poems, was inspired by the poet's empathy for the workers' dignity,
courage, and honor. Symbolizing the modern industrial world's horror and
beauty and the poet's rage at the terrifying energy of tyranny that devours

human hopes and aspirations through exploitation and prejudice, the poem's images merge in a mysterious revelation.

While living in Detroit, the poet encountered racism and anti-Semitism, and he became angry and afraid. Over the years, Levine has come to believe that nations and governments are responsible for the violent oppression that has plagued the Jews and other minority peoples throughout the world. The poet has long been interested in Spanish anarchism and its leaders previous to and during the Spanish Civil War. Many of Levine's poems are in honor of these men and women and their cause.

The one continuous element in the poet's work deriving from his Jewish heritage is his concern with tyranny and suffering. In "Baby Villon," the narrator describes meeting the tiny ex–prize fighter Baby Villon, who speaks of himself as a ubiquitous but plucky victim:

> He tells me in Bangkok he's robbed
> Because he's white; in London because he's black;
> In Barcelona, Jew; in Paris, Arab:
> Everywhere and at all times, and he fights back.

This tiny man of pain and courage epitomizes much of the humanity that underlies Levine's art. He may be a victim of prejudice and tyranny but he is prepared to defend himself.

"Uncle" celebrates a man who combines the earthy sensibilities and skills of the workers with aspects of Jewish religious tradition:

> Prophet of burned cars
> and broken fans, he taught
> the toilet the eternal,
> argued the Talmud
> under his nails.

In our interview, Levine stated that his uncle and his grandfather were "the real Jews." Like Baby Villon, they were tough, self-reliant, proud Jews who were not afraid to fight against discrimination.

In several of his best poems of recent years, Levine merges the spiritual faith of the Jewish people and the secular faith of the anarchists. In both systems of belief there is prophetic rage at suffering and injustice and affirmation of human freedom and oneness. In his poem based on a drawing of the rabbi of Auschwitz by Flavio Constantini, the poet recalls the horrifying specter of suffering and death. The only solace is the courage and dedication of individual people and their link to others. When the poet looks at the rabbi, he sees that the rabbi's face resembles his own.

THE INTERVIEW took place on Thursday, March 20, 1996, in Philip Levine's Greenwich Village apartment. Levine is a tall, slender, wiry man with curly hair and dark eyes with a blue tinge. When he speaks in his gravelly voice, his right eye sometimes closes (like Popeye). He gives the impression of great intensity and energy contained by stoic reserve. He had asked not to see the questions before the interview.

GP: What have you found the hardest thing about being a poet?

PL: I think the hardest thing is easily the constant need every morning to take myself away from everything except myself, go into a room—if I happen to be living where there's a room where I can do this—shut the door and sit patiently hoping something will happen. And as you know, usually nothing happens, but if you're not there for sure nothing's going to happen. So it takes a great deal of staying power to do that consistently as I have for fifty years, actually more than fifty now. That is the hardest thing.

GP: Okay, let's turn it around. What's the most enjoyable thing?

PL: Well, the most enjoyable thing occurs on those days it happens, and you've been sitting there saying to yourself, what am I doing? I could be doing something useful like picking onions or talking to one of my friends or taking a walk with my wife. And then suddenly my mind is invaded with words or images or ideas, usually words and images, and the words start falling into a rhythmic pattern, and I start to follow them and something unexpected happens. And oftentimes it requires hours and hours to get it as close to right as I am capable of getting it, and sometimes it happens quite miraculously. An hour passes, and I look down and there's "They Feed They Lion," which I don't think took me more than an hour. Three or four or five years ago I sold my papers to the Berg Room here in the New York Public Library. I was going through a lot of things, and I came across the original manuscript of "They Feed They Lion." And it was incredible how right from the first draft I seemed to know what I was doing. Somewhere between the third and the fourth stanza, I went off into a direction I didn't like for six or eight lines, crossed them out, found my way back to what I wanted, and then wrote the rest of the poem. I also found the original manuscript to the poem "What Work Is," and this involved practically the same thing. I'd written a few lines at the top of the page that really had to do with my feelings about Detroit that day, which were boiling in me, because I'd just seen a horrible program on public broadcasting the night before about two guys, a father and son, who killed a young Chinese man in Detroit. They thought he was Japanese, and they had this animosity to-wards him because they were blaming the Japanese for the decline in the auto industry or the decline in their jobs or whatever marginal relationship they had with the auto industry. And they beat the guy to death. And there was this immense anger in me. I had completely forgotten what the poem came out of. But I had written at the top of the page, "Detroit is shit." And then I went off on this wholly different tangent. I had a very specific memory of waiting for a particular job and racism never entered into it, although that was what was in my mind when I sat down. I just went off on a memory of waiting in the rain and not getting the job finally because of my own impatience. So those are the glorious moments, and in both cases I knew I had a good poem. I knew this is about as good as I can write at that particular time, so I said, "Wow!"

GP: Ginsberg hated it when I used the word *inspiration*. Is it fair to say you were inspired when you wrote those poems?

PL: I was all there. I don't know why Allen would object to the word *inspiration*. Maybe because it's connected with some kind of voodoo that has to do with very romantic notions of how poetry comes to be. But I think anybody who spends as much time writing poetry as he has or I have is aware of the fact that you're not the same every day of the week or every week of your life, and that there are some days when you're stupid and what occurs to you is trite and what you write is what you've already written, and there are other days when you have breakthroughs and something happens. Whether you apply the word *inspiration* or not, it frankly doesn't bother me in the least. I don't believe in the Muse. I have never sat down and prayed to some power outside of myself to come visit me and bless me with language, because I think the power is re-ally within me. And I think there are special days when I seem very much in command of my memories, of all the words I know. Your best poems are really smarter than you are, and they certainly have a vision that you can rarely claim. They seem less distressed by the trivial than I myself am oftentimes. I think my best poems present a "me" that's really an individual superior to me: calm in the face of dreadful things, wise beyond my years, et cetera. So if that's not being inspired, I don't know what it is.

GP: A lot of that must come from the unconscious, but what about another subject that lots of people are really obsessed by: craft, which to me has to do with conscious, controllable things. When I say craft, I think oftentimes the first thing that comes to mind is traditional craft: meter and rhyme. What about the element of craft in the process that you've been describing? Is it all free and organic? I know you've written some formal poetry, but in the two marvelous poems that you've mentioned, I don't detect that. Should a young poet be trained to know about the traditional craft or not? Did that kind of conscious craft enter into those marvelous moments when you wrote those two poems?

PL: Well, yes and no. That is, I have every assurance that I wouldn't write the way I do if I hadn't spent a number of years, maybe ten or more, working with traditional forms, trying to master them. When I started writing, the poets that I admired the most—Hart Crane, Hardy, Dylan Thomas, W. B. Yeats, Emily Dickinson, Robert Frost—were all poets who worked in traditional meters. And I loved the way they sounded, and I loved the effects they got, and I worked very hard to acquaint myself with the tradition that they came out of, which gave them this strength that I didn't have. In so doing I went back as far as Chaucer. I remember when I first got married, I lived in a small mountain town in North Carolina—Boone, North Carolina—forty-three years ago this summer. One of the lovely things that I found in the local public library was an uncut version of the history of English prosody by George Saintsbury, a man whose opinions I didn't necessarily share. It was a wonderful collection. I was much more interested in the poems themselves than the comments he made about them. And I studied it and studied it. I didn't have many books with me. I was reading Williams at the time too.

I would have to say that the students who don't acquaint themselves with the craft are the losers. When I was younger, I'd force them. Then at a certain point in the sixties, two things happened. One is if you forced them in the sixties, they called you a pig or a cop. Who needed that? The other thing was it took energy; it took my own energy. By this time I'm in my forties. I'm losing the energy. If they don't want to do it, they don't have to do it. Let them do what they want. The best students I ever had, people like Larry Levis, David St. John, Greg Pape, Roberta Spear, Sherley Williams, they did the work. They did what was necessary. I didn't have to push them too hard. All I had to do was make suggestions. To David St. John: I think you'd really like Philip Larkin. There's something in the way he expresses himself that you would find useful. To a guy like Larry Levis, who was already mad for Hart Crane, well, why don't you get an antidote to Crane? How about Hardy, a much tougher and firmer poet? To Greg Pape I said, you know, you need lyricism: Yeats. One of these poets is going to lead you to other poets. They'll lead you back to their origins, and finally you're going to wind up with Chaucer and then come all the way back again. I think these are tools.

I remember back in the sixties I had a lot of friends in the art department back at Fresno State. What was their answer to the question "What do you need for art?" You need a canvas; you need paint; you need inspiration. How about the ability to draw? Well, come on, we're not in the nineteenth century anymore. I think they were shortchanging their students, frankly. I just went to a show yesterday with my wife to see Bonnard and Rothko. It struck me looking at the two together [that] Bonnard was a far more daring painter than Rothko. They used the same palette and that's what the show brought out. But Bonnard's paintings were both more daring and more accomplished. I found them much more interesting. Rothko's art for that kind of painting is terrific, but if I could have one in my house, I'd take a Bonnard. These little seascapes that were maybe a foot wide and eight inches high: I would have taken one instead of a massive Rothko. I could look at them day after day after day, and they weren't the best of the Bonnards. The students may put up their hands and say, we don't want this corny shit. But I don't think you're there to just make the students happy. You're there to try to make them better poets. Here at NYU I asked them the first night, Why are you here? I asked each student, and several of them answered, I want to become the best poet I can become. Once one of them says it they all say it. Then I say, okay, that means a lot of reading on your part, even memorizing, and I make them memorize poems. And one of the things they discover, of course, is that it's much easier to memorize rhyming, metrical poems. They help you memorize. So then pretty soon they're into rhymed poetry. It's Emily Dickinson, it's Frost, it's Hart Crane— these are the people they're memorizing—Dylan Thomas. Very few of them memorize Whitman or William Carlos Williams.

GP: What is free verse and can it be taught? Are there methods for teaching it?

PL: I think there are methods for teaching it, but I haven't found them. I rarely write free verse. Most of my stuff has a kind of guiding pattern to it. I remember being on a radio program in Berkeley, and this guy opened the book *What Work Is,* and he said, tell me, why isn't this prose just cut up into lines that you figured were convenient? I said, well, for openers prose doesn't rhyme. He said, rhyme? I said, yeah, that poem you're pointing at is rhymed. He looked down the right-hand margin of the page and he realized it was. He said, I didn't hear any of the rhyme. I said, I couldn't care less whether or not you heard it, but I put it in there. Some portion of you probably was more aware of it than you may think.

I said, count the syllables. He counted them. Every line's got the same number of syllables. I said, there are a couple of exceptions but by and large that's right, and the end-stop positions are with a few exceptions places where I'd want you to rest for a moment. Twice in the poem I end a line with an adjective, but I'm really doing that on purpose. I'm trying to gain some kind of speed to get you into that next line faster because I want the emphasis of that speed to get you to arrive at that noun that I think is crucial.

I said, I've thought about what I'm doing here. It's not prose; it's verse; let's call it free verse, but it's not that free. It's governed by a syllable count and it's governed in this case by rhyme, which I don't always use, but which I use when I feel like using it. I wanted that lyrical effect at that moment. Now that's a poem that's maybe eight years old. I was working on a poem yesterday. It had a very rigid syllable count. I think I varied one line. I always vary one line just to be ornery or something, but I don't expect the reader to hear this. I don't think people really hear syllables. They do hear the clusters of stresses. From line to line I'm managing the stress pattern differently, so that on certain occasions where I really want a lot of attention to a line—I was using an eleven-syllable line—I might have seven stresses in that line, as many as seven stressed syllables. I'm working really with patterns of iambs and trochees.

I think the great masters of free verse—Stevens and Williams, the greatest in American poetry, and D. H. Lawrence, the greatest in British poetry—all wrote in traditional meters. Williams not very well but Stevens and Lawrence exquisitely. I think their ears were tuned very sharply to the language. Roethke is another one who's in a class with them as a versifier. He may not be as great as Williams or Stevens or Lawrence but God knows just the verse itself is absolutely stunning and intensely musical free verse. Yeah, it's free verse. It doesn't have a predictable governance. You can't go to a particular line and say line eleven is going to be a variation on iambics. Well, I'm sure that someone could say it is, but it's not as predictable as a sonnet by Shakespeare. Everything in the poem is iambic pentameter or a variation on iambic pentameter. Not so with Roethke. It's not that predictable. Is it any less musical? Well, it's not any more. You can't be any more musical than Shakespeare. It's a standard for us all, but Roethke's pretty extraordinary. So I'm pushing my students to stuff like that, saying, all right, you want to see what free verse can do. It doesn't sound like prose; read it; study it; steal from it. Learn your craft.

GP: You've written of the influence and example of your teachers. I'm thinking of John Berryman and Yvor Winters. What did they teach you, and what can a teacher bring to the teaching of writing and reading poetry?

PL: Well, it's interesting because they were very different types, and one of them was a flop as a teacher. I think Yvor Winters was good for me in spite of how bad a teacher he was. He was good for me because I wasn't a kid anymore. I turned thirty during the year I worked with him. I was not particularly upset when he didn't like what I wrote. I didn't like a good deal of what he praised and liked himself, so it didn't really matter. I was there on a grant. I was happy not to be working. He helped me a lot with nineteenth-century French poetry and Elizabethan and post-Elizabethan poetry. He knew that stuff incredibly well—and early American poetry.

As a teacher of creative writing he was fickle, and I think essentially dictatorial, and though he said he wanted independence in his students, the ones that he praised the loudest were the ones who wrote the most like him. Thom Gunn made a remark that all of his best students finally wound up writing poems he would have despised. I don't know if Thom put it exactly that way, but he said something like that. And I think Thom's right. The people who were his best poets, Thom, for example, finally wound up writing poems that I think he wouldn't care for. But he was a standard; he was there; and he was constant. When you had a problem and you wanted to work on it and you needed some help, say, with a nineteenth-century poet, he'd spend a lot of time with you. Time was no option, no problem with him.

Berryman was a guy who didn't want you writing like him. He considered himself, and rightly so, as a rather eccentric poet, and he urged me away from that kind of eccentricity in other poets. He saw I could be eccentric enough without imitating John Berryman. I was not tempted to imitate him anyway. Of the two it's clear that Berryman is now obviously the better poet. He's just far more interesting. There's far more variety, energy, life, emotion in his work than in Winters's. But the thing about Berryman was he was alive to such a great range of poetry, such a variety of poetry, whereas Winters's vision was very limited by his theories. He wanted answers to all questions, and he had them to his own satisfaction. John saw that life was a lot more mysterious than that and in that sense he was a much better teacher. He was also fun in class, whereas Winters could not only put you to sleep, he could put himself to sleep.

GP: In the poem "Coming Home, Detroit, 1968," you say at the end, "We burn this city every day." You show Detroit as a modern inferno. How long did you live in Detroit and how did your poetry grow in such a place?

PL: I was very lucky. My father had died when I was five, but he had been a great reader and he got my mom reading. So there were books that I turned to even as a young guy, and I lived near a branch library. I was over there all the time. I loved to read. I just loved immersing myself in lives other than my own, which seemed pretty dull by comparison. And so my early poems were composed when I was thirteen or fourteen years old. Then I put poetry aside for a while. I think I discovered girls or something. I don't remember the exact reason I stopped, but then I started again. At about age seventeen I discovered Wilfred Owen. World War II was still going, and I suddenly realized that the kind of emotions I had about the war I shared with this poet Wilfred Owen. He was writing in 1916 or '17, even '18, and this was 1944–45, but I saw there was a kind of universality here and his poems were a great help to me. They showed me I wasn't nuts. That you would go out and kill somebody in the name of the state or be killed by them: *That* was nuts, and nothing was more obvious once you read Owen. All that propaganda that might get you to do it was just that, bullshit.

GP: The workers of Detroit whom you met in the factories are at the center of "They Feed They Lion" and a lot of your other important poems. You write of their suffering, their poverty, earthiness, and heroism. And I think you even say you take at least some of your vision from them. Were they your friends?

PL: Oh yeah. I got very close to a lot of them. I spent weekends with them, took the women out, tried romance and what have you. The men became my friends; the women became my friends; not always romantic, just friendships. Yeah, I got close to them and realized that their lives weren't that different from my own. They found out, for example, after I'd finished college, I worked another four years in Detroit. I didn't leave until I was about twenty-six. They said, What do you want to be, Phil? Well, I'd like to be a poet. Ain't that some shit. You want to be like Edgar Allen Poe? They knew Edgar Allen Poe but that was about it. They had a very good-natured attitude toward me. You graduated from Wayne? Yeah, I graduated from Wayne. And you're working here on the night shift with me. Well, I never went to college. I guess I wasn't so dumb after all. You wasted four years and you're here with me. We're both making $1.85 an hour. College wasn't that good for you, was it? I don't know what they thought about my poetry. They never saw it; they never even asked to see it. I don't think they gave a damn. They didn't seem to think it was nuts that I was doing it, or if they did, they kept it to themselves. I guess they weren't doing anything any more noble in their own eyes. It didn't interfere with our friendships.

GP: When you wrote "A Walk with Tom Jefferson" did you return to Detroit to do research for that poem? It's so detailed; you have so much real stuff in the poem. Or did you write largely from memory and imagination? Did you do research on your poem?

PL: Well, in one sense I did research. I had no notion that I was going to write that poem. I went back to Wayne for the retirement party of one of my old teachers. Wayne wasn't paying me. Wayne was just going to pay my airfare; I was living in Boston at the time. I said, yeah, I would do it; I liked the guy a lot. When I got to the Detroit airport, I expected someone to meet me—here I was giving them a day. Well, nobody did meet me there. A woman from Northwest Airlines handed me an envelope, and somebody at Wayne had sent instructions as to how to take the bus into Detroit and so on. It turned out that it was a great stroke of fortune. It pissed me off, and I said to myself, I think if this is how they're going to treat me, I'm going to torture them. What I'm going to do is show up for this guy's retirement party one minute before I'm due. They said at 3:30 or something in the afternoon we want you to read poetry. I said, I'll show up at 3:29. I'll stick it to them. I'd gotten there at about 10 in the morning. So I went into these old neighborhoods that I knew well and spent hours walking around talking to people. I didn't have anything in mind. I got back to Boston and a great deal of that imagery really stuck in my head. I keep a journal, so I put a lot of details in my journal that night when I got home. And three or four weeks later I started writing this poem. Now Tom was really an amalgam of several people that I knew from childhood. I shouldn't say childhood—young manhood. I had met a guy who reminded me of a guy I knew very well, so there wasn't any single character that was Tom. He was a fiction who was made up out of fragments of different people. And, of course, that wasn't his name, but he could be a descendant of Jefferson. So in a way there was research but it wasn't intentional. It was a poem that took me a long time to write. I wrote the first draft of it in two days. It was nine hundred lines long. I cut it to about three hundred and twenty and then stalled. About a year and a half later I got an idea, and in one day I finished the poem.

GP: Would you have found your way to anarchism without going to Spain?

PL: Yes, one of the reasons I went to Spain was to learn more about it.

GP: So you knew about it before. How did you come into contact with anarchism, then: the idea of anarchism or the historical phenomenon of anarchism?

PL: Well, partly through a guy who figures in one of my poems, Cypriano Mera. That wasn't his real name. I got to anarchism through him and then through reading and through meeting people. There are anarchists all over the place, and I met them. I met guys who were in the Wobblies, International Workers of the World; they were out West when I went out West originally. They were old guys then. There used to be an anarchist press not far from here. I forget the name of it. It was in Union Square. I used to go up there and talk to the guy who ran it. Anarchists love to argue. I remember one time there were these two much older guys who I think had been to Spain in the civil war; they didn't want to talk about it. But they got into a terrible argument about what happened with some anarchist movement back God knows when. And they were brothers, and of course they argued like mad. And I thought, God, they can't agree on anything. Little wonder anarchism is not advancing. Here are these two guys who share a common faith and a vision. They're brothers and all they can do is argue with each other. It was a gas.

GP: You've said somewhere, "I don't believe in the validity of governments, laws, charters, all that hide our central oneness." How did you develop the faith of anarchism?

PL: I don't know how I developed it, frankly. It just seemed like the only answer, especially in a nation like our own in which politics is so immensely corrupted and in which the state and business have merged into one greedy conglomerate. I grew up in a world in which our central oneness was the last thing you were supposed to recognize. I grew up in a world in which Henry Ford, for example, was spending a lot of money to let the world know about the "Protocols of Zion," so people would hate Jews and also to pit white people against black people for the same jobs, so he could intensify racism and use that. I grew up in a world in which it was clear to me that Blake was a visionary and had seen all of these dangers, and for me Blake was a great anarchist poet. But I don't know how I got to the point where I felt it almost with a religious fervor, which I do not anymore, because it now seems to me impossible that it's going to be realized. But what the hell? You give yourself to a struggle; you don't expect to win anything in your own time.

GP: Phoebe Petingell believes that you "make the witness of the anarchist Ascaso a brilliant symbol for man's unquenchable spirit," but she also surmises that "the martyrs are merely aspects of Levine's death haunted imagination." She goes on to posit that for you "identifying with suffering is as much wholeness as we can hope to achieve." Do you think she's right?

PL: No, I think she's wrong. I don't agree with her there. I think we can achieve more, and I see the problem essentially as a celebration of an indomitable courage, a will to bring justice to a country, Spain, that had never known it. Essentially my poem is a tribute. What am I going to atone for in a poem like that? The crimes against Spain were not mine. I don't know anybody asking forgiveness for what has been done to Spain.

GP: Okay, you identify with the victim, the oppressed minority, in the poem "Baby Villon." Does this concern with oppression, exile, suffering come from your Jewishness, your sensitivity to anti-Semitism, and the whole Jewish tradition of social and political justice?

PL: Certainly in that poem it does. That is the driving force of that poem. Again it's a tribute to this guy, this little guy who will not be taken for less than a man, a full man. No matter how the world may try to define him, he will define himself as a man. They can call him whatever they want—Arab, Jew, whatever—but he fights. He's the despised; he is a North African Jew, a Sephardic North African Jew, and he's also a very small guy. He's just a little 118-pounder, but he's got the heart of a lion. He's like a mentor. If I had to describe him, it would be as a teacher; he's a spiritual teacher to me.

GP: You knew him?

PL: No, I made him up. I knew people like him. Again, he's an amalgam, and I didn't know anybody quite as remarkable as I think he is. I take it back. I did know people who were as remarkable as he was. I just put him in a very dramatic situation. I did find my French-Jewish family after World War II, actually in 1965. I had imagined what they would be like. Well, they weren't like that except that my cousin was about his size. He was about five feet tall, and he was a guy who had survived the Nazis by walking at night from Nîmes to the hills above Florence and living with the anti-Fascist guerrillas in Italy. He and his wife walked all that way and survived the war and came back to Nîmes. I wrote the poem before I found them. I knew he existed or had been eliminated by the war, and I had the good luck to locate him, and so in a way the poem is prescient. It's like predicting who he was. He wasn't a prizefighter but he had this indomitable, undefeatable spirit about him.

GP: In your poem "Lost in America," the narrator is surrounded by discrimination and violence but never mentions his Jewishness until he's been branded by another as a Jew. Has anti-Semitism been at the source of your identity as a Jew and in your identity as an anarchist?

PL: No, not really. I don't think so. I knew a lot of anti-Semites as a kid, and it certainly helped form me and did form me. It made me aggressive; it made me touchy; it taught me that I had to fight back or fight first. We had a motto back in Detroit: "We will not go quietly!" For a number of years I was a guy who got in a lot of fights when people opened their big mouths, and I won them. Most guys you fought were drunk, and I didn't have a booze problem. If you're sober and you're fighting a drunk, it's pretty easy to win. I could defend myself pretty well. Of course, I was reacting to the myth that as a Jew I was going to be this highly intellectual physical wreck, whom anybody could just demoralize with a few words and gestures. I remember even when I went out to the University of Iowa, I had trouble not with faculty but with students. I cleaned one guy's clock and that was the end of that. He was a guy who'd just gotten out of the army and thought he was very tough, and I took one look at him and knew he wasn't. He challenged me, and I beat the shit out of him. You only had to do it once in a town the size of Iowa City and people would leave you alone.

GP: Do you agree with Harold Bloom that there cannot be strong Jewish poets in America because they cannot identify with the dominant Protestant sublime tradition, or what he might call the great Christian father poets? In other words a Jew can't identify with Emerson, with Whitman, etc.

PL: Well, I'm taking your word for what he claims. It sounds odd to me. The greatest Whitmanian poets seem to me to be Hart Crane, Galway Kinnell, Allen Ginsberg, and Gerald Stern. Those are my four favorites of the poets who come right out of Whitman. Two of them are Jews.

GP: Do you consider yourself a Jewish poet? In the poem "Who Are You?" the voice remembers a tradition which he and his son share, Israel and centuries of exile. Do you feel that tradition is in your poetry?

PL: I'm Jewish and I write poetry, so I'm a Jewish poet. I'm not big on bagels and cream cheese and lox and all the accouterments of Jewish life. A friend of mine from Detroit wrote some outfit down in Miami. They were giving a prize in Jewish poetry, and I got the National Book Award that year. How come you didn't give it to Levine? my friend asked. He got this letter back. Well, he's not Jewish enough. There are not enough talliths and not enough bagels and Passover feasts in his poetry. And he said to me, what do you think of that, and I said, well, if that's what they're looking for they'd better find somebody else.

GP: How did you find out about the art of Flavio? In the poem "On a Drawing by Flavio," you say the rabbi "has my face / that opened its eyes / so many years ago / to death." How did you find Flavio?

PL: There's a magazine published, I believe, in Switzerland but distributed here in the United States and probably all over the world. I think it's trilingual in German, French, and English, called *Graphis.* It's a magazine that studies and presents graphic arts. One of his large graphic pieces was on the cover. It was a depiction of something I recognized right away: a famous anarchist. I wrote the magazine in an effort to reach this guy Flavio Costantini. And the guy wrote me back. In fact, he sent me two large seriographs that he'd done that probably sold for a thousand bucks apiece. They arrived on my birthday, and I couldn't believe it. Then I get a letter from this cat in Italian, which I got translated. So I write him back in English and tell him it arrived on my birthday, and he wrote back that he did not believe in accidents: All has a motive behind it, and I've looked into it, and you live in Fresno, California. There was a famous free-speech fight there conducted by the Wobblies in 1910. He knew more about the history of Fresno than I did. He said, What I need to know is what Fresno looked like back in 1910, so maybe you can help me with that. I went down to this guy named Charles Eaton, who was a banker who had published a volume on the history of Fresno, and I knew he had this library of photographs. I told him I wanted photographs of what Fresno looked like in 1910 because a friend of mine wanted to do a painting of Fresno in 1910. I didn't tell him anything about anarchism because I immediately sniffed out the fact he was a political conservative. He loaned me ten photographs of where the free-speech fight would have taken place with all the stores and the cars and the horse-drawn buggies and what have you of 1910, 1911. I sent them to Flavio and, oh God, he was so happy, and he sent me a small photographic reproduction of the painting he'd made, and then I decided I was going to go to Italy, take my youngest son to Italy with me and my wife. My other two kids had grown up and left home, and we stopped off and saw Flavio, and I walked into his apartment. We shook hands. He embraced me, brothers in anarchy, and he said, I want to show you something. He took me into his study. At the time I had a beard and there was this drawing that he'd made of this rabbi in Auschwitz, and he said, He's you; he looks just like you. It's true. He gave me the drawing. He was on the cover of *Ashes*.

GP: In "They Feed They Lion," do you identify in any way as a prophet? You seem to imagine a dread force that makes all of Earth's creatures holy and yet devours their hopes and ideals at the same time. You're writing about some kind of divine force or overpowering force, as I read the poem. Do you see yourself in the writing of that poem as a Jewish prophet?

PL: I see myself as a witness to a great American crime. It's a poem about American racism. It's a poem that comes out of the riots of 1967 and my going back to Detroit and realizing that in Eldridge Cleaver's term I'm part of the problem, not part of the solution. I'm white, I'm middle-class, I'm middle-aged, and the neighborhoods that I grew up in are no longer home to me. I had identified at a great distance with the black rage that was exploding in what they called the great revolution, but when I went back my emotions were much more complex. I saw how I was viewed as exactly what I was: a guy who'd made his peace with America—working in a state university, taking the state's money, paying my taxes, being a good citizen, and all that. There was no reason that I should be seen in any other way. It's out of that firestorm of emotion that the poem arises, an effort to come to terms with being that guy.

GP: The men in the poems "Uncle" and "Zaydee" combine sacred and profane qualities: "Prophet of burned cars / and broken fans, he taught / the toilet the eternal, / argued the Talmud / under his nails." Did these men combine the earthy sensibilities and skills of the workers with aspects of the Jewish religious tradition, or did you ever think of them that way?

PL: Yeah, that's exactly how I thought of them, as the real Jews. My uncle was a guy who could fix anything. If a radio was broken, he fixed it. He was a tough kid; his father was a bootlegger. He was my uncle through marriage. He was a terrific guy, a tough American Jew. He was a wonderful man, and I thought he was indestructible. But of course old age and God knows what got to him and he finally died. My grandfather was a hearty little guy. He was five feet tall. He was a lot like the cousin that I found in France—very tough and a real gambler and a guy unafraid to lose his shirt and a proud little cat. They were very Jewish guys, spoke Yiddish. Neither was conventionally religious. My grandfather occasionally would go to shul, and he knew Hebrew. He wasn't a devout man. On the other hand, he was a great lover: he loved women; he loved life. He had a lot of vitality. Like my uncle, he was a fun guy to be with. They were worldly men. My uncle was born in the States. My grandfather, like my father and my mother, was born in Russia; he never quite got comfortable in America. My uncle was very comfortable here. He'd lost an eye fighting, and no one screwed around with him. I see him as reinventing the Talmud, putting it into a kind of context of Detroit.

GP: In the poem "Goodbye" from *1933*, the son encounters a sparrow outside his window. When the sparrow says, come here, the boy goes to an alley and sees a peddlar's cart piled high with refuse. And then the sheenie man appears, "pissing / into a little paper fire / in the snow." The bird performs a ritual. It looks three times over each shoulder and then shakes its head. Then it "rose in a shower / of white dust above / the blazing roofs / and telephone poles." The poems says, "It meant a child / would have to leave the world." Was that a vision, and if so where did it come from, and what does it mean for you who wrote it? Are you a mystic there; are you having a mystic vision?

PL: Yes, I am, and the vision is that deprived of your father you must become a man. It's that simple. That's how the child leaves the world. He doesn't die: he stops being a child; he has to grow up and be a man.

GP: In the poem "On the Murder of Lieutenant José del Castillo by the Falangist Bravo Martinez, July 12, 1936," how do you envision so much of that scene of what happened as if you were there? Had you seen photos, prints, paintings, films of this or similar incidents, or do you imagine it?

PL: Well, I invented it. It happened in the park near the railroad station in Madrid. I put it on another street, one in Barcelona. I took the liberty that Renaissance painters took. They didn't know what Palestine looked like, so they had Christ crucified on a hill outside Amsterdam. I didn't know that park. I'd been there once; it didn't impress me. But that street in Barcelona, the Ramblas, is a place of enormous energy. I think it's the most beautiful street I've ever seen in my life, and it has the flower sellers and the animal sellers and dog sellers and the bird sellers and it's very colorful. And I wanted that contrast between all the vitality and the life the street represents at the same time that you get the dying of the other man. I wanted that contrast in the poem.

I had read about José del Castillo's death. I read it in an old history of the Spanish Civil War. He was a man who died because he had killed some *señoritos*. *Señorito* is a Spanish term for a wealthy young man who is a playboy, and these playboys were attacking strikers in Madrid. They would drive up to these building sites and just shoot these strikers and then drive off. And of course the police with their mutual affinities made no effort to find out who they were or what have you. José del Castillo was a guy who had sympathies for the working class, and he saw one of these events take place. He pursued a car full of these *señoritos* and he had a gun fight with them, and he killed one, and he captured the rest. A famous, powerful newspaper columnist had been writing that the strike was an insult to Spain. He, Calvo Sotelo, was a columnist for a right-wing newspaper; in fact, a descendant of his later became the head of government. His was a very powerful family. The fascists hired this guy to kill del Castillo. His comrades identified his death as one caused by this newspaper writer. They went out and arrested him with a phony warrant and murdered him, and in an old history of the Spanish Civil War I read that García Lorca's death was the result of this chain of killings. Because one writer from the right had been killed, the right determined they were going to take the most famous writer from the left, and when they got the chance to kill him, they did. Some years later I read a book that showed that García Lorca was killed by petty little small-town shits that hated him because he was a genius; hated him because he was bisexual; hated him because he was flamboyant and he was the most famous person around. They were just determined to kill him and they killed him. The whole world mourned the death of García Lorca; he was a great man, a great poet. But no poet had written one word, as far as I knew, about del Castillo, so I said, I'll go to the loss of this beautiful cat who gave his life for working-class people. So that's where a lot of the charge came from. Then I decided I'd put it in Barcelona. All that detail comes out of the hundred times I walked the Ramblas; I lived in Barcelona for a year.

GP: In the poem "Ashes," you conclude with a prayer: "Do you want the earth to be heaven? / Then pray, go down on your knees / as though a king stood before you, / and pray to become all you'll / never be, a drop of sea water, / a small hurtling flame across the sky / a fine flake of dust that moves / at evening like smoke at great height / above the earth and sees it all." What are you trying to suggest there?

PL: I'm suggesting, pray to gain the wisdom you can only gain by ceasing to be merely yourself, which will come with your dying.

GP: You mean the knowledge comes from dying?

PL: In your dying you'll join the rest of the universe. Your ego will be gone. Your identity will be gone. You'll merge with everything, with creation, and you'll understand.

GP: Is that something to be desired?

PL: No, I like being myself.

GP: It doesn't sound bad.

PL: It's a very hopeful vision of what dying would be like.

GP: In the poems "Fear and Fame" and "Growth," you reveal a kind of total recall. If that's true, do you have a photographic memory, and if it isn't, how does your process of composition work in the creation of those poems?

PL: In those two poems the memory is almost photographic, yes, especially "Fear and Fame," which has an enormous amount of detail. But I'm describing a job I worked at for exactly one year and did at least once a week. Let me see: fifty-two times I performed the cleaning out and the refilling of these acid tanks in all that equipment and armor that I wore. I was only twenty-five years old when I did it and probably fifty something, maybe sixty, when I wrote the poem. It wasn't something I'd forgotten. For the other job in "Growth" I'm even younger. I'm just a kid about fourteen, but I remembered that job very well. Going into those ovens where the soap flakes were drying and the immense heat that suddenly hit me and the knowledge that you had to do this fast. They weren't going to turn the heat down for you so you had to get in and get out as they dried out these soap flakes. It was a very crude process. I'm sure today it's done much more efficiently, but at the time it was just a little dinky operation where they made soap, and then they made these soap flakes and dried them. I used to watch the process starting with the trucks driving up, and they would dump off these barrels of fat from the restaurants and then later on the stuff would come out. They sold it to laundries.

GP: You call García Lorca and Hart Crane the two greatest poetic geniuses alive in your poem "On the Meeting of García Lorca and Hart Crane." What have you learned from their examples?

PL: Well, number one I've exaggerated. They probably weren't the two greatest poetic geniuses alive because Vallejo and Neruda and Mayakovski were all alive too and so were Williams and Stevens. Oh hell, let's exaggerate. What they both had for me is something I lack; they had unbelievable language. I am very envious of Crane's incredible phrasing. I don't know anybody who phrases better than Crane when he's really hot. You could say the same for Lorca. When he's hot the phrasing, the language, is just terrific. There's a line in that poem that makes some people laugh. I've never figured it out. I say "even the ants in your own / house won't forget it." That's a line I've adapted from Lorca. He's talking about the bullfighter's dying in that great elegy. He's telling him how dead he is, and he says "even the ants in your own / house don't know you." How does the imagination see something like that? And Crane looking at New York from his apartment over in Brooklyn says "the city's fiery parcels all undone." I look from a high building down at the city, and I think of that line and say, God, what language, what imagery, what music.

GP: What has poetry taught you about language?

PL: That I can never know enough about it. That I can never exhaust the need to know more and more about using language. It's also taught me that if you don't control language, it will control you. That's a kind of Freudian insight in some ways. I tell my students if you don't control the language, it will reveal you in ways you don't want to be revealed. So you have to become the master of it. You have to work with it. You have to become cozy with it. People are constantly saying, Oh, it's so limited, our forms of communication are so half-assed, etc. To me they seem all right; they're not perfect, but my God, when handled with the skill and devotion of someone like Crane or Williams or Shakespeare or Chaucer, it's amazing how much we can bridge the enormous separation between one human being and another or from one time to another, from one culture to another. The possibilities for language are inexhaustible.

GP: The Language poets have become very prominent certainly in academia, making language the essence of the poem, all based on postmodernist theory. Do you have any thoughts about them as a movement?

PL: What I dislike about the stance of most of the Language poets is the manner in which they define the poetry scene: they tend to see it as a war in which they represent experiment, the future, the struggle against an entrenched and wealthy imperial power. In truth they are an important part of the American scene; their influence in the writing programs, the publication industry, and all the rest of the "church temporal" of poetry is enormous. I know for a fact that they dislike my work, which is fine; in truth theirs has meant very little to me, but I am sixty-nine. The young may find their vision very useful, and in the long run they will undoubtedly enrich our poetry, but I dislike that heroic, em-battled stance. I am glad to have had poets as different as Creeley and Wilbur as contemporaries, and I've never believed I had to choose one and despise the other. I love the work of both of them. I would hope these Language poets don't go into workshops with the old nonsense: This is THE way to write. There is not THE way. A young poet is lucky to find A way to cope with his conflicting emotions in a composition of words that can mean something to someone else.

GP: And the last question. What's the most amazing thing about your life?

PL: The most amazing thing is probably my marriage. I will have been mar-ried forty-three years come this summer. And people say, boy, was that smart. But let me tell you, I was not thinking with my head. My wife and I were driven to each other for irrational purposes. We've been able to live together a long, long time and still enjoy each other's company a great deal. I'd rather be with her than anybody else in the world, and so it's been a great blessing for me, that and fatherhood too, which has its difficulties, but it's been terrific too. I feel very close to my kids, so I guess that whole thing, marriage and having children, has been the great surprise of my life, because I was a guy who grew up believing that marriage was a trap and having children was a greater trap. What I've discovered is that's not true at all. It makes a human being out of you, and the rewards go on and on and on. So far it's terrific. You never know. Don't count your blessings too quickly.

ELAINE FEINSTEIN

BORN IN 1930, Elaine Feinstein has made her living as a writer since 1972. In that year, she was made a Fellow of the Royal Society of Literature. She has written fourteen novels, of which *The Border, Loving Brecht, Dreamers* and *Lady Chatterley's Confession*—a sequel to D. H. Lawrence's novel in the spirit of Jean Rhys—are all currently in print. Her work has been translated into French, Spanish, German, Italian, Danish, Hungarian, Romanian, Portuguese, Hebrew, and Chinese. Her versions of the poems of Marina Tsvetayeva, for which she received three translation awards from the British Arts Council, are available from Oxford University Press in both England and the United States. In 1990 she received a Cholmondeley Award for Poetry and was given an Honorary Doctorate of Literature from the University of Leicester. Her *Selected Poems* came out in 1994. She has written radio plays, television drama, and three biographies. She was writer-in-residence for the British Council in Singapore in 1993 and in Tromso, Norway, in 1996. She was chairman of the judges for the T. S. Eliot Prize for poetry in 1995. Her latest book of poems, *Daylight,* is a Poetry Book Society Recommendation.

BEING A WOMAN and a Jew from northern England, Elaine Feinstein is an English poet with a sense of being different from most of her contemporaries. She noted in our interview that she identified with the language and voices of such twentieth-century American poets as Pound, Olson, Ginsberg, Paul Blackburn, and Ed Dorn. "It was natural for me to look across the Atlantic to a culture, a rich culture, an energetic culture, with an immigrant base, and that's why American poetry was very influential for me."

Her poems, however, do not resemble Pound, Ginsberg, Olson, etc., as much as they do her female contemporaries, including the American poets Sylvia Plath and Anne Sexton. Like them she writes frankly and openly of her personal life. When I asked her what the hardest thing is about being a poet, she answered, "I suppose the hardest thing about being a poet, my kind of poet, is exposing your own life intimately and particularly family members."

According to Feinstein, the poet she most identified with and has learned the most from is the Russian poet Marina Tsvetayeva. Feinstein first became familiar with the Russian poet's work when she began to translate her poetry. She found in Tsetayeva a kindred spirit; both poets were women who had to work and bring up children, even though neither was well suited for domestic life.

There is, however, a deeper level of empathy between the two poets, for as Feinstein said of the Russian poet, "She had all this passion, this sort of propositional assurance that she gets into her poetry and a wholeness of self-exposure. . . . She had a very direct voice from her own being, from her own passions, and in the process exposed some rather humiliating things in herself."

When I asked her about Tsvetayeva's suicide, Feinstein defended the Russian poet because she wrote with such passion and energy and never gave up, despite the terrible circumstances of life in Stalinist Russia. According to Feinstein, it is unfair to compare Tsvetayeva's suicide with those of Plath and Sexton. "She was alone, really, in a Soviet Russia whose terrors were far greater than most of us will ever be called upon to bear, so she's not in the same bracket as Anne Sexton or Sylvia Plath. She was an accidental suicide."

Because of the example of Tsvetayeva, her teacher of courage, Feinstein has been able to go beyond the restraints of her English background and training to "a wholeness of self-exposure." Feinstein's candor and her lucidity can be seen in "Bathroom":

> My legs shimmer like fish
> my hair floats on the water:
> tonight I observe that my
> skin is no longer smooth
> that blue veins show
> in my arms that my
> breasts are smaller . . .

Several times in our interview Feinstein spoke of the tension between "song and the speaking voice." In "Bathroom," Feinstein writes without pretense and with lyric precision and directness about the universal subject of aging. While the poem is unremitting in its self-exposure, it is also "as memorable as a tune."

I was struck by the differences between Feinstein's view of herself as a Jewish poet in England and the situation of Jewish poets in America. As she stated in our interview, just being Elaine Feinstein typecast her as a Jewish poet in

England. "Even if I had never made a single note of allegiance, I would be Jewish in this country."

In addition to being pigeonholed as Jewish, Feinstein and other Jewish writers have been subjected to anti-Semitism. When she mentioned getting anti-Semitic hate mail, I said that I was shocked, because this would not occur in the United States. She described receiving a Christmas card "featuring a lot of gas canisters and limericks saying if six million, why not six million and one." She admitted being quite worried about such vile mail when her children were young; her tone became more intense as she said, "Then I was worried all the time about it."

·

THE INTERVIEW took place on October 14, 1996. It began in Groucho's Club at 45 Dean Street in the West End of London, but when the club proved too noisy for taping, we took a taxi to the poet's townhouse in Hampstead. We sat at a living room table near the front window overlooking the street. Feinstein spoke extemporaneously. After the interview, she showed me her study with its crowded floor-to-ceiling bookshelves and the window overlooking a garden.

GP: What have you found the hardest thing about being a poet?

EF: I suppose the hardest thing about being a poet, my kind of poet, is exposing your own life intimately and particularly family members, which they may not always welcome. I think that is the hardest thing about being a writer, whereas with novels, you can hide behind fictional characters. In poetry I speak very much in my own voice.

GP: Now, since you mentioned that, have you had difficulties with revealing personal elements of your life in poetry?

EF: Well, I've had a long and very fruitful marriage but very often I've talked about it in ways that haven't always been friendly; I know that. My children, too, I've talked about very intimately, but they have always felt loved.

GP: Do you see your fiction and poetry as complementary, that is, are your fictional characters extensions of the self that's in some ways the central voice of your poems, or does your fiction come from a different source?

EF: I think the voice, the cadences, the rhythms are very different; since I impersonate people whose life experience I haven't shared, it's bound to come from a different part of myself. Fiction is after all invented. Novelists use themselves in a way, whether dispersing themselves through a variety of characters or in one particular character.

GP: What does a poet need to know about the craft of poetry, and are rhyme and meter still important enough to be part of the young poet's training—since so much poetry, certainly in America, is written in free verse and sometimes students (at least my students) seem to feel that rhyme and meter impede them. What do you think a poet needs to know about craft?

EF: Of course, poets need to know about craft. It *is* a craft and you have to be soaked, really, in the poetry of the past—I would think—four hundred years to be able to use the English language at its richest. I would certainly insist that you need to know and love that poetry. My own poetry is, as you can see, written in a free form, though I use rhyme, sometimes internal rhyme, sometimes to make clinching points from time to time. I depend enormously on rhythm and shape, and these things are all part of a poet's craft.

GP: You talked about interest in the poetry of the last four hundred years. Can you think of a few poets who have been your teachers, who have taught you about the English language?

EF: Well, let's think. There are two very extreme poles, George Herbert and D. H. Lawrence. I mean, George Herbert had that marvelous quiet, contemplative sort of voice of piercing lyrical directness, which I aspire towards. And Lawrence has that marvelous gritty, detailed apprehension of the world, which I think is enviable and possibly emulatable.

GP: You have poems in tribute to Emily Dickinson and Elizabeth Bishop. Have those poets influenced you and if so how?

EF: I don't think so. Not really. I mean, Elizabeth Bishop is a lovely poet, but I don't thinks she's actually influenced me. I enjoy her. Emily Dickinson, similarly. Emily Dickinson's more borderline perhaps, but I mean the real influences on me have not come from those two poets, though they were wonderful precursors.

GP: Have there been any other American poets who have been influential for you?

EF: I was very influenced by American poetry in general in the fifties when I was very bored with what seemed to me to be the New Movement's caution and tightness, and I felt myself of a very different spirit from that. I looked across to America because of language, of course, which seemed to be the same one that we shared. I was passionately involved with it through Pound and Black Mountain poetry and Olson and Ginsberg and Paul Blackburn, Ed Dorn. People of this kind seemed to be writing with a music which I could pick up with my voice. I have a very odd voice in England, in English terms, because when I began to write, I was from the North. Many people who were involved in the New Movement were also from the North. But they were men, and I had a woman's voice, I came from the North, I was additionally Jewish, and I really did not fit into people's idea of a poet and my voice was not that which people had in Cambridge very often; so it was natural for me to look across the Atlantic to a culture, a rich culture, an energetic culture, with an immigrant base, and that's why American poetry was very influential for me.

GP: You had said earlier that being a Jewish poet in England would be different probably from being a Jewish poet in America. I gather you've already started talking about that. Is there anything more that you can say about that subject?

EF: Well, it's a very small Jewish community here, and although it has art festivals, it's quite a Philistine community. I mean, if one looks to see where the intellectual vigor which exists here goes, it goes into law, into science, to a certain extent into business. It does not on the whole pour into literature. I mean, I can think of immediate and obvious exceptions. You know, there's Harold Pinter, who will no doubt be Sir Harold Pinter, whatever, in due course, and there are others. But a Jewish English writer is doubly exiled. He's an exotic in the host culture, you know, an exotic figure. He'd come from somewhere *outside* the predominant culture of England. And you're pretty much an exotic as a writer within the Jewish community, so one way or another you don't have a constituency in the same way an American Jewish writer has a constituency.

GP: I see what you mean, although it may be somewhat similar for the American Jewish poets, really. With all the richness of contribution of American Jews to even world culture, there isn't all that much of a place and a voice for the Jewish poet in America. You've been extremely attracted to the Russian poet Tsvetayeva, and I'm sure you've spoken about this before, but I'm still curious as to why her influence on you was so profound. Since for one thing it seems as if, from the little bit that I know about you, her life had been quite different from yours. I mean, she was a suicide, I take it, and writes a kind of rather bleak poetry.

EF: No, she doesn't write bleak poetry. That's for a start. She's very life-loving, in fact, though she did kill herself. I'll come first to what attracted me towards her. I didn't have an enormous number of women role models when I began to write poetry. In the English scene, I had rather spinsterly figures like Stevie Smith, I mean, who was still alive when I began to write, and country poets, like Patricia Beer. And when I found Tsvetayeva, I was really very excited, because she seemed to have all that I wanted. She had all this passion, this sort of propositional assurance that she gets into her poetry and a wholeness of self-exposure. I mean, no "probably's" and "it may be" and all these carefully hedged bets of the New Movement that we all remember and I personally disliked. She had a very direct voice from her own being, from her own passions, and in the process exposed some rather humiliating things in herself, which I suppose all confessional poetry does. Especially a sense of loss and abandonment. Certainly her life has been very different from mine, but there was one thing we did share. We had a living to earn, and we had children to bring up, and we kept that show on the road even though we were really much more suited to a nice privileged life. Just writing poetry would have suited us both fine and that isn't the way it worked out for us, as it happens. I don't claim to have been as poor as Tsvetayeva was. I've never been that poor. Nobody has in the West, actually.

GP: So, you made your living by teaching?

EF: Three years. After '72, I lived as a writer. That's a long time.

GP: Tsvetayeva worked?

EF: She also made her living as a writer, but she couldn't have done that without an enormous number of begging letters to her friends.

GP: Are you the first person to have translated her?

EF: The first book, yes.

GP: And you told me that it's had an impact.

EF: Enormous impact. I think one of the reasons why women poets are so excited by her was that she offered this role model of somebody who didn't actually *give up* like Sylvia Plath. She put up with a lot of pain and rejection. She wasn't everybody's idea of the beautiful young poet who, you know, served as the muse of Robert Graves. She was herself the poet figure who fell in love, who was not the beloved but the one who loves, and that's quite important really.

GP: How would she be different from Akhmatova, for example?

EF: In the way I have said. I mean, recently there's been a lot of work on Akhmatova, and I was very struck by the fact that both of them had in common this marital problem—that their poetry was seen as an act of adultery—but the big difference between them is that Akhmatova was enormously beautiful. She had three unhappy marriages, that is true, but she was enormously beautiful and had enormous numbers of men who loved her. Whereas on the whole Tsvetayeva writes of her own heartbreak. The only person who really stayed true to her right through to the end was her husband, and he was in jail in fact and probably shot at the time she was on her own. She didn't kill herself because she was in love with death at all. She was alone, really, in a Soviet Russia whose terrors were far greater than most of us will ever be called upon to bear, so she's not in the same bracket as Anne Sexton or Sylvia Plath. She was an accidental suicide.

GP: You're originally from Liverpool.

EF: Yes, so indeed I am.

GP: Does it give you a connection with other Liverpool writers?

EF: Well, I know them all. I know Brian Patten and Roger McGough and Adrian Henry, but I don't know that we have much particularly in common because of that. I analyzed that in a little essay that I did in an anthology called *Liverpool Accents,* and I was saying there what I thought Liverpool gave me. I left it when I was just about a year old. It gave me a family who came from Liverpool and a voice from there, and a Liverpool voice is very skeptical. It doesn't like the pretentious. It means that you don't pretend to like things you don't like, which is a very good thing, but the downside is it means if you don't immediately like something you often don't think there can be anything in it and you're kind of suspicious of it. So I'm suspicious of things that I don't respond to, and I think that's part of the Liverpool inheritance.

GP: You went from Liverpool to Leicester?

EF: Yes. Well, that's another voice; the Midland voice there is closer to, you know, "If you're so clever, why aren't you rich?" I mean, it's a very rich town, Leicester, unlike Liverpool, which is a poor one.

GP: And where did you go to school? Where did you go to college?

EF: Oh, school. Ordinary school, I went to the Wyggeston Grammar School, a very good school. I think they've now closed it down, but it was a very old semipublic school at which I won a free place. I went to college in Cambridge for three years to read English.

GP: Can you describe the experience behind the poem called "Survivors," in which you seem to be talking about the Roman Italian Jewish community? Do you remember that?

EF: I do. It came out of—well, it's a bit of tourism, really. We went to Rome, and wherever we go, we always go and look for the synagogues because everybody, I think, with any interest in Jewish affairs finds that's how they can discover what happened to the Jews of this particular city. You don't often get the Jews who are most like yourself because, of course, people who are still going to synagogue are often very much more religious than I was certainly when I went there, but I was very struck by the fact that the old joke "If there are two Jews on an island they have two synagogues" seems to be really true. And in Rome there is a huge synagogue, but if you happened to come in a different wave of immigration to Italy there's this kind of poky little hole just underneath. I was just affected by that.

GP: Now you've got another poem in the *Selected Poems,* which is called "New Year," and you're talking about Rosh Hashana, of course, the celebration of the Jewish New Year, and you have a line in there saying "somehow I find it easier and easier / to pray." In regards to that is there anything you can say, and then I would follow that up with, do you consider yourself a Jewish poet?

EF: Well, I have a poem in this new selection—which is going to be called *Daylight*—called "Prayer," and it acknowledges the anomalous act of prayer. When you are in great need, danger, or when someone you love is very ill, it seems to be a human instinct to pray—actually human, not particularly Jewish, just human. And yet when you think about what you're actually doing and the enormity of it out there and the numerousness of us down here, it makes kind of no logical sense, so it's a very funny thing for human beings universally to have evolved, a sense of prayer as an effective thing to do. Well, I noticed—I think the thing about poets is they have to bring out and say what other people don't necessarily bring together in their minds. I think people do pray; they also are often totally agnostic, sometimes atheistic. And so when I said I found it easier and easier to pray, I went with that feeling that prayer, in some way I haven't entirely worked out, helps and it's sort of what that new poem is about.

As to whether I'm a Jewish writer, I'm not a writer who uses many Jewish themes in her poetry. I mean, I'm just not. If you look at the bulk of my poetry, I think there are about three or four or five poems which have an explicitly Jewish content, which is odd because in my novels I do have a strong awareness of the Jewish past and the way it presses on the future. Sometimes I seem to feel a sense of the future pressing on the past. I'm quite aware of the whole Jewish dimension, but I don't think poems are written about anything but direct experience, and I have no direct experience either of persecution or of a kind of Jewish involvement which could go into the poems. You know, my entire family was not brushed by the Holocaust, through a series of accidents. So I've been very interested in the whole phenomenon, but I don't write poetry out of it.

GP: I remember in your introduction to your section of *The Bloodaxe Book of Contemporary Women Poets* you talked about the fact that you were very much influenced and struck by the Holocaust experience. So you say then that you have not written poems about the Holocaust?

EF: Nothing.

GP: Would it be accurate to say then that you write about the Holocaust in your fiction, but not in your poetry?

EF: No, I never write about the Holocaust at all. I write about people who have survived it. I feel very strongly that I have no wish to and no right to explore material such as the Holocaust, which other people have experienced on their own flesh. I feel that would be wrong. So, in my novel *The Border* (still in print in both the UK and the USA), the three people I'm talking about in the center of *The Border* are approached by the Holocaust in the sense that they are in Vienna just before the Anschluss and their story is played out in prewar Vienna. Again, in *Loving Brecht* the central talking voice escapes to Russia and lives a section of her life in Russia as someone who is in love with Bertolt Brecht. That's the story. I make her Jewish because I couldn't imagine being a German in that time very easily, but I could imagine what it felt like to be Jewish in that time. She's an invented figure; the rest of the people are real. In both cases, the actual Holocaust is not an area that I enter. I don't want to.

GP: But you imply at least that you identify with being Jewish, or being a Jew.

EF: Oh, yes. I was brought up in an Orthodox Jewish home, and like most people in the forties I threw all that on one side for the length of my time in Cambridge, but I encountered a lot of very interesting Jews who were very

Zionistic or left-wing or kinds of things like that, which was thought to be a Jewish decision.

GP: Do you see yourself strictly as a poet; are you one of these people who don't want to be categorized as a Jewish poet, or as a woman poet, or as a poet per se, or do you see yourself as an English poet?

EF: Well, in a funny kind of way, as I've got older, I've seen all the difficulties. In a way, I suppose what I would like to be is part of the English tradition of poetry. That is, I'd like to exist in that tradition of English poetry in its widest sense. The trouble with categories, for an English Jewish poet, is that they aren't sufficiently inclusive. I'm not a Jewish poet; there are no forebears. And there aren't enough of us to constitute a tradition, really. Three or four poets is not a tradition.

GP: Do you think there's room then for an English woman Jewish poet to become part of what the critics would call the English canon?

EF: Yes, I do think so. Of course there is, but it will be quite hard. I think that whenever I'm invited to somewhere like Chelsea, people are very well aware of my Jewishness whether I'm reading from poems which make any mention of it or not, because in England one is categorized all the time in a way that you aren't in the States. Anyone called Feinstein is Jewish. It's just as simple as that, so I'm perceived to be Jewish. Even if I had never made a single note of allegiance, I would be Jewish in this country.

GP: And does that label come along with some implicit anti-Semitism or not?

EF: I have been lucky in the last thirty or forty years of writing because there has been less anti-Semitism in this country as a result perhaps of the Holocaust, which created an umbrella of protection. So there's been less anti-Semitism in this country than there would have been at any other time.

GP: There does, however, seem to be fear, if not a paranoia, about the National Front. I gather there is real fear in the Jewish community about these protofascists.

EF: Well, there are a lot of protofascists, but they're not yet very menacing. I myself would think a scenario where they would become menacing would be, say, if Labour wins the next election, if the Tory party split, then goes to the right, it might possibly come back into government with the aid of the National Front. That's the only scenario I can imagine which would make it very dangerous. As far as the lunatics at the moment are concerned, I've had my share of hate mail, of course, because everyone has.

GP: Hate mail?

EF: Yeah.

GP: So you've actually gotten anti-Semitic hate mail in regard to you as a Jewish writer in England?

EF: Well, I suppose so. My guess is what they do is they go through the *Jewish Yearbook,* something like that, and I'm in that as a Jewish writer. I mean, that's the way in which they find out I'm a Jewish writer. For example, I got a Christmas card featuring a lot of gas canisters and limericks saying if six million, why not six million and one. But I don't know anyone who didn't get that among the Jewish notables, so I wasn't particularly anxious or, if you like, I didn't take it personally. I didn't think they were out there waiting to get me.

GP: See, now from my point of view, I'd take that as alarming, as shocking. Has this happened over a period of years, or is it a new phenomenon?

EF: Once or twice it's happened and it is a new phenomenon, and when I first heard it, I immediately rang, I think it was, Bernie Rubins, and found that we'd all got the same card, and I just thought, well, they can't go for all of us really. They can't be after all of us very significantly. I felt more paranoid when I was younger, if you want to know, when I had small children. Then I was worried all the time about it.

GP: So, you've had to identify as a Jew, certainly in terms of anti-Semitism.

EF: How else can you? If you are not able to get rid of that label, then you think what it means to be Jewish and it's actually quite an interesting thing to be. It means I come trailing a whole lot of stuff which the ordinary English writer does not have to draw on and quite an interesting family and history. I'm not sorry to be Jewish. I'm delighted to be Jewish but yeah—you can't mistake it.

GP: All right, let's shift the emphasis a little bit. In a poem called "A Letter from La Jolla," obviously La Jolla, California, it seems to me that the poem is quite personal, and it talks about your marriage. Do you see this as a confessional poem, or what is the poem's purpose? Is it for a therapeutic purpose to get something off your chest?

EF: It really *was* almost a letter. A very strange thing to do, but it was at a rather bumpy period in my marriage, and I was thinking about other people that I'd been involved with and wondering what had happened to them. I had no intention or indeed an address of communicating directly. I wrote this poem as a sort of letter to the world—like Emily Dickinson—that never wrote to me, something like that, and have thought of it like that ever since, really.

GP: In answer to my question about what is the hardest thing about being a poet, you said the hardest thing is writing about painful personal elements of your life, so I wonder if this would be an example of it?

EF: Yes, because he was the first man I wanted to marry. We did get engaged, in fact, as people did in those long-forgotten days. Now people don't even get married, but in those days people got engaged, formally engaged, and there was a big party. And it was a very long engagement because he was in the air force, and it broke up. And I was really quite devastated by that breakup, which was almost the first adversity, if you want to think about it as adversity or pain—why not just call it pain—that I'd experienced in such intensity. You know, I'd been used to getting my own way. How could something like this go actually wrong?

GP: So it's an autobiographical poem.

EF: Sure.

GP: Now you've talked, again in the very nice introduction to your selection of poetry in the Bloodaxe anthology, about how writing served as a rebirth for you as a beleaguered mother. Can you address that issue again?

EF: I have almost forgotten that state of mind, but I was a very beleaguered mother. One thing I did have in common with Tsvetayeva, which I forgot to point out, is that I am not a great housekeeper or organizer domestically at all. I'm really very bad at it. So there were three small children and a university job in prefeminist days when a man expected decently to pursue his own career and left all that to the woman, of course, since it was expected. I was pretty beleaguered. In the end I never sort of got my head above water, really, for many years in order to do anything. Poetry was wonderful because it was short and fierce. I thought, yeah, I could control the world.

GP: Did you get to know other poets who were women?

EF: Oddly enough, not for a long time after I started to write poetry. All the poets in that group around Jeremy Prynne when I knew Andrew Crozier and when I was writing my first book, *In a Green Eye*—all the poets, with the exception of Veronica Thompson, who rather tragically died young, were men. It was rather freaky to be a poet at that time.

GP: Freaky for a woman to be a poet?

EF: Yeah.

GP: That's interesting.

EF: Oh, there was Denise Levertov, actually.

GP: Denise Levertov, who moved to America.

EF: Somewhere there were people like Fleur Adcock and Anne Stevenson, because we're largely contemporary, but I didn't know them.

GP: So, when did you start writing novels—was that after you wrote poetry?

EF: Yes. My first novel, *The Circle*, came out in 1970, so that's after my poems.

GP: And you've published how many novels since then?

EF: Twelve.

GP: Twelve novels. But you still see yourself primarily as a poet—or do you see yourself as both?

EF: I see myself as both. I don't know what people mean by "primarily." "Primarily" is whatever I happen to be doing at the moment. I've just finished a book of poems that's taken a long while to put together and it's quite an important book to me, and that seems to be my primary concern at the moment.

GP: In the same preface to that excellent anthology of contemporary women poets, you say you wanted poems that were genuinely trying to make sense of experience but you also wanted "plain propositions, lines that came singing out of the poem with a perfection of phrasing like lines of music as in the poetry of Pound and Stevens." Do you still feel roughly the same way about your aims as a poet?

EF: Yes, I do. I think there's always a tug between song and the speaking voice, and the speaking voice is that effort to get things natural and direct, and nothing fancy, nothing that would embarrass my Liverpool forebears, you know, with their mockery of the pretentious. That's the speaking voice, and then at the same time, no poem lasts unless it is as memorable as a tune.

GP: Anything again about how you get that tune, how you get that memorable music? You know, a lot of poets, especially in the past, in the English tradition said there has to be meter in there somewhere.

EF: Quite often when you look for it, you can see that I'm just off the iamb by a beat or two. There is meter. I'm very conscious of meter, but I don't use meter to get the tune. The tune comes across the iamb, really.

GP: So you would see yourself essentially then as a free-verse poet?

EF: That's right. That's right. Not open form, though. I like to feel something to pull against. I use stanzas. I find that helps control the way the poem sounds.

GP: What do you see as the main difference or differences between twentieth-century English and American poetry, or the different scenes in the two countries?

EF: I'm completely at sea in the American scene. You must tell me about that. I really don't know enough about it. I've only been there all together, what, four or five times. Some of my novels have been published there. Some of my poems have been published in this Norton anthology which I'll find for you. On the whole, I'm not a presence there. I can tell you about the English scene. The English scene is fragmented. This week, an Irish poet, Sean O'Brien, described it as poets in a barrel, and I agree that is what it's like. There are very few prizes for older poets—there are lots of prizes for younger ones. There are more and more younger poets and there's a beleaguered lot of older ones. I'm not complaining, but the fact is that it is a very odd situation. There's a readership I would say of about 10,000 for poetry in this country, not more, and about—if you've ever judged one of these major competitions, as I have, you'll know there are many poetry writers out there and there must be about 60,000 of them, so it's a very funny situation.

GP: Well, the numbers may be greater, but I don't think the ratios are all that different in the United States. In other words, you're implying that there are more poets than there are readers of poetry.

EF: Far more.

GP: And I think we have the same problem in the United States.

EF: There's nothing wrong with that and that's not going to change as far as I can see.

GP: How does one face death, and can poetry help?

EF: It does help, I think, but I must say it doesn't help much if you're feeling ill. I'm very struck by the difference between health and illness because about two weeks ago I had a very high fever for a few days and my gall bladder was infected, a totally minor thing, but it totally laid me out. I suddenly realized that nothing would help if you had a temperature and couldn't sleep. Nothing would get through to you. You just feel so awful. Assuming it will not be like that and you're conscious that you're getting older, you're bound eventually to die, then poetry does help. It's one of the things that does, yes.

GP: All right, now can you tell me how? Any specifics? Any particular poems or poets, or do you mean the writing of it?

EF: No, I meant the reading of it. I don't know about the writing of it. Yes, I guess that helps too, but I meant the reading of it. Which poems? Well, Ecclesiastes is a great help as a matter of fact. I recommend Ecclesiastes. You see things, I think, more from the other side, and all the things that are rattling you and making you feel exasperated and irritated, they seem to drop away. And, of course, it makes things more beautiful and you can respond to the golden day more.

GP: In continuing along that line, does poetry add to life's meaning? Wallace Stevens, for example, saw poetry as a possible form of faith. He talked about poets creating what he called the supreme fiction, which would be something like myth, a new kind of myth. He actually has a great poem called "Sunday Morning," which is at least an attempt to show this.

EF: Marvelous poem.

GP: You know, as he said, poets should write a great poem of the earth. We've had enough poems, he said, of heaven and hell; it's time to write the great poem of the earth. Do you think poetry can help one with, not only with coping with death, but also with enjoying life more and creating a kind of faith?

There is a lot of poetry attached to Judaism, the Psalms, for example, the prophetic books.

EF: Not to mention Ecclesiastes, of course. There is a lot and I do think that poetry has always made this too much loved earth more lovely, so it adds a poignancy, really, to the beauty that it celebrates. It isn't a substitute for religion, but it's the closest I get to feeling religious, really. That is how I feel religion. I feel it inwardly and through prayer as a matter of words. I mean, there's a real overlap between lyric poetry and prayer.

GP: What has poetry taught you about language, about words? You've already talked eloquently about how it teaches you to appreciate language more. Has the craft of writing poetry day by day and/or fiction taught you about the making of words or about the composition of language?

EF: No generalizations has it taught me, but I suppose that all it's taught me is how to hone and to prune and to clarify and to get clean and to shape. Yes, I suppose that's what I've been doing for about the last thirty or forty years most days.

GP: What do you wish to still accomplish, I suppose I mean in particular as a poet and writer?

EF: Well, I think what I want to do is to write my last poems well. I don't know what they're going to be yet. I don't have an ambition to do a particular thing, but I want to make this next decade or so count. Of course, one can't count on the decade, but if I were given such a decade, I would want to make it count in the body of my work and I'd want to write more poetry. I've almost stopped writing journalism now, but I can't pretend that it might not come back, and I just want to make this really a decade where what I've learned can be turned into poems. "Why poems while they have such a small readership?" is another question. It's just I think they last. I've noticed that they last.

GP: So that even though you've published all those novels, you still value the lasting import, perhaps the religiosity, of poetry.

EF: I value, yes, I value the lyrical emotions of poetry, and that lyrical emotion is close to the kind of surge of emotion that you get from music. That's why it is aesthetic.

GP: What place do you most identify with, what city, town, region?

EF: Oh, London. No question about it, London. London and particularly Belsize Park, which is where we are now. I love these streets; that's where I identify and have lots of friends all around: John Lahr, Ruth Padel, Fay Weldon.

GP: Any other reasons besides the friends?

EF: It's the place I've felt most at home, really.

GP: If you could do it again, if you could live it again, what if anything would you do differently?

EF: Oh, I don't know. I don't know what I would do differently. That's too hard.

GP: What's the most amazing thing to you about life?

EF: That we should be here at all and conscious and able to think and feel and enjoy.

GP: And what is the most amazing thing about your life?

EF: I think it's that I've been enormously fortunate in being able to do what I want, that I've been able to be a poet. Well, I'm a poet in the sense that that's what I do. Or a writer, let's call it a writer, and I do that everyday and that's a great fortune. I would add to that that I have been very fortunate in my children, who have been very supportive and generous, you know, and have lived their own creative lives very fully. One of them is a lovely musician, and one of them writes, and one of them is a good mathematician, and all of that is really probably due to the fact that I've had, for all its ups and downs, a marvelous marriage, really.

GP: Marvelous in what sense?

EF: That I'm married to a man who's very clever and very rich inside.

RUTH FAINLIGHT

RUTH FAINLIGHT was born in New York City in 1931 and has lived mostly in England since she was fifteen. She has published twelve books of poems, including her new *Selected Poems* and *Sugar-Paper Blue,* as well as two volumes of short stories. She has also written opera libretti, and books of her poems have been published in French and in Portuguese translations. She is married to fiction writer and poet Alan Sillitoe.

IN THE preface to her poems in *The Bloodaxe Book of Contemporary Women Poets,* Ruth Fainlight begins by saying that "writing poetry is what I do to make contact with my spirit and the spirits that inhabit me." She goes on to describe her writing process, beginning with the "almost continual monologue or soliloquy inside my head." Tapping into key words, she finds a "ground-rhythm of the poem presenting itself." At some point she discovers "this phrase, or node, or cluster, of words" that "includes every essential element of the poem: its consonantal and assonantal sound-colour, style of vocabulary, and pace; as one cell can contain the information necessary to grow a complete organism."

The poet's preoccupation with spirit can be seen in her sibyl poems. Since sibyls were women regarded as oracles or prophets by the ancient Greeks and Romans, they seem a natural subject for Ruth Fainlight, but in fact the poems began as an assignment, when Leonard Baskin asked her to collaborate with him on a book of poems and drawings of sibyls. "He showed me some of these drawings that he was doing, drawings and watercolors, and I started writing poems. I showed him poems, and he did drawings from them, and we worked back and forth like that. And those are the poems that were published in my book *Sibyls and Others* (1980)."

When she writes poetry, Fainlight says, "I go into a different state of being and also have a different sense of time passing." Many of her poems touch on inspiration, possession, and the figure of a muse. The narrator of "Gloria" says,

> I won't forget
> How space expands

> Until it can include
> A million goddesses and concepts.

However, she goes on to say, "My muse is in myself." It is as if the muse personifies the poet's urge to realize her imaginative vision. The muse is an awesome figure:

> She makes me dance,
> She frightens me at night
> With horrors,
> Leads me to the burning-place.

The poet's task is dangerous: to see beyond ordinary human perception.

By fully utilizing her imaginative powers, the poet challenges boundaries and limits:

> But
> I am released by language,
> I escape through speech:
> Which has no dimensions,
> Demands no local habitation
> Or allegiance, which sets me free
> From whomsoever's definition:
> Jew. Woman. Poet.

The poem "Vertical" shows how language liberates the poet from society's stereotypes into a higher realm of experience dominated by openness and mystery.

This theme appears also in "God's Language," which begins "Angels have no memory, / God's language no grammar." After these two audacious statements, the poem pictures divine speech in which

> . . . each consonant
> Proclaims a further meaning;
> The unacceptable
> Also the true, beyond
> Time's bondage.

Both in her *Bloodaxe* preface and in our interview, Fainlight compares poetry to dance. "So it is a sort of expression of exaltation to me, dancing. In the same way that the highest form of verbal expression becomes poetry, the highest form of physical expression becomes dance."

THE INTERVIEW took place on Monday, November 11, 1996, at Ruth Fainlight's home in Notting Hill Gate, West London. Fainlight is short, wears very thick glasses, and has frizzy hair. Despite this, there is something commanding about her stature. There were hundreds of books lining the walls of the entire apartment and large separate studies for her and her husband, Alan Sillitoe. Because she had just returned from their cottage in the west of England, the heat was not operating properly, but she and I were able to get the problem solved. We also had to move from the living room to the kitchen because of construction work going on in the building. After the interview was over, she showed me the collection of prints by Leonard Baskin accompanying her sibyl poems in a sumptuous limited-edition folio volume published by the Gehenna Press.

GP: We shall begin with question number one, which I've asked everyone. What have you found the hardest thing about being a poet?

RF: The hardest thing about being a poet is sustaining the faith that I'll write another poem after I've finished one and I'm not writing any poetry. And I think, will I ever write another poem? Just enduring those periods is probably the hardest.

GP: Have you gone through long periods when you haven't written poems to your satisfaction, or even when poems haven't come?

RF: I'm talking really about when poems haven't come, rather than "to my satisfaction," because even writing poems that later I think are no good is better than not writing at all. I suppose a couple of months is probably the longest I've ever gone without doing anything connected to writing poetry, and that's quite hard.

GP: You have a poem called "The Noon Day Devil." Do you remember that poem?

RF: The demon of Accidie, indeed. Yes.

GP: That seems almost like a "Dejection Ode." Is that about how hard poetry can be to write? I mean, it almost seems like that.

RF: Well, it certainly could be. It's very appropriate to that, but it's more about a whole state of mind, a complete joylessness with regard to every aspect of life as much as poetry.

GP: What's the most enjoyable thing about writing poetry?

RF: I don't know how to answer that question. It is an extremely enjoyable—*process* isn't the word, *activity* isn't the word. I mean it *is* a process, it *is* an activity, but I really do believe that classical description of inspiration and being possessed by the muse. That seems an appropriate way to describe it. I go into a different state of being and also have a different sense of time passing, because it seems that when I'm writing poetry, I always have time to do it. Time just organizes itself around this different state of being.

GP: I have some more questions about this subject, but first of all, what does a poet need to know about craft? Now, you write eloquently about the muse, about inspiration, which is kind of a romantic notion, I suppose. There's still and always will be the classic notion of a formal metrical approach to poetry with or without rhyme. Just out of curiosity, do you think that rhyme and meter are still important enough to be part of the young poet's training, or do you think it's better to go to free verse? Can free verse be taught?

RF: These are a lot of questions.

GP: Yeah, all right. Let's start with "What does a poet need to know about craft?" Since you're so interested in inspiration and even possession, do you think a young poet should still learn about rhyme and meter?

RF: Absolutely, absolutely, because I think that's the seed. Well, to go back to the previous answer I gave, I said I believe in the classical idea of inspiration. I didn't say the romantic idea—I was going back to classical times, to the *pneuma,* which is a Greek word for inspiration, breath. I believe in that sense of inspiration, which to me is a classical idea. Of course, you could say it's romantic as well, so I won't quibble about that. I think the seed germinates when it's dropped into prepared ground. By which I mean, yes, I do think the young poet should learn about the craft. I wish that when I was a young poet I had learned more, that I had existed in a different atmosphere in which it was absolutely accepted that one had to learn as much as possible about the craft. I think there's much more interest in craft now than when I was a young poet, and I think that's good.

GP: You mentioned something interesting that Ginsberg talked about almost obsessively in our interview, and that is breath. Now, the Black Mountain poets and Ginsberg are very much into what they call the breath unit.

RF: Yes.

GP: Almost an oral approach to poetry.

RF: Yes.

GP: And he talked even about Greek meters. So, just out of curiosity, do you equate inspiration and possession with breath as spirit?

RF: I don't mean specifically and precisely what the Black Mountain poets meant when they talked about breath units. I'm very interested in what they have to say, and I write in pulse units, I suppose. No, this is leading me off into vaguenesses that I don't really want. I write to rhythm and sound, and of course it's to do with breath, because when I write, I then repeat it to myself and say it to myself over and over again, and it relates to breath, but not in the way that the Black Mountain poets used it.

GP: In the *Bloodaxe Book of Contemporary Women Poets,* in your preface to your poems, you eloquently state, "Poem and dance are the most primitive and most enduring expressions of the sense and joy of being alive." And I'm curious, do you have a close connection to dance, or what do you think is most poetic about dance, or vice versa? Because most often poetry is compared to painting or music: *ut pictora poesis.* But you have that beautiful statement about dance. Were you a dancer?

RF: Like many little girls and young girls, I went to dancing class, and I loved to dance and I used to dance a lot. I've never been a professional dancer. Movement seems to me the first thing, the first expression of emotional states. One sees it with very young children, and then of course there's the whole business of dancing to change mental states, dances used in connection with religion—whirling dervishes, for instance. This is a Jewish thing as well, or one aspect of it—Hasidic dancing, dancing before the ark, King David danced before the ark. So it is a sort of expression of exaltation to me, dancing. In the same way that the highest form of verbal expression becomes poetry, the highest form of physical expression becomes dance.

GP: Are the sibyls that you write about literal presences to you? Is Lilith a sibyl in your poem "Lilith" in the *Selected Poems*? Do you identify with her rage? In fact, you write a lot about anger and rage, among other emotions. I keep circling around. Are the sibyls a literal presence? Do you see them?

RF: Let me explain about this sibyl project. I've always been interested in ethnology, anthropology, religion, psychological states connected with these lines of thought. When Leonard Baskin, an American Jewish artist, was living in

England, we became friendly. And he said to me one day in the late seventies, "I've started new drawings of sibyls. Would you like to write some poems, and we'll do a book?" That's how it all began. Then I discovered that earlier poems of mine could be called sibyl poems, but it hadn't been a conscious project at all. And I ended up writing twenty-seven sibyl poems. I worked on this for about a year or about fifteen months, something like that, just doing nothing except writing sibyl poems. I was in this hot state of excitement, because I was doing a lot of reading and research, and it tied in with all sorts of things that I already knew about but hadn't put together. And it was also at that time that Leonard introduced me to Rabbi Albert Friedlander. He's a Reform rabbi, and he's the editor of *European Judaism*. And, incidentally, that's why I'm the poetry editor of *European Judaism*, because when the former poetry editor, Edouard Roditi, a surrealist, died, Albert Friedlander asked me if I would take it over. So that's how it happened, through my introduction to him in order to read the Hebrew sibylline books and any information he could give me, and we have remained in contact.

GP: So the sibyls come out of a Hebrew tradition, Hebrew mystical tradition?

RF: No, the Hebrew sibyl was only one of them. Supposedly, there were nine, ten, or twelve sibyls, and most of the classic authors give information about sibyls, and there are various sites around the ancient world which are connected to sibyls. And there is also a tradition of a Jewish sibyl. In the sibylline books, there is a section about the Hebrew sibyl, but as this is all . . . The sibyls weren't real people, or maybe they were. This is a very interesting question. It was all in connection with Leonard's images. He showed me some of these drawings that he was doing, drawings and water colors, and I started writing poems. I showed him poems, and he did drawings from them, and we worked back and forth like that. And those are the poems that were published in my book, *Sibyls and Others* (1980). I don't know if you've ever seen that.

GP: No, I'd like to.

RF: All of those sibyl poems are there, the complete group.

GP: It'd be nice to see the poems and the art work.

RF: And then we did another. We did a beautiful book, which was only published in about '92 or '93, of twelve woodcuts and twelve new sibyl poems, which are also in my 1994 collection, *This Time of Year*. So, were the sibyls real? To me, the sibyls are concentrations of ideas, ideas about prophecy, the position of women, power. They became the most marvelous focus for me to deal with and explore all these ideas.

GP: Well, we'll come back to the sibyls. What about the muse? You write a lot about the muse. In a poem called "Gloria," on page 10 of *The Selected Poems*, she sounds like a cult source. You say there, "She makes me dance, / She frightens me at night / With horrors, / Leads me to the burning-place." You know, it almost seems like you're involved in some kind of pagan ritual.

RF: Well, I suppose it could sound like that. Earlier today I was sitting on the train coming up from Somerset. I've just started to read Gibbon's *The Decline and Fall of the Roman Empire,* and he describes this wonderfully accepting, tolerant, inclusive attitude to religion of the Roman Empire at that time—about 180 A.D.—to all religions. When I say, "leads me to the burning place," I must have been thinking about that whole aspect of woman the destroyer. You can call it pagan if you like. I'm very interested in all religions. When I read that bit from Gibbon this morning, I thought, "That's how I feel." I'm very respectful of everyone's religion. I don't object to going down on my knees if a Catholic procession goes by. I don't object to taking off my shoes going into a mosque or a temple, and I will certainly do everything appropriate when I go into a synagogue. Because I do believe, in the same way Gibbon said the Romans did, that everyone is worshipping the same God, even though following different routes.

GP: Is this God female or male or both?

RF: Oh, both of course. Yes. You know the joke. She's black? Yes.

GP: Switching it again a little bit. You mentioned movement in dance before. This is a pun on "movement." Do you see yourself as part of a movement, school, or tradition of poets?

RF: I suppose the simplest answer is to say no. I don't see myself as part of a movement or a school. I see myself as part of a stream of poetry that's always been there. I'm part of a group of poets whom I hope are good and authentic.

GP: Sylvia Plath has dedicated a poem called "Elm" to you. The poem implies to me that, at least in the beginning of it, she's speaking to you as having survived some kind of fearful experience and come through it whole, which has inspired her in some way. What do you make of the poem, if anything, and how did you and Plath come to know each other?

RF: Well, to answer the second part of your question first: We came to know each other in a wonderfully literary way, because my husband had been awarded the Hawthornden Prize for *The Loneliness of the Long Distance Runner,* and it was the tradition for the holder of the award to pass it on to the person who was getting it the next year. And the person who got it the next year was Ted Hughes, so, on that occasion, the four of us met for the first time. An exemplary literary meeting, wasn't it? Sylvia and I took to each other and felt we had a lot in common. I mean we both wrote poetry, we were both American, we were both pregnant. Our husbands were both Englishmen from the North and very well known and we weren't. There were lots of parallels which made us immediately feel that we wanted to get to know each other better. I didn't know Sylvia for very long actually, because this was only a couple of years before she killed herself. And for the last year of her life I wasn't even living in England. But soon after these two babies were born, when my son was about a month or two old, and hers was a couple of months older, we went down to Devon to visit her and Ted. Sylvia had just been working on that poem, and she said, "I want to dedicate this to you because I think this is right for you." And that's all I can say.

GP: In the poem "Dawn Chorus," you write, "There comes a moment when the tide turns. / Light has won again." Is this the moment when the muse comes? When the inspiration for the poem comes?

RF: Well, I'm actually enchanted by that interpretation. That's never occurred to me. I mean, it's about insomnia.

GP: Uh-huh—I just had it last night.

RF: Yeah, really. When you're lying there, and then there is a moment when the birds do start and the light changes, and somehow that seems the moment when at last you can go to sleep. But that's a wonderful metaphor for when the muse comes, and I shall probably adopt it now. That will be the new official interpretation!

GP: In the poem "Moon," you say, ". . . Old reliable Moon, who / Always makes me write poetry. / My sister Moon." Now there's a feminist mythology based on the moon and the lunar cycle. Are you thinking of that at all when you invoke the moon? Literally, a kind of feminist moon, or is it the muse, or is it just the moon?

RF: Well, I don't have any thoughts at all in my mind now because the poem is so old. But I wrote a whole book called *Another Full Moon,* which is where I really let it rip. And certainly, for all sorts of classical and traditional reasons, the moon has always been associated with dreams and lunatics and poets and women and menstruation.

GP: Is the poem "The Sibyl of the Waters" a midrash—that is, a retelling of a traditional Jewish text?

RF: I don't really know whether it is. What I know is that when Noah came out of the ark, according to Genesis, he gave thanks. That is in one of the lunettes, one of the small sections of the ceiling in the Sistine Chapel, which I studied in great detail, because Michelangelo painted the sibyls all around the ceiling. One of the sections is Noah and his sons and his daughter-in-law at the altar. And my poem is a description of that painting. Or not a description, but the image I had in my mind's eye was of Noah's daughter from the ceiling of the Sistine Chapel.

GP: That's interesting; so it's a painting poem, too. When she, the sibyl, crushes the dove against her breast, is that part of the Michelangelo?

RF: No. No, that's me.

GP: Well, we were talking about "The Sibyl of the Waters," and she crushes the dove against her breast. Is this an act of rebellion against God?

RF: I can't just say yes, it's an act of rebellion against God, because as you know that isn't the way poetry works.

GP: That was my reading of it.

RF: Yes.

GP: My guess.

RF: Mmm.

GP: Okay. Does "Miriam's Well" come from a tractate of the Talmud?

RF: Yes.

GP: Do you remember reading it?

RF: Yes, but I can't give you chapter and verse.

GP: No, but there the basic premise is something that you read.

RF: That's right. That's how I get most information.

GP: And she said the children of Israel . . .

RF: The story is that when the children of Israel were crossing the desert during the forty years, Miriam was transformed into a source of water for them, so they would not perish of thirst—a miracle. So, probably, I got my inspiration from that. I'll tell you something that's very interesting about the end of the poem. The last line is, "Remember to fill your mouth with water." Well, that wasn't the original last line. The original last line was much less interesting. It was, "Remember you must be silent," or words to that effect, and that poem was translated into Hebrew by a very good Israeli poet named Moshe Dor. And he said to me, you might be interested to know that when I translate this into Hebrew, the phrase I would use, if I were to retranslate it back into English, would be "to put water in your mouth," because that's a way of saying to keep silent in Hebrew. And I was absolutely thunderstruck, and I said, well, I'm going to change the last line of the poem now in English on the basis of this Hebrew translation. Don't you think that's fascinating?

GP: Yeah, because there you're talking about the collaboration between a translator and a poet leading to a change in the original text.

RF: Yes. That's the only time it's ever happened to me, and the only time I've ever heard of it, actually. Have you ever heard of it?

GP: No. Let me ask you about revision. Do you revise a lot? I mean, do you do it as a regular activity, or are you one of these people who are almost obsessed by it, or are you usually pretty happy with the first or second draft? What about revision?

RF: Oh, I revise and revise and revise, and poems go through ten, twenty, thirty drafts, and they might change radically from the first. There's something in the very beginning that one has to stick with. The poem's there in the beginning, but you have to find where it is. You must know this yourself. I do certainly revise a great deal. Of course, occasionally a poem comes and I hardly have to change it. That's to say, if I can just go through some three or four drafts, as far as I'm concerned, that's unrevised. But that's rare.

GP: Again, in that eloquent preface to your poems in the Bloodaxe anthology, you speak of a "continual monologue or soliloquy inside my head," and you go on to say that "this phrase or node or cluster of words includes every essential element of the poem." So that must have been what you just alluded to.

RF: Yes. I still see it like that.

GP: There's something in there that you can't change. Can you speak any more about the process? In other words, you've got this node or cluster. I already asked you about meter or breath units. Anything else you can say about the process of composition? Of taking that original seed and making a poem out of it?

RF: Well, one thing I can say in relation to one of your earlier questions, What is the thing that makes me most unhappy about being a poet? It's when that monologue ceases that I become unhappy. When I'm working on a poem, I'm working on it all the time, twenty-four hours a day. I know that it's continually in my mind and revision is going on in my head below the level of my conscious mind sometimes. I don't mean that's how all of the work is done by any means, but suddenly, it might happen. You know, when you're writing a poem, there's a section you're sure you haven't got down yet. There's something wrong. It doesn't sound right, the rhythm's wrong, or you haven't got exactly the word you want. The word you've used isn't the most appropriate word for a variety of reasons. It's a substitute, filling in until you find the real thing. It's not the most precise way to say what you want and it's also not exactly the right sound. It doesn't have the right associations. Its main meaning is correct, but side associations mean that it's unsuitable, and you still have to find another word to take its place. That word is limited by the number of syllables or the sound, the assonance, or the alliteration. There are all these prescriptive aspects to revision. Do you follow what I mean? So when I'm working on a poem, that sort of work must be going on in my head, because suddenly a line comes. I know that what I want is dot dot dot, but I haven't been thinking about it. I might have been peeling the potatoes.

GP: Do you usually work on one poem at a time, or do you have many in your head?

RF: Almost always one at a time. Sometimes a couple, or I might be working on the current poem and recent poems that aren't quite finished will be trailing behind and I might have an idea for one of them, but not with the same concentration as the one I'm working on.

GP: Okay, I've got some more questions about a few of your early poems that are in some way religious. You say something fascinating in the poem "God's

Language." You say, "God's language" has "no grammar," and you go on to say "all words" are "variations of his name," and that the angel's purpose is "to gaze / Upon God's work, and listen, / Until the day that he / Pronounce the name: Messiah." All of that is very interesting. Do you remember anything of the kernel or node behind that extremely interesting religious poem, where you're talking really about language, religion, and art?

RF: It's very difficult for me to remember. I know that there was this sort of *true-lie* aspect to it. That's to say, I came across a sentence or a phrase, "Angels have no memory." It struck me with enormous force, and everything seemed to come out of it, as if a meteorite hit something and all this stuff splattered up. Do you remember that there was a film in the sixties called *Barbarella* with Jane Fonda, a sort of science-fiction film, and there was a quite unforgettable visual image of angels trapped in rock, and I think something in the film must have been the origin of the idea that angels have no memory. You see, my sources are much more . . . *catholic* isn't quite the appropriate word!

GP: Eclectic.

RF: Yes, eclectic. If you think about "angels have no memory," the implications are staggering—or were to me at the time. And, of course, what else would you say after saying that angels have no memory? The next line *has* to be "God's language has no grammar." There's no alternative.

GP: You're way up there. Well, you're way up there in a poem called "Vertical," where you long to be free of the earth, and you're released as language. I don't know if it's language that has no grammar, but language nonetheless. You must mean some kind of sacred language again—God's language—that you're in touch with in some way? And then you say that this language sets you free from definition as Jew, woman, poet. But then I wonder how you cannot be those three things. What are you if you are not a Jew, woman, poet? Well, I think I have a feeling that what you were thinking of is that you don't want to be categorized. You want to rise above categories.

RF: That is it, of course.

GP: That is it, but still. Yes, you're a poet. You're a human poet, but you are also a Jew and a woman.

RF: Yes.

GP: So there must be a conflict between being those things and wanting to rise above them into some higher dimension.

RF: I was asked to write something—not very recently but, say, within the last few years or within the last decade, which is recent in comparison to the poems that we're talking about—about, Am I a Jewish poet? And as you can imagine, I was keen to say, no, I'm not a Jewish poet, I'm just a poet. I ended up saying that the only definition I would be happy to accept would be related to my language. That's to say I'm an English-language poet, because the language is the most important thing. So that's just a comment to add into this.

GP: Well, we're certainly back to the question of "Do you consider yourself a Jewish poet?"

RF: What I say when people ask me that is that I'm Jewish and I'm a poet, but you could say I'm a poetic Jew as much as a Jewish poet. I think most people try to escape the constraints of those sorts of definitions. When I was younger, I objected more strenuously to these categories. Now I'm getting older and more easygoing. At one time I wouldn't agree to be included in an anthology of women poets, or Jewish poets, or anything. And now I let it happen, because I know it's rather silly and infantile to have a little tantrum, and scream no no no. As you say, I'm Jewish and I'm a poet and I'm a woman and that's that. That's the way it is.

GP: What was the impact of the Holocaust on you, if any? I know you've got some poems that touch on it.

RF: When I was a teenager, when I first learnt about the Holocaust, I had nightmares about it all the time. It obsessed me and it terrified me and I'm sure it affected me horribly—disgust and fear, and a horrible mixture of wanting to find out more about it and trying to avoid learning anything more about it. It affected me totally, that's all I can say.

GP: Well, you know, I don't want to be presumptuous, but it might have affected you so strongly because you're a Jew.

RF: Of course, yes.

GP: Okay, another of these questions. Have you been to Israel and has that had any impact on you?

RF: I have been to Israel several times. My feelings about Israel are very complicated. I don't really think this is the appropriate place to go into a political discussion about it. I don't have a mystical feeling that this is the land that God promised. The attitude of the extremists, the religious extreme right in Israel at the moment, I find totally unacceptable. It's complicated: I've been to Israel; I have Israeli friends. I went to Israel first with my husband, who was invited there as a friend of Israel, a non-Jew who was a friend of Israel, to the extent that he had defended Israel at various times when there was a lot of anti-Israeli material in the press and so on. That's how I got to Israel, and sometimes I've wondered if I would ever have gone if I hadn't been taken there by my non-Jewish husband.

GP: Was he famous when you met him?

RF: No, not at all. We'd been together since long before he published his first book.

GP: Well, that first book became famous, right?

RF: That's right.

GP: Called *Saturday Night and Sunday Morning.*

RF: That was published in 1958. And here we'd been together about five years then.

GP: So he was a struggling writer until he published that book.

RF: Yes. Absolutely.

GP: Your poems contain several references to your passionate relationship with your father, but very little that I've seen about your mother, at least in terms of a passionate relationship. Does that accurately reflect your relationship with your parents? It seems a little bit unusual. The warm poems, like the one called "Learning about Him," on pages 262–63 of the *Selected Poems,* seem to be about your father. Any thoughts about that? In other words, you write about the muse and the sibyls, and all these mystical female, if not feminist, beings, but there isn't too much about your mother that I've caught.

RF: I'm fascinated that you say that because I've written more poems about my mother than about my father. I think my most anthologized poem is one called "Handbag." There is a group of poems, "Love Feast," "Handbag,"

"Wartime," "Or Her Soft Breast," all of them about my mother. Then later, "The Crescent." I didn't write poems about my parents until they were dead. I had a difficult relationship with my mother. Since her death, I've been writing more and more poems about her. In my most recent book, "This Time of Year," "The Coptic Wedding," "Lineage," "Choosing"—that's a group of poems centered very much on my mother. I usually read these poems when I give a reading, because they get a very strong and immediate audience response. They're direct and full of emotion. So I'm really a good girl who loves her mom!

GP: I must be giving your poems a male reading, a male chauvinist reading. It just struck me that there were several about the father that I thought were very passionate. Another question. In "A Discussion with Patrick Kavanagh," I assume the famous Irish poet, he advises your narrator to "be / passive, observing with a steady eye," which seems to be pretty good advice, but he seemed anything but passive and steady as a person and as a poet. His poetry seems filled with rage and bawdy, and I think he pretty much destroyed himself, from what I've heard, with drink, etc. So I'm kind of interested in that. Was that when he was quite old, or when he was quite close to the end of his life when he gave you that advice?

RF: I never met Patrick Kavanagh. I didn't know him. That's a line from a poem called "Intimate Parnassus," and the line impressed me very much. Probably the reason it had such a freight of significance is because he was describing this ideal of behavior which he could never hope to achieve. And it struck me in exactly the same way because I'm a very passionate person and to be passive, to be whatever . . . What is it? What's the quote?

GP: "To be passive, observing with a steady eye."

RF: Observing with a steady eye—that's an ideal for me as well, which is what the poem's about, but, no, I never met him.

GP: In several poems in your new book, *This Time of Year,* you describe women involved in abusive relationships with men. And in one of those poems you call yourself lucky. Lucky, I gather, for being in a good relationship. Were you describing Plath as a victim in those poems, or were you rather generalizing?

RF: Oh, no, nothing to do with Plath at all, and nothing to do with my own personal life. I suppose the reason that I'm hesitating is because you say "generalizing." Do I accept that; is that how I would describe it? I suppose they're the fruit of observation and introspection and speculation. I don't know. I'd have to look at the poems before I talk about them.

GP: On page 8 or page 16.

RF: Yeah, 8—"My Lucky Star."

GP: I mean, you seem to be talking about literary relationships.

RF: Literary relationships, that's right. It's an expression of a moment of rage against the whole male establishment as a woman writer. I was thinking about that type of writer—late nineteenth century/early twentieth century, the man who lives alone in a rather squalid room in a hotel or a bed-sitting room and spends a lot of his time in cafés and smokes a lot and drinks a lot and is a bachelor and idealizes and fears women, the way I describe it in the poem "My Lucky Star." And that was the only model of an artist that seemed to be valid when I was a young girl, and of course, to be a young girl who feels that she's an artist, and the only model of an artist you have is a man like this, and you just think, how on earth? What does that have to do with me? And, therefore, how can I ever be an artist? Or what is an artist? Etc., etc. It's to do with that sort of identity problem, let's say, of being a young woman artist. That is part of it. And then I suppose it's just high-spirited spleen after one literary party too many.

GP: When did you first feel that you wanted to be a poet?

RF: I've always written poetry. I can remember writing poetry when I was ten and eleven. I don't know. I've always known that I was a poet.

GP: Where did you go to college?

RF: I didn't go to college. I didn't have any higher education. Well, I went to art college. I went to art school, but I never finished the course. I got married when I was eighteen, and I ran off from that marriage into my present marriage when I was all of twenty.

GP: So did you run off to England, was that it?

RF: No, I was in England already. I came to England when I was fifteen. My father was English. My mother was born in what's now Moldova, and she went to America when she was six. The actual classical American "bring me your huddled masses" story. Her family had a grocery store. In what's Harlem now, I think. My cousins took me up to show me where my mother had lived when she was a little girl. It was north of Columbia University. My father went to America when he was a young man and met my mother and they got married. And then he got tired of living in America and wanted to come back to England.

GP: What do you see as the main differences between twentieth-century English and American poetry, or the scenes, the poetry scenes in England and America?

RF: It's fascinating what the differences are. I think that American poetry is having a much stronger influence in England in the last five or eight or even ten years than it did before. The young poets I know—I'm not talking about poets my age, I'm talking about poets in their thirties and forties—are all very knowledgeable about American poetry. They're interested in American poetry in a way that, unfortunately, young poets weren't when I was a young poet. But luckily, because I lived in France and Spain all through my twenties, I met lots of American poets and writers who had come to Europe. Because of not having gone to university, I really don't have many connections with English poetry. I don't have that sort of nexus of university friends, and I've noticed how important it is. Many of the people I know are American Jews. The apple finally hasn't fallen very far from the tree.

GP: Well, there's that strange, that intriguing quote from the Russian poet.

RF: Tsvetayeva.

GP: "All poets are Jews."

RF: Right.

GP: I've never been able to figure out what that means.

RF: Well, it's like Sylvia Plath, "I must be a bit of a Jew."

GP: Right, the victim.

RF: They mean victim and outsider.

GP: Which isn't the only definition.

RF: Exactly, but that's their meaning. It's the stereotype. They think they're being friendly, but you could, if you wanted to really be paranoid, say that they were being anti-Semitic.

GP: Right. That's true. Well, then . . .

RF: Well, you see, there's no pleasing Jews, is there?

GP: Do you think that you're pretty much alone as a poet, then? I mean, without a gang, without friends. You haven't had people you've sent your poems to? Groups of poets you've met with?

RF: No. Nothing like that.

GP: You've been your own support system?

RF: Yes, I suppose so.

GP: So, no one has read those poems but you before you send them out? I mean besides the editors.

RF: I've never had an editor in that sense. My relationships with editors have always just been technical.

GP: All right, now we have some daunting questions, beginning with, How does one face death, and can poetry help?

RF: Writing poetry is a response to death. It's a response to one's consciousness of death, the contemplation of one's coming death.

GP: Does it help you to prepare for it by being conscious of it and writing about it and not trying to put it out of your mind, or perhaps taking a religious approach to death, rather than facing it on a daily basis as it comes to you?

RF: I don't know about anyone else, but a basic belief of mine is that my reactions are absolutely standard; that I'm a standard human being and have the same reactions most people do. On one level, I think about death all the time. Writing poetry is a way of (*a*) thinking about death and (*b*) confronting death, accepting death. In a recent poem I wrote: "Elegies must be the oldest art form." That's my response to your question about death.

GP: Does poetry add to life's meaning above and beyond death? Can you build a faith, a way of life around it? Do you see it as a religious activity or having religious meaning, or would you rather keep it as a strictly secular activity?

RF: I don't accept those definitions—religious, secular. They imply a specific sort of religion, but I think that writing poetry is a religious activity in the sense that a lot of things people have done from the earliest times are what we could call religious or spiritual. I think *spiritual* would be the better term. Art is a way of trying to puzzle out one's position in the universe and discover the meaning of it all, beyond the basic business of brute survival. So, art is a religious activity, but it's not the same as being Christian or Jewish or any other religion.

GP: What has poetry taught you about language?

RF: It goes on teaching me about language. I mean that poetry is language. More than the thought that's expressed, poetry is the language in which it's expressed. You could say the same thought can be expressed in different sorts of language, from the most banal to the most piercing and original On the other hand, you could say that if you don't express it in exactly the same way, then the thought is different. Poetry is language. Poetry isn't just noble thoughts or good thoughts. It's language.

GP: There is, of course, a school in America called the Language poets, who want the language to be the meaning of the poem.

RF: Yes, and I don't understand that.

GP: What do you wish to still accomplish as a poet?

RF: I just want to keep writing poetry, and I hope it will get better, whatever "better" means.

GP: What place, what geographical place, do you most identify with?

RF: I love being in the country. But actually I'm a city person. I'm the cosmopolitan, that pejorative term for a Jew—rootless cosmopolitan—and I suppose London is the place I've lived in longest and where I feel most comfortable, in England. But I love being in the countryside; I need to be out of the city and to be in touch with nature—natural rhythms, a different sense of time.

GP: If you could do it again, what would you do differently?

RF: I couldn't possibly answer that.

GP: What is the most amazing thing about life?

RF: The most amazing thing is that it's here at all—that life arose, and exists.

GP: And, finally, what is the most amazing thing about your life?

RF: That I'm still alive, I suppose. You know, everyone when they're young thinks they're going to be dead by the time they're thirty and then forty and fifty.

GP: I always thought I was going to be dead by the time I was thirty-three, because that's when Hart Crane and Jesus both died.

RF: That's right. As my husband says, "I'm too old to die young." Yes.

MARGE PIERCY

MARGE PIERCY was born in 1936 in Detroit and attended the
University of Michigan. *The Art of Blessing the Day: Poems with
a Jewish Theme* is her fifteenth poetry collection. She has also
published fourteen novels. In 1990 her poetry won the Golden
Rose, the oldest poetry award in the country. Her book of craft
essays, *Parti-Colored Blocks for a Quilt,* is part of the Poets on
Poetry series of the University of Michigan Press, and she has
edited a poetry anthology, *Early Ripening.* Her poetry is repre-
sented in many anthologies. For many years now she has made
a living as a writer while residing in Wellfleet, Massachusetts.

MARGE PIERCY is a feminist poet who has made a gradual return to Ju-
daism. In our interview, she revealed, "My struggle to merge feminism and Ju-
daism began in early adolescence." She found that she "couldn't be seriously
satisfied with modern paganism, because it has such a made-up, patched-
together feel to it," so she began to explore Judaism. When she "realized that all
the Jewish holidays have a natural and an agrarian level (as well as a historic
and a religious), they became more meaningful to me." She is one of the few
contemporary poets to write liturgical poems in the tradition of *piyyutim* and
she has been engaged in writing religious verses for the Reconstructionist
Seder (*Or Chadash*).

Piercy's Jewish poems in her volume *Available Light* render religious
meaning within nature. In "A Candle of Glass," she describes associations that
come with the light of the *yahrzeit* candle, burning in memory of her mother
during Passover. Piercy's strong bond with her mother may well be her main
link back to Judaism. She energizes her religious vision with nature's fertility
and sensuous cycles.

In "The Garden as Synagogue," she views nature as sacred and writes of a
"goddess / rooted in animal power and grace, the sacred / that connects us to
the green flesh / of the grass." It is the spiritual, personified as earth goddess,
that connects man and nature. As the narrator eats the ritual food at the Seder,
she says she is "healed / to the sprouting earth that bears them all in me." She
knows she is of the earth and the earth is holy.

In the volume's final poem, "The Ram's Horn Sounding," Piercy calls attention to Rosh Hashanah, the New Year, at the same time that she defends her return to Judaism. She says it is hard to reconcile being woman and Jew and goes on to grapple with the conflict in terms of being a Jewish poet. Although she serves the word, she can only "wrestle the holy name" and knows she cannot contain or control the divine voice, yet she appears, nevertheless, to be an oracle for the "fierce / voice whose long wind lifts my hair / chills my skin and fills my lungs / to bursting."

She ends by praying to the Shekinah, the female manifestation of God, to use her "for telling and naming." Again, Piercy acts as an instrument for the divine voice. She is the prophetess inspired and fulfilled by that visionary presence, Shekinah,

> Stooping on hawk wings, prying into my heart
> with your silver beak; floating down
> a milkweed silk dove of sunset . . .

Piercy's religious poetry is written out of a romantic love for and faith in nature but centered in the Jewish vision of God and Shekinah (goddess) and the sacred cycle of holidays and rituals. In "My Mother's Body," she shows her fascination with the mother figure, Shekinah, earth goddess, and vows to carry on her mother's life as well as her own. The death of her mother may have inspired her to imagine a new feminist vision of her religion.

∎

MARGE PIERCY has a fierce Tartar face and a darkly formidable presence. I have seen her read her poetry three times, and each time she has attracted a large crowd and held them spellbound with a dynamic performance. I'll never forget how tirelessly she read and responded to student and faculty manuscripts when she visited Wright State University. She told a large gathering at her lecture that you have to be driven to succeed as a writer.

Piercy answered my questions in writing in August–September 1996.

GP: What have you found the hardest thing about being a poet?

MP: The hardest thing about being a poet is overcoming people's belief that poetry is not for them. Once you get them to a reading, you have won the battle.

GP: What is the most enjoyable thing about being a poet?

MP: The most enjoyable things about being a poet are writing poetry and performing it.

GP: Do you see your fiction and poetry as complementary? Are your fictional characters extensions of the self that is the central voice of your poems?

MP: Fiction and poetry are very different genres. They exercise different parts of the brain, really. Narrative impulse is strong but seldom has much to do with poetry. Much of my poetry comes directly out of my life. Almost none of my fiction does.

GP: What does a poet need to know about craft? Are rhyme and meter still important enough to be part of the young poet's training? What is free verse? Can it be taught?

MP: It is reasonable to have some training in rime and meter, but it helps much more to read a great many kinds of poetry from the last four hundred years, including and especially current poetry. I like Denise Levertov's term "organic verse" better than "free verse." Of course it can be taught, as much as any poetics can be taught. When I have sufficient time in a workshop, I always work with the class on line lengths and line breaks, as they are critical to the power of a poem and its flow. I always work on oral effects also. Rime is only one of those and not my favorite.

GP: In "The Ram's Horn Sounding," you write, "A woman and a Jew, sometimes more / of a contradiction than I can sweat out...." When did your struggle to merge Judaism and feminism begin, and what inspired it? Also, a related question: You have turned to both Jewish mysticism and to paganism for your symbols and myths. Is this part of the contradiction that you sweat out as a Jewish feminist poet?

MP: My struggle to merge feminism and Judaism began in early adolescence and has gone on ever since then. You give up, you give in, or you struggle: i.e, you abandon Judaism as so many Jews have; you become Orthodox and live in a set of rigid rules and strong community; or you attempt to create a Judaism you can live with your entire mind and body and brain, knowing everything that you know and not compromising. I mistrust anything, whether it is a love affair, a friendship, a business arrangement, that I have to go into pretending not to know what I know, having to be naive, having to censor any part of my intellect or experience.

I used pagan myths and holidays in the seventies, before I had begun to reexplore Judaism. It attracted me because in its present incarnation, it is women-centered. But the reason I used the Celtic names instead of the Hebrew names for the months in the lunar calendar was, as I thought I had explained there or in some essay, partly in homage to Nancy Passmore and her annual lunar calendar, which I have up in my office. I always have three calendars: a "straight" calendar, a Jewish calendar, and her lunar calendar.

I couldn't be seriously satisfied with modern paganism, because it has such a made-up, patched-together feel to it. Once I realized that all the Jewish holidays have a natural and an agrarian level (as well as a historic and a religious), they became more meaningful to me.

I have been studying Kabbalah on and off for about ten years. Ha-Shem of course is both female and male. I relate more to the female emanations. But in, for instance, the Haggadah I have been working on (every year I modify it), I used alternate forms for female and male in the blessings. A lot of people do this, I am sure. All that holds some others back is probably not knowing enough Hebrew to change the blessings accordingly.

GP: In "To Be of Use," you celebrate people who "jump into work head first." Why is work so seminal? Does the best person work the hardest?

MP: I am not much of a hierarchy maker. I am naturally and devoutly pluralistic. Therefore, there is no "best person" for me. I respect hard work, probably partly because I grew up stone working class at a time when the pride in hard work and doing something useful was still strong, when the media still celebrated ordinary work and not only the celebrity and the gorgeous façade.

GP: In your powerful poems "My Mother's Body" and "Crescent moon like a canoe," your mother is your muse. "My muse, your voice on the phone wavers with tears. / The life you gave me burns its acetylene / of buried anger, unused talents, rotted wishes, / the compost of discontent, flaring into words / strong for other women under your waning moon." Does anger define you, does it overpower your other emotions and thoughts?

MP: I think you are misreading the last lines of "Crescent moon like a canoe." I am talking about my mother, rather than myself, or rather of the energy that came into me from my mother because of *her* buried anger. She had the usual amount of suppressed anger that the weak and powerless contain. Since I have chosen to fight openly, I don't suppress or contain anger.

GP: How does your father and the Father fit into your mythology? He doesn't fare well in "Burial by salt."

MP: My father is not a mythological figure. If he does not "fare well," it is because he was who he was. He was a violent man. Now, there's someone who had plenty of anger. It is one of the characteristics I associate most with him, and probably one of the reasons I am relatively calm. We were not close and did not have much communication. He was not an educated man, but he was naturally bright. However, he read little beyond the newspaper almost cover to cover, newsmagazines like *Time* (which my mother hated), fiction of the sort the *Saturday Evening Post* published. Once he got a TV, except for the paper, basically he stopped reading. He never read any of my books. He was not interested. He did not believe a woman could produce any writing he would find worth his bother.

As for my brother, to whom I was very close when I was a child, probably you can get a pretty good picture of my individual and slanted take on him and our early and later relationship from the series of poems in the new book, *What Are Big Girls Made Of?* One section is called "The Brotherless Poems."

GP: In "A candle in a glass," you write movingly of Passover and the candle lighting and of your beloved grandmother Hannah, but you end the poem on a cynical note: "We lose and we go on losing as long as we live, / a little winter no spring can melt." There's a similar reference in "Summer mourning"—"the cost / of what is, is the bone rotting from within." Why such negativity?

MP: As for the poem "A candle in a glass," I don't understand how you can consider observing the reality of death "cynical." To be clear and unsentimental is nothing like being cynical. I respected and loved my grandmother. To recognize that she is utterly gone is not being cynical but being simply factual.

Such negativity in "Summer mourning"? That is a poem for the holiday Tisha b'Av, saddest days of the Jewish year, which concludes and culminates the mourning period for the destruction of the first and second temples in Jerusalem. The history of the Jews is largely a "negative" experience for anyone contemplating it. This poem is a contemplation of history and the cost of trying to change its direction. Is Yom Kippur a negative experience? I don't think of things in that grid. That is not a meaningful distinction to me, positive experiences, negative experiences.

GP: On the other hand, in "Nishmat," you say, "Let silence still us so you may show us your shining / and we can out of that stillness rise and praise." And in "Amidah," "All living are one and holy." So you must see light as well as darkness.

MP: I don't understand this line of questioning about light and darkness. I write poems about roses and rivers; I write love poems; I write gardening poems; I write political poems; I write religious poems. "Nishmat" was written specifically to be used as liturgy. It was written to be part of the P'Nai Or Siddur, Or Chaddash. I wrote several pieces for the siddur, as well as a few other pieces designed as parts of services. It is a "nishmat," as it says; a morning prayer designed to put a person in a frame of mind to experience holiness. That is its function.

GP: In your introduction to *Circles on the Water,* you say, "My work is of a piece. I can do more and try more, but the voice is the same voice." Can you speak of your poetic voice and how it remains constant?

MP: My poetry is more personal than my fiction, since it comes out of my life and out of the lives of others I know sometimes directly, sometimes through persona, sometimes even more indirectly than that. But it issues from the life. It is very different from writing novels, in which I create a particular world peopled by particular characters going through a set of actions specific to that world. In that sense, it is of a voice, my own voice in my poetry. I am aware I have a pretty wide range and that the voice differs. For instance, in some poems it is an intimate voice; in others it is more of a "we." In others it is more prophetic or incantatory. But it's all the range of an individual voice.

In fiction, if you are asking me to contrast the two genres, as I understand you are, every character has a "voice." In *Gone to Soldiers,* for instance, where there are ten viewpoint characters, I would hope that if you read from any given page, I could immediately tell you which character it is, because their individual voice would be strong enough to suggest their name and identity. I maintain that you could read me a page of any of them and I could identify the characters from the language, the rhythms, the idioms of that personality. There are writers, like Grace Paley, who have a consistent voice in fiction, but I am not one of them. I try to enter each character and to create a voice for that character from the inside.

GP: Do you consider yourself a Jewish poet?

MP: I consider myself a Jewish poet, although it is more important in some poems than in other poems. I consider myself an American poet, although it figures more in some poems than in others. I consider myself a feminist poet, although it is present in some poems and not in others.

GP: What place do you most identify with?

MP: Obviously the place I most identify with is Cape Cod, where I live. I have lived here for twenty-five years. I would not stay if I did not love it here. As I answer you, a hurricane is lashing us. We are far out to sea, and we suffer from that even as we usually enjoy that. It is not a landscape that permits you to ignore the nature that we are part of, to ignore the phases of the moon, the season, the winds, the tides. It is a fragile land and the impact of people and their technologies shows. It is a place I love and a place that has taught me a great deal.

GP: What is the most amazing thing about life?

MP: The most amazing thing about human lives is people's ability to regenerate after disaster, to turn around and change, to grow, to go on from devastation to a life intense in some new way. When I see that, it fills me with wonder and joy.

GP: What is the most amazing thing about your life?

MP: The most amazing thing about my life is that I have managed for at least a good portion of my life to make a living doing exactly what I want to do. I don't need to be rich to enjoy my life and I will never be powerful. If I can make enough to live comfortably where I want to live and with the person I want to live with, then I am a success. The other amazing thing is that after many, many, many relationships and collisions and misprisions and experiments, I have been together with Ira Wood for roughly twenty years. I think it's absolutely unlikely to find someone with whom you can live in a friendly and loving manner, to be sensual and intellectual, to be creative and playful, to share all manner of ideas and quirks and tasks.

ALICIA OSTRIKER

ALICIA OSTRIKER was born in 1937. She is the author of eight books of poetry, including *The Imaginary Lover*, which won the 1986 Williams Carlos Williams Award, and *The Crack in Everything*, which was nominated for a 1996 National Book Award. *The Little Space: Poems Selected and New, 1968-1998* was a finalist for the 1998 National Book Award. Her prose work includes *Stealing the Language: The Emergence of Women's Poetry in America* and *The Nakedness of the Fathers: Biblical Visions and Revisions.*

AS POET and critic, Alicia Ostriker communicates clearly and forcefully in response to complex questions. For example, I asked her about the apparent inconsistency in her statements that (*a*) women writers have been imprisoned in an "oppressor's language" while (*b*) she sides "with those who see language as inexhaustibly multiple, full of change and layering and contradiction, rather than those who see it as monolithic."

In answering my question, Ostriker described what Adrienne Rich may have meant by using her phrase "oppressor's language" to depict "forms of discourse created by and for male privilege." Yet Ostriker rejects the idea that traditional language is male: "But I think it is completely absurd to reduce language—human language, which is like God, with its center everywhere and its circumference nowhere—to the tiny orderly emissions of academic men." She believes that language is created everywhere, including "the kitchen, the butcher shop, the factory, the prison." Since language is everyone's "birthright," women must "transform and morph the tradition. . . . Language is not a brick wall. It's a swamp of unpredictable new growths, it's a stew, it's an ocean."

Like Marge Piercy and other feminists, Ostriker insists on the importance of the Shekinah, the feminine goddess found in Jewish mystical sources. Yet she realizes only too well that throughout history Jews of all persuasions have faced hostile forces, "Spoiling paradise / Spoiling even the dream of paradise." Despite tragedy, the down-to-earth importance of the mother of households and the mystical Sabbath bride offer moving and hopeful images to the narrator of "A Meditation in Seven Days":

And in my sleep, in my twentieth century bed
It's that whisper I hear, *go away,*

Don't touch, so that I ask
Of what am I the vessel

Fearful, I see my hand is on the latch
I am the woman, and about to enter

Nothing is too deep, serious, agonizing, twisted, puzzling for this poet who expresses herself with what I would call clairvoyance. "Finding the truth that lies beneath or behind the truth you already know, finding a form for it, creating a piece of beauty—that is the poet's task. . . . Poetry is a diagram of reality. A distillation of reality, that may make us free." Ostriker's definition of the poet's task could well apply to her own efforts as a poet.

▪

OSTRIKER responded to my questions in writing in August–September 1996.

GP: What have you found the hardest thing about being a poet?

AO: The hardest thing about being a poet is loneliness. Who cares about poetry? What does poetry matter? And even if poetry matters, who cares about one's own poems? Writing is a lonely affair in which you commune with the deepest and strangest aspects of your own mind and feelings—things that seem to have no place in the practical world. You struggle with the never-ending attempt to find the right metaphor, the right sound, the right cadence. "We poets in our youth begin in gladness," as Wordsworth says. "But thereof come in the end despondency and madness." The despondency of solitude, of rejection, of despair about the world, together with despair about perfecting your craft. When I was a student, there were always other student poets around. We read each other's work, we competed with and advised each other. The hardest period of my life as a poet began in the mid-sixties, when I started teaching English at Rutgers, with two children in diapers at home, and no colleagues who cared about living poets. Creative writing was something like basket weaving in my department. Something for the feeble-minded. My own poetry was in the closet. I had nobody to talk to about poetry for years and years. It was devastatingly lonely. I had to fit my writing into the chinks between motherhood and teaching freshmen. And of course when you are just getting started, you have to deal with all the rejection letters you get from magazines, and persist. There is a wonderful stanza in an H. D. poem: "In me (the worm) clearly / is no righteousness, but this— / persistence." The miasma of loneliness began to lift in the mid-seventies, when I began to find poetic companionship, at first in Berkeley in the Berkeley Poets' Co-op, then in Princeton in US 1 Poets' Co-op, which I helped found, and the New Jersey Poets and Writers Association. Many of the people from these groups are still among my closest poetic companions. No writer should be without writing cohorts. You go mad. Even Emily Dickinson, famous for weaving a web of solitude round herself, had numerous literary friendships. In fact the only poets I know who truly flew solo are William Blake and Walt Whitman. But of course they were towering geniuses. And though I don't know if Whitman suffered from loneliness—from having nobody understand what he was doing until he was an old guy—Blake certainly did. He agonized about it. Today I have peers, I have an audience, in fact several audiences. I write as a poet for a general audience, I write as a woman, I write as a Jew, and there are communities of readers for whom these identities are deeply important. Still, I never permanently shake the old sorrow of feeling in some way essentially isolated. I suppose it goes with the territory of any creative life.

GP: What is the most enjoyable thing about being a poet?

AO: Oh, nowadays, everything. The writing, the revising, the performing. I love the way a poem moves me from what I already know, into the unknown—how exploratory it can be. How, when something confuses or disturbs me, I can come to understand it through the act of writing. I love performing. I like to make people in an audience laugh and cry. Revising can still be hell, of course. Not finding the right word, the right flow of sounds, to make the poem come. But it is, so to speak, a holy hell. Everything connected with the actual making of poetry is a joy, and I am infinitely grateful for it.

GP: You have referred to William Blake as "first among poets in my life." Is he still so, and are there other poets who have influenced you profoundly?

AO: I wrote my doctoral dissertation on Blake's prosody; the dissertation, "Vision and Verse in William Blake," was published as a book in 1965. I also edited Blake's *Complete Poems* for Penguin. That was published, with my two hundred pages of notes, in 1977. For all those years, Blake was my guru, my main man, my spiritual and moral guide, my encyclopedia. The richness of not only his lyrics but his prophetic poems is incalculable. I've written about my long and stormy relationship with Blake in an essay called "The Road of Excess," published in a collection of essays called *The Romantics and Us.*

At the same time, as an American poet coming of age in the sixties and seventies, I was powerfully influenced by the Whitman, Williams, and

Ginsberg line. My early training was traditional; I wrote in fixed forms all through school, and developed my ear that way. But open form meant the radical necessity of improvising the music of poetry the way a jazz soloist has to improvise. You know where you've just been, but you don't know where you're going. The poetry has to have that feeling of newness, freshness, openness to the future. It is a way of responding to time, to history—your personal history, and the world's. A way of writing a kind of hopefulness into the form of your work. I never think of open form as being "free verse." Eliot says, "No verse is free to the man who knows his business." In fact, open form is harder. You have to create your own rules as well as play with them. Traditional forms are in a real sense easier to work with. Like Yeats, I like "the fascination of what's difficult."

In the mid-seventies I began being influenced by American women's poetry, and then the sources began to explode. H. D., Plath, Sexton, Swenson, Rich—I wrote essays on them, they changed my work, but so did numerous others. Marge Piercy, Carolyn Kizer, Maxine Kumin, Diane Wakoski, Sharon Olds, Eleanor Wilner, Judy Grahn, Marilyn Hacker, Ntozake Shange, Sonia Sanchez, Lucille Clifton, Toi Derricotte, Ai—I could go on and on. There is a sense in which every one of these writers is visionary. Every one is charting new territory, traveling where no poet has traveled before. This is an extraordinary time to be writing as a woman. We follow centuries of silence. The world is all before us. And it is within us. Half the experience of humanity remains to be explored and lifted into language.

GP: You say women writers have been imprisoned in an "oppressor's language" (*Stealing the Language*), and yet you also say, "I stand with those who see language as inexhaustibly multiple, full of change and layering and contradiction, rather than those who see it as monolithic" (*Feminist Revision and the Bible*). Is there an inconsistency in those two statements?

AO: The phrase "the oppressor's language" is not my invention, nor does it represent my personal experience. It comes from an Adrienne Rich poem, "The Burning of Paper Instead of Children," written in 1968, a crisis year for our country and for Adrienne herself, who at that time was teaching in an open admissions program at the City University of New York, an experience that marked for life everyone who taught in it. "The Burning of Paper Instead of Children" is like a response to Arnold's "Dover Beach." An anti–"Dover Beach." Where Arnold proposes love as an escape from a meaningless, cruel world, Rich makes clear that love is itself a problem, not a solution. It is as real and painful a problem as poverty and racial prejudice. When the speaker in this fragmented, tormented poems says to her lover, "[T]his is the oppressor's language / yet I need it to talk to you," there is a sense of hope wrestling with despair. And we know that Rich has brooded on the question of language throughout her career. A few years later, the nascent second-wave feminist movement in America took it for granted that "the oppressor" was male, and that culture is dominated by forms of discourse created by and for male privilege. In France, and to a certain extent in America, the concept of an "Écriture feminine" became fashionable in the 1970s. I am condensing a great deal of complicated cultural history here, as you can well imagine. A great deal of complicated analysis of language, spoken and written, and the ways in which it encodes gender relations. But the idea behind "Écriture feminine" is that language itself is wholly and irredeemably male, that it excludes female reality, and that therefore a wholly female language needs to be invented. I think many women did believe that.

My own view is different. For me the idea of an "Écriture feminine" is nonsense. It's true that the various discourses of high culture have indeed more or less thoroughly excluded female participation, for at least two thousand years. But I think it is completely absurd to reduce language—human language, which is like God, with its center everywhere and its circumference nowhere—to the tiny orderly emissions of academic men. Nonsense! Language is generated everywhere. In the kitchen, the butcher shop, the factory, the prison, it sprouts and flourishes. Language is our birthright: we find the loopholes in authoritative systems, we twist the lion's tail, we drill down to the water table, we steal and mask, we transform and morph the tradition. Every creative person does that. Women as a class do it too. Yes, of course, every marginalized group comes up against an "oppressor's language." The language of authority, whose main message for us is "thou shalt not." We need to recognize that. But we also need to see how full of complication language is, how full of potential for us. Language is not a brick wall. It's a swamp of unpredictable new growths, it's a stew, it's an ocean. Rich in another poem, "Diving into the Wreck," speaks of wanting to explore "the damage that was done / and the treasures that prevail."

Throughout *Stealing the Language,* I try to show that there is a submerged tradition of women's writing in this country that partly parallels, partly deviates from, the mainstream of male writing. In my last chapter, I make the claim that what I call revisionist myth making is one strategy women poets employ to transform the meaning of gender in our culture. And really, I go on from there, from that point in *Stealing the Language* to my biblical work in *Feminist Revision and the Bible* and *The Nakedness of the Fathers.* Both those books spring from an absolute faith that women can wrestle a blessing out of the tradition that has come down to us. The language of our fathers is also the language of our mothers, and it holds the seeds of a future. As Sylvia Plath says in "Mushrooms," "Our foot's in the door."

GP: You write that women are indignant at the assumption that masculinity represents "superiority of mind and reason" over "female emotionality, subjectivity, and corporeality" (*Stealing the Language* 132–33). Yet doesn't that dichotomy force a choice between difference and similarity that you oppose because it perpetuates a "slave mentality" for women (*Feminist Revision and the Bible* 106)?

AO: The whole point is that the mind-body dichotomy is stupid. It's old, it's philosophically enshrined, but it's stupid. Mind and reason aren't superior to emotion and the body. Read Blake, who was the first poet in the English language able to say this in poetic form. Read Whitman. And men are not in fact particularly rational, nor are women in fact particularly emotional. These are myths. Self-fulfilling myths which need a little alteration. I seek to be a rational and spiritual and emotional and physical creature. So do you, I hope. I'd rather not have someone tell me I'm forbidden to be cerebral because I'm a woman, and I'd rather you didn't think you're forbidden to experience deep feeling because you're a man.

And please, how much insight does it take to perceive the obvious fact that men and women are partly alike, partly different from each other? What can perpetuate a "slave mentality" for women is the insistence that we are always and totally different from men. There are some bright women who think so—Luce Irigaray, for example—but they are wrong. They are too shackled to the dualisms of the past to recognize a simple reality.

GP: "A Meditation in Seven Days" is a moving, consummate poem, about which I have several questions. Is it an example of feminist revisionary mythology? Does it exemplify your perception that the common denominator of the women's spirituality movement is sacredness of the body? You quote Judith Plaskow in your note to the poem. Do you believe that images of the goddess will indeed be incorporated into Judaism? The Orthodox certainly don't seem revisionist. Finally, what moved you to write this beautiful poem? Was the process of creating it different from your other poems?

AO: "A Meditation in Seven Days" in *Green Age* is a poem that broods about the significance of women and femaleness within traditional Judaism, and ends in a prophecy or dream of change. I began the poem in 1986, in the notebook I was using for Jewish reading. I had already begun *The Nakedness of the Fathers*, my own midrashic work, and I was reading wildly. Buber, Wiesel, Yiddish stories—I was casting my net freely, to gather in as many different meanings of the word "Jew" as I could. For Jewishness is not a single thing, it is multiple and full of inconsistencies. And I remember very clearly the moment when I began the poem. I was in the middle of reading Adrienne Rich's

"Sources," when some mysterious energy in that poem sent me suddenly to my own notebook, where I began writing fast and furiously, beginning with the paradox of the idea that Jewishness from God on down seems to be so much defined by its male heroes, patriarchs and prophets, male rabbis and their male students and disciples—yet Jewishness in biological terms comes through the mother's line. Sarah's line. The chain of birth is matrilineal. So the first line of my poem is in italics: "*If your mother is a Jew, you are a Jew.*" And then I found myself going on to explore the layers and complexities of women and female symbolism within Judaism. The power of the first matriarch, Sarah—but also the defining of woman as sexual temptation. The denial and rejection of the feminine aspect of God, about which you can learn in Merlin Stone's *When God Was a Woman* and Raphael Patai's *The Hebrew Goddess.* Patai claims that the goddess who was intermittently worshipped in ancient Israel alongside Yahweh goes underground, as it were, but reappears in such figures as the Matronit and the Shekinah, in Jewish mysticism. But then there is the exclusion of women from male worship and male study, from the time of exile onward. As a woman with intellectual and spiritual yearnings, this is unbelievably painful to me. But then again, in the Enlightenment, in *haskalah,* the education of women becomes important, and in all the movements associated with social justice and Zionism women have a role, a part in the dream. And then again there is the down-to-earth importance of the mothers of households, there is the mystical welcoming of the Sabbath bride, and ultimately there is the hope that feminine images of divinity will once again be reincorporated within Judaism.

Obviously this won't happen tomorrow. But it is already happening in many non-Orthodox congregations and *havurot,* especially in the Jewish Renewal movement. Ultimately, even Orthodoxy is bound to change. Every tradition remains alive by changing, even though every tradition likes to represent itself as permanent and changeless. Orthodoxy itself has changed over the centuries, and will go on changing as Orthodox women become more active as students of Talmud, which is already starting to happen both here and in Israel. And yes, I do believe with the theologian Judith Plaskow that a purely male God is nothing but an idol made in man's image, so if we want to avoid idol-worship, our understanding of God has to change.

But back to the poem—of course it works by images, not theories. It is a poem, not an essay. And the images arise partly from dreams, from the unconscious, maybe even from the collective unconscious, if Jung is right. I have been deeply influenced by the poet H. D., who trusted the spiritual significance of dreams and myths. For her, the Holy Spirit—the third person of the Christian Trinity—makes itself known to us in dreams. I love that idea. For me, the vision of the barefoot woman knocking at the door in the final poem of "Meditation in Seven Days" is mysteriously associated with the coming of spring, images of fiddlehead ferns unfurling, snakes unpeeling, mushrooms arising from the moisture of the forest floor. Who is she? She is nameless. I dreamed her, or perhaps she dreamed me.

GP: In "The Eighth and Thirteenth," you say "art destroys / silence." Is art ultimately a political act? And do you agree with Tsvetayeva that "all poets are Jews?"

AO: "The Eighth and Thirteenth" is about two symphonies of Shostakovich. The Eighth Symphony commemorates the siege of Leningrad during World War II, during which three million people died. The Thirteenth Symphony is based on Yevtoshenko's poem "Babi Yar." Both are deeply strong, deeply painful works. But Stalin forbade the playing of the Eighth Symphony in the Soviet Union after its first performance, because it was not cheerful enough. Patriotic art, socialist realism, was supposed to be cheery and uplifting. So it was not performed again until after Stalin's death. Similarly, Yevtoshenko could not have published "Babi Yar" until the thaw following Stalin's death. The statement "Art destroys silence" comes from Shostakovich's autobiography, and refers specifically to the breaking of the silence about the massacre and mass burial of the Jews of Kiev at that site. Shostakovich, by the way, is a ferociously brilliant writer as well as composer. He claims that people knew about Babi Yar before the poem, but were silent. Yes, for him art is the hammer thrown at the glass house of fear. It breaks silence. I find it moving and gratifying that this Russian man could compose great music out of the suffering of his fellow Russians, but also out of the suffering of Jews. Part of the task of the artist is to reach across boundaries, to love and empathize with the other, the stranger. All Jews, by the way, are enjoined to do exactly this, whether they are artists or not: "Love ye therefore the stranger, for you were strangers in the land of Egypt."

Yes, all art is political. Either it is political or it is wallpaper. I like to say that poetry which takes no risk is like wallpaper. It makes a pleasant background. But after all, even wallpaper is political! You have to have a certain amount of money to afford wallpaper. You have to belong to what Veblen called the leisure class—the middle class, that needs to engage in conspicuous consumption to demonstrate its prosperity. And where does the money come from? No, it doesn't grow on trees, it grows in specific social and political environments which protect it. The garden in which money grows is fed and watered by politics; politics builds the fences that keep out the poor, keep them from walking on the grass and tearing up the shrubbery. And poetry—at least the poetry that gets into the anthologies and textbooks—has almost always been the property of the leisure classes that support it. Homer is political. Dante is political. Shakespeare is political. Milton is political. But it is usually only the art that comes from dissenting or revolutionary movements that gets called political. So we know Milton is—the man was the great propagandist for regicide, after all, as Cromwell's Foreign Secretary after the hanging of Charles I, and *Paradise Lost* is so antimonarchical that Milton was in danger of arrest and execution himself after the Restoration of Charles II. We don't think of Shakespeare as political, but of course he was. It is just that he supports monarchy instead of attacking it.

Of course, art is not merely political—it is many other things too. That's what makes the difference between art and propaganda. Propaganda is good for the moment, but art stays good, stays fresh, when the moment has passed.

Tsvetayeva is a beautiful example. So is Akhmatova. What Tsvetayeva actually said, by the way, was "Poets are Yids." She used a term more demeaning, more pejorative, in a Russian context, than "Jews." It was her way of saying that poets are despised, and live at the whim of the powerful. How lucky we are in America. We are merely a despised, not an endangered, species.

GP: In "The Book of Life," you write of those who stand on holy ground "outside the synagogue" in a "perennial garden / Jews like ourselves have just begun to plant." Is the essence of Judaism for you outside the synagogue? What forms does it or should it take to reach you and others who share your views?

AO: I do not believe there is such a thing as "the essence of Judaism." There are multiple strands, multiple layers, dynamically related to each other. My own background is Eastern European. All my grandparents were Socialists, non-observant Jews, but very real Jews nonetheless. Moral Jews, ethical Jews, Jews who believed in justice and in the brotherhood of man—that was what I got from my parents. My religious training consisted of being told that religion was the opiate of the people. But my moral training came straight from the prophets of Israel. Forget about ritual. Feed the hungry, clothe the naked. Care for widows and orphans. Free humanity from oppression. My husband's family was Reconstructionist. Presently I'm a member of a P'nei Or congregation, part of the movement of Jewish Renewal. I think it's inevitable in any religion that some people are psychologically and emotionally attached to past tradition, while others have one foot in the past and want to take that next step into the future. Does this produce tension? Of course it does, and that tension is healthy. It is a sign of life. The same is true of American democracy. Where would the radicals be without conservatives, and vice versa? We push and pull at each other, we call each other bad names, and somehow we move forward. In spite of tragedy.

GP: In *The Nakedness of the Fathers,* you say, "I am and am not a Jew." Is it possible to resolve the contradiction, the tension, that you feel as woman, poet, and Jew?

AO: "I am and am not a Jew." That is the opening sentence of *The Nakedness of the Fathers*. I love that sentence. I think it grabs people, and it should. I want my readers to feel the kick of contradiction, the torsion of tension. Not only in myself but in themselves. Contradiction and tension are part of life. Where would poetry be without tension? There is tension even in the music, the rhythms of poetry, between the pull of traditional meter and the urge toward open form. And what's wrong with contradiction? You don't hear Whitman saying he wants to resolve his contradictions. Not at all. "Do I contradict myself? Very well then, I contradict myself. I am large, I contain multitudes." Life is like that. Face it. Denial is death.

GP: You are a feminist poet bent on changing Judaism and patriarchal culture in general, yet you say you must remember that "I am my fathers, just as much as I am my mothers" (*Nakedness of the Fathers* 15). You are a feminist yet you glorify your relationships with your husband and children in very traditional ways. Does your art come from these kinds of conflicts, or do you see no conflicts or contradictions here?

AO: See above!

GP: What was the impact of the Holocaust on your poetry?

AO: I believe that the most important homage one can pay to the dead is to try to help life prevail: to love the great whirlwind of life, to praise it, to nourish it, never to try to reduce it to something less than life. I hope my writing shows this. When I was pregnant with my first child, I found myself thinking often about the vileness of war in general and the horror of the Holocaust in particular, and wrote the line "whoever has died, I make this child for you." Adorno is exactly wrong, I think: after the Holocaust, one not only can write poetry, one must. Hatred and death are to be fought against with all the strength of one's life—and in my case, that means through art. But I've really only written two "Holocaust poems." One is "Poem Beginning with a Line by Fitzgerald-Hemingway" in *The Imaginary Lover*, which is about three men who saved thousands of Jewish lives during World War II: Otto Schindler, Raoul Wallenberg, and the French Protestant pastor André Trocme. The poem is a meditation on the true meaning of heroism. My other "Holocaust poem" is "The Eighth and Thirteenth." But I can't say I'm comfortable with the term. My piece on the Book of Esther in *Nakedness* meditates, among other things, on the long history of the persecution of Jews, and the way my grandfather introduced me to that history when I was a small child. And my piece on Noah treats him as a man suffering from survivor guilt.

GP: You address death in your "Mastectomy Poems." Was it tough to reveal so much of your pain, grief, anguish, anxiety, etc.? Can poetry such as "The Mastectomy Poems" help to heal pain? Can the writing of such poetry be a therapeutic act?

AO: Frankly, writing that sequence of poems was a pleasure, because I knew intuitively that they were going to be very good poems. I worked hard on those poems, polishing and scraping, for about six months; they went through several sweaty drafts, I got advice from several friends—but all the while, I knew they would turn out well. It was like modeling from clay. The life experience is the raw material. Doesn't Coleridge tell us that? I'm afraid I don't think of poetry as therapy for the poet. Poetry can be therapeutic for its readers, by articulating for them what they cannot say for themselves, and enabling them to understand their experience as belonging to a larger pattern. But not for the poet. Spilling one's guts isn't what it's about, either. Finding the truth that lies beneath or behind the truth you already know, finding a form for it, creating a piece of beauty—that is the poet's task. You might say that poetry is diagnostic, rather than therapeutic. Poetry is a diagram of reality. A distillation of reality, that may make us free. You might also notice that there is a fair amount of joking in those poems. I think it is important to leaven tragedy with levity. That's something I learned from Allen Ginsberg. Did you ever notice what a funny poem "Howl" is?

GP: You were nominated for a National Book Award for *The Crack in Everything*. What does the title mean?

AO: I lifted the title from a refrain of a Leonard Cohen song. It goes, "There is a crack, a crack in everything, / That's how the light gets in." Beautiful line. A friend sent me the tape, and when I played it for the first time driving to work, I knew I had my title. It's metaphysical, it's kabbalistic, and it is also very simple and ordinary. Light comes through the cracks. Illumination comes through the flaws. As Sylvia Plath says, "Perfection is boring." Imagine living in a world without cracks, a smooth, perfectly closed world. It would be like a padded cell. Or a womb for the unborn. Thank heaven for the cracks and the craziness.

IRENA KLEPFISZ

IRENA KLEPFISZ was born in Warsaw, Poland, in 1941 and emigrated to the United States in 1949. Educated in New York City public schools and Workmen's Circle Yiddish schools, she attended City College of New York and received her Ph.D. in English literature from the University of Chicago. An activist in lesbian/feminist communities, she has published many books, including *A Few Words in the Mother Tongue: Poems Selected and New, 1971–1990* and *Dreams of an Insomniac: Jewish Feminist Essays, Speeches and Diatribes.*

IRENA KLEPFISZ is haunted by memories, but how could she not be? Born in the Warsaw Ghetto in 1941, she was fated to witness a world of suffering and death. Her father was killed when he hurled himself on a Nazi machine gun to protect his comrades in the Warsaw Ghetto Uprising. The poet and her mother survived because her mother was able to pass as Polish. After the war, mother and daughter emigrated to the United States when Irena was eight.

The venerable Polish-Jewish culture that Irena Klepfisz was born into was destroyed by Nazi genocide. She has committed herself to the cause of keeping Yiddish (the mother tongue) and *Yiddishkayt* (the Yiddish way of life) alive. Much of her poetry, essays, and plays as well as lectures, teaching, and social and political activism is devoted to this end.

One of Klepfisz's best-known works, titled "*Bashert*," combines poetry and prose, memory and imagination, dream and reality to depict key events in the poet's life. Sections 1 through 4 of "*Bashert*" are written in prose blocks. The poet views them as prose poems: "I think there's that element that to me is a poetic force, that pushes the poem so that by the end of the poem I have become a keeper of the accounts." "1: Poland: My Mother is walking down a road," describes the war-torn Poland faced by the poet and her mother. Klepfisz has so much to present that her lines must stretch to the right-hand margin:

> My mother is sick. Goiter. Malnutrition. Vitamin deficiencies.
> She has skin sores which she cannot cure. For months now she
> has been living in complete isolation, with no point of

233

reference outside of herself. She has been her own sole advisor,
ompanion, comforter. Almost everyone of her world is
dead. . . .

There are those who say that poetry after Auschwitz is not possible, but
there are also those of us who would claim that the literature of the survivors
has given us something invaluable and at times powerful and unforgettable.
Klepfisz's poetry is part of this literary achievement. At the margins of poetry
and prose she writes with clarity and precision about cataclysmic moments
that occurred in her very young life, bringing the reader into her nightmarish
world.

Klepfisz's harsh view of America comes from the poet's loyalty to the so-
cialism of the Jewish labor movement; her vision is that of a secular Jew. "I was
taught that capitalism oppresses the working masses and all poor people, that
it has to be smashed, and that we are to work toward building a classless
society."

Besides standing for the values of the Jewish Labor Bund, Klepfisz is also a
leader of the lesbian/feminist movement. Proud of her Jewish legacy, she faced
a painful conflict. "I knew that the moment I declared myself a lesbian, I would
become a stranger." When she did come out in 1973–74, there was little chance
of reconciliation with the Jewish community, but she found support and en-
couragement within the lesbian/feminist movement. Twenty-five years later,
she believes there is hope that gays and lesbians may find acceptance within
some sectors of the Jewish community.

Even in the remarkable dual-language poem "*Etlekhe Verter oyf Mame-
Loshn*/A Few Words in the Mother Tongue," there are references to "*di
lezbianke* / the one with a roommate" as part of a catalogue of types of Jewish
women. This poem differs from the poems of "*Bashert.*" Instead of making its
impact via concentrated description, the poem is a skillful interweaving of Yid-
dish and English equivalent words and phrases that creates its effect largely
through sound. To this reader it seems almost natural when the last third of
the poem is written almost entirely in Yiddish, heightening the poem's audi-
tory power. It is one instance of Klepfisz's deliberate use of Yiddish as a way of
keeping the language alive.

■

ON SATURDAY, February 8, 1997, I interviewed Irena Klepfisz by phone via
answering machine with tape recorder.

GP: What have you found the hardest thing about being a poet?

IK: Earning a living.

GP: Anything else?

IK: The hardest thing about being a poet? I don't know whether you experience this, but I feel a chasm between what I experience internally as a writer struggling with poetry and what other people perceive a poet is. I experience pressure to "poeticize," be prolific, to be constantly "a poet." For me poetry is private. I always feel like I am different from what a poet is supposed to be. You're with a group of people and something happens. And someone says, "Oh you should write a poem about that." They think they recognize the substance of poetry, of a poetic moment. But a lot of my own struggle is to discover the poetic moment. Also I'm a very slow poet and an obsessive rewriter. I do endless revisions. Yet people always seem to want to know when your next book is being published.

GP: Where does that pressure come from that you're talking about? From the literary community?

IK: I think it's both from society in general and from the literary community. At the book party for my collection *A Few Words in the Mother Tongue,* which represented more than twenty years of work, some people already wanted to know when my next book was coming out. I said, well, in twenty years or so. In some ways it's a compliment. They like your work. They want more. Still, it's hard not to experience this as pressure.

But I think there's also a professional component here. It's a kind of consumerism because poetry and poems are viewed as products—like everything else—and you're supposed to keep "making" more and more of them. But my poetry is intensely private, about my internal process and how I'm adjusting my life to the broader life and where I am in my life and what I'm thinking about and what's happening in the world and how it is or is not in sync and so on. So I'm simultaneously flattered, stymied, and offended by questions about my writing. I feel like I'm on one planet and the readers, meaning everybody else, are on another.

GP: I've always thought that poetry wasn't part of popular culture or middle-class culture in America, and you're making it sound like it is. You think of a best-selling author as turning out a product because it is distributed in a big way and sometimes it gets made into a movie and all that sort of thing. But you're saying even without those big carrots out there, poetry is still like that for you.

IK: I don't think that poetry is part of popular culture, but I think those who practice the art of poetry are affected by the values of the culture. I think the "poetry world" is a small world, and I think it's a world that's very aware of itself. It's not like the big screen and it's not like big sellers, but it's a defined world. It's not that different from the academic world where academics are expected to publish at a certain rate in order to continue teaching. And if poetry hasn't entered popular culture, it *has* entered the academic sphere. Most poets, if they are able to earn a living at all, usually earn it in academia. In other words, academia acknowledges them as poets and allows them to teach and survive as poets. There are always poets who remain outside of it, but generally that's where the money's going to come from: teaching or giving lectures and readings at universities and other well-paying institutions. We're not going to earn money by reading poetry in our local coffeehouse. And we're not going to earn money by publishing because our royalties aren't going to amount to anything. I'm more aware of that because my academic teaching has been so erratic; I'm constantly looking for work. In searching, I sense others' expectations about what I should be "producing."

Today, I do a lot of different kinds of writing. But when I began, I wrote nothing but poetry. So in the early years when I said I was a writer—I'm not even sure I said that—I think I said I was a poet. That's changed over the years, and I do a lot of different things now. I've written a play for five voices; I've written a bilingual (Yiddish/English) performance piece; I have developed a passion for Yiddish and have in the past translated and continue to translate Yiddish poetry and prose; I co-wrote the narration for a video documentary. I work as an editorial consultant on Yiddish for the Jewish feminist journal *Bridges*. I've written critical articles about Yiddish women's literature and Jewish Eastern-European women activists, and I've done political work and political writing. So over time, my sense of my writing has changed in terms of who I am as a writer and what I write.

So now, I really feel more like a writer than a poet. I think some people—many people—stick with poetry. But for whatever reason, that didn't happen with me. There are well-meaning friends and acquaintances who regret this development in my life. They say to me: "It's too bad you haven't been writing at all"; and what they really mean is I haven't been "working on my poetry"—or haven't published any poetry. In fact, I *have* been writing poetry (but not publishing it). It's also true that I've been working more on other kinds of writing during this period.

GP: So you've become a professional writer.

IK: Well, you know, I still don't earn my money by writing.

GP: Right. You still earn your money by teaching.

IK: I earn my money by teaching or lecturing or giving readings.

GP: We've got a book in the making, because we've only covered one question out of forty. The second question is, What is the most enjoyable thing about being a poet?

IK: The most enjoyable thing about being a poet is sitting alone in a room thinking about what you want to write and working on a poem and having the sudden realization that you thought you were writing about one thing and instead you are actually writing about something else, and this occurs in this silence where you're dialoguing with yourself or talking to yourself. As extremely frustrating as this can be at times, it's also the most satisfying and the most peaceful and the time that I'm least distracted by the world, even if what I'm writing about is outside of me. That kind of moment is always the best. It's what always wows me, what I want to return to; and when I don't do it enough I always feel off-kilter.

GP: So when you write prose, it's a little different? It's not as private and personal as poetry?

IK: Some of it can be, but for the most part it's much more externally directed. It usually has a point. The goal usually remains the same in a piece of prose for me. If I decide to write on a certain topic, I may end up taking a different route than I thought originally, but the aim is the same and remains the same. In prose, I believe the most exciting moment is finding out what I think and feel, and as soon as I do, I always despair because I know I now have put it down on paper; whereas with poetry, the whole process becomes the poem and that's always satisfying.

In the last few years, I've learned to merge poetry and prose. I've been writing parables and they're not really fiction and they're not really poetry, but they're certainly a poetic kind of prose. They're in between an essay and a story and a poem. They do have points to make, but I'm never quite clear what those points are until the process is over. So they're different from essays in that sense, but they're certainly not laid out on the page like poems; they're laid out like prose.

GP: Sections 1 to 4 in "*Bashert*" are written in prose paragraphs or blocks. Are those pretty similar to what you just talked about?

IK: Those are actually a little different because I was experimenting when I was working on "*Bashert*." In that poem, I really was trying to push the limits of poetry. The last section is much more rhythmical than the others in terms of the prose. There's one parable in my essay collection *Dreams of an Insomniac* called "The Lamp." It was the first one I wrote and it's part autobiography and part fiction. The other parables have gotten more complex since that one. I stuck it in the essay book because it really didn't belong in the poetry book, but it probably doesn't even belong in the essay book either. It's a kind of weird genre for me that I made up for myself, which I'm comfortable with at the moment, but it's clear to me this is not poetry.

GP: Getting into craft, although you write free verse, do you believe that rhyme and meter are important enough to be part of the young poet's training? Do you believe in the metrical tradition? Is it a vital part of the poetry of today or not?

IK: I make students try various forms using rhyme and meter, whether it's a villanelle or a sonnet. And I play around with them myself. I think form has become a bit more important to me today than it was twenty years ago. I'm not even quite sure why. I have this series called "Work Sonnets," which was a deliberate move against the self-consciousness of the form. And I'm experimenting with Yiddish and English. A lot of the Yiddish poetry that I was raised on was in fact rhymed and metered and some of it was proletariat, or what we would call today working-class, poetry. As a child, I was required to memorize it in my Yiddish schools. I totally internalized it and it was very important to me in terms of shaping me as a poet. When I teach, I want young writers to understand that when they choose free verse it is a conscious choice. I want them to be able to recognize when form helps and when form inhibits. They need to understand when they're choosing one or the other and for what reason.

GP: If you're going to write free verse, you have to know what you're free from.

IK: Right, exactly.

GP: The next question is, What is free verse and can it be taught?

IK: I'm conscious of line breaks even if they don't follow a pattern of spacing, of how words look on a page, and I may stop working with the words of a poem and not stop working on the way I lay it out. I ask students to become conscious of that. I teach them that even if their poetry comes out "in a gush," and they don't touch it, they're still making a choice to leave it as it is. The poet has to make that decision; it's deliberate. They have the option of changing it, and if they take the option of not changing it, that is a choice as well.

GP: What do you think inspired you to be a poet? And do you remember writing your first poem?

IK: I don't remember writing the first poem. I remember writing the first poems or groups of poems.

GP: You were young?

IK: I was very young. I was in my mid-teens. I think I was fourteen or fifteen. I think I started writing because I was so frustrated. By the time I came to the United States, English was my fourth language. I was angry at having been dislocated for a third time. I was quite a poor English student. I was a great math and science student, but I think I failed everything in English.

GP: Well, math is a kind of universal language.

IK: Right. In math, I didn't have to verbalize. When I got into high school, I was an honors student. I was in an honors section in all subjects. But eventually I was thrown out of honors English—a tremendous humiliation. I think I really turned to poetry and writing in general because it could be private. I didn't want to show it to anybody, and I didn't want to fail anything. I really needed to try to articulate. I couldn't speak up in classes, I grew more silent. They didn't know what to do with me. Finally, I stopped speaking in class altogether. The teachers would call on me, and I would stand there—not saying anything. So I probably turned to poetry because I didn't think it needed to be grammatical. I could do anything I wanted; it represented a kind of freedom.

There were two phases. During the first phase, I wrote what I thought would be considered poetry. There was no control of any sort. I never even knew what it meant to rewrite anything. That was very important to me and it was a tremendous relief. I started rewriting much more consciously when I was in graduate school and then later I had a realization about craft and about spacing and words and those kinds of issues. It was a long process for me. I wrote volumes before my first book came out, and then my first book came out when I was thirty-three. It might have been my tenth book.

I wrote a lot but I never showed it to anybody. I was very secretive. I just didn't want it touched. I was really burned by teachers and school and so I was kind of a late bloomer.

GP: So, who encouraged you or who became your contemporaries, your peers in poetry?

IK: For the first seventeen years or so, almost no one even knew I was writing. I told one friend in graduate school in Chicago and showed her my work. In the early seventies in New York I began to show some of my work. I even sent out a couple of pieces. I was surprised that I got into *The American Poetry Review*. Armand Schwerner published a couple of things of mine, and the *Chicago Review* published some. This was sort of hit-or-miss. At that time, I really had no idea where to send my poems.

But ultimately, my becoming public with my work and admitting I viewed myself as a poet had a lot to do with feminism and the lesbian/feminist movement. It was interesting that these parts of my life converged. When I came out, I happened to meet some lesbians who were forming a writing group. I'd never attended workshops or groups because I was so private, but I went into this group not for feedback but really just for social contact with other writers. In the mid-seventies and late seventies, there was an explosion of lesbian and feminist alternative presses and publications and there were a lot of journals and reviews. That's really how I got the courage—not so much by refining my poetry, which I never did in this group, but by just getting used to being more public about it, by showing it. I can't even describe the terror I felt at the start of that group. But it wasn't anything high-powered. We were all unpublished.

GP: So you see yourself as a lesbian feminist poet.

IK: I see myself also as a Jewish poet.

GP: I have a quote from Adrienne Rich from the beginning of your *A Few Words in the Mother Tongue*. She says that "'*Bashert*' takes its place (as does Klepfisz' poetry as a whole) in a multicultural literature of discontinuity, migration and difference. Much of this new literary flowering is of course also lesbian and feminist." My question is: Can your poetry be what Adrienne Rich says it is and also in some way an extension or an expression of Jewish literary tradition?

IK: I don't shy away from the labels. I think partly because my lesbian/feminist commitment is very strong, and so I'm comfortable in my poetry being in that context as well as being in a special Jewish issue of *Prairie Schooner*. Either of those contexts is fine with me. I don't feel either limits me. The way things have played themselves out makes me feel grateful to the lesbian/feminist movement because it really did help me get out there. I'm not sure whether I would have ever really been picked by a university press or by other presses to be published. The one thing about the lesbian/feminist movement is that we had a lot of room to do whatever we wanted to do, and so I'm very grateful because the movement really gave me the impetus, and now of course I'm anthologized in very mainstream anthologies, including Jewish ones.

GP: Another question. Your father lies in an unmarked grave, killed as he threw himself in front of Nazi machine-gun fire while fighting in the Warsaw Ghetto. In some ways, your Holocaust poetry is a memorial to him, yet your primary allegiance is to the lesbian/feminist community. So I'm wondering, is there a paradox there? I'm thinking of the poem "Searching for My Father's Body." I'm saying that the Holocaust poetry in many ways is about your heroic father and yet your primary audience and allegiance are women. So it seems to me there's a tension there.

Let me go on, and maybe I can clarify it with another question. In the poem "The Widow and Daughter," you write of your father, the missing one, as "hero and betrayer / legend and deserter— / so when they sat down to eat / they could taste his ashes." It almost seems to me that there's a resentment there against your father for his death, for being a martyr, and for leaving you and your mother behind. Do you identify at all with Plath's love-hate relationship with her father, who dared to die when she was a child and who became "Daddy"?

IK: I confess I've never liked Plath's "Daddy." In any case, I think it's hard to be the child of a martyr. The public perceives it one way, and the child experiences it another way. And I think certainly as I was growing up there was a tension—though it remained unstated, perhaps even unconscious. My father was very well known and much admired and eulogized in the community I grew up in. And I was supposed to like that and I did in a certain way. But there was also a real contradiction for me in that on some level I understood that he might have done a great thing for the Jewish people, but it wasn't so great for me. I don't feel it now, certainly. But when I was growing up I think there *was* a sense of abandonment.

My father is honored at the U.S. Holocaust Museum, and my mother and I helped with that. I'm not sure I would have put in all that time about twenty-five or thirty years ago. I was more resentful then of his reputation and his absence. I have no ambivalence now and memorializing him has become much more important to me now. But I think that ambivalence about a public parent is always there, whether he's alive or dead. It's usually a mixed bag for the children. My father's reputation was something that I had to live up to and I was very shy, very timid. So that was a pressure for me which was hard to live with.

Now in terms of the lesbian/feminist community, I will disagree with you.

I don't think my audience is mainly feminist or women, because I know *A Few Words in the Mother Tongue* is used in a lot of English classes, American poetry classes, in Jewish poetry classes, lesbian and women's studies courses. And my work is included in many, many mainstream poetry anthologies. Heterosexual scholars—men and women—are writing about my work. In some ways it surprises me because I came out of such a specific context. So I think I have a truly mixed audience now.

As to what my father would think about me, I suspect that he would probably have a typical response to my lesbianism. Why should I believe he would have been any different from anybody else of his generation when he discovered that his daughter was a lesbian? But I also can fantasize that he would have changed his initial reactions because I've watched change happen. And this change is quite evident in the Jewish community. Even the Holocaust Museum has had a small exhibit about gays and lesbians during the war.

Certainly the gay community and the lesbian community have found my work meaningful. I didn't know the late Audre Lorde all that well; she was one of my role models when I first came out as a lesbian. Audre was an extraordinary African American lesbian writer. It really meant a lot to me that she wrote to me on three different occasions that the dedications to "*Bashert*" were important to her. I've been told that those two dedications have been read for gay men who died of AIDS. They were included in a gay and lesbian oratorio. They've also been included in endless Passover Haggadahs and all kinds of Jewish and non-Jewish rituals. A lot of people from diverse backgrounds have responded to those dedications. I feel honored that the poetry has been meaningful to so many people.

GP: In the dedications to "*Bashert*"—"These words are dedicated to those who died" and "These words are dedicated to those who survived"—are you setting up a false dichotomy by making two poems out of a shared and interrelated experience? In other words, they were all in the death camps together, and you've made one poem for those who survived and one poem for those who died?

IK: I don't view these as separate poems or even separate sections and don't allow them to be published separately. Some people have actually asked if they could just publish one of them, depending on how they felt. They're missing the whole point because I think they're totally intertwined. You can't get the meaning of one without reading the other.

GP: They could almost really be published side by side, literally intertwined. I was thinking that "those who died" also struggled, took risks, had faith, as you say about "those who survived."

IK: The dedications actually came after I had written the rest of *"Bashert."* Among survivors and scholars, there's been an ongoing argument about what was possible and who gets credit for surviving and who doesn't and who didn't resist and so on. And I know to my bones much of it was luck. In the dedications, there's a trick. If you read the first dedication—"those who died"—you say, oh, these are the reasons they died. But some of the reasons appear also in "those who survived." I wanted these to merge in some way so that the reader is lulled into a false security of thinking there is logic and there's cause and effect. I'm hoping that by the time they finish "those who survived," they realize that the cause and effect is nonexistent.

GP: Sections 1 through 4 of *"Bashert"* are in prose paragraphs or blocks. Do you view these as prose poems or poetic prose?

IK: I view them as prose poems. They're not stories. They're clearly not stories. I think there are internal rhythms to them. I tried to mirror things in each section: my mother walking down the road; my walking around Chicago. I think there's an element that to me is a poetic force that pushes the poem so that by the end of the poem I have become a keeper of the accounts—that's definitely not a story.

GP: All right, in number 3 of the poem "Brooklyn 1971," you say, "I am almost equidistant from two continents." Do you mean Europe and America?

IK: Yes.

GP: And then is America not more than "Just a spot where it seemed safe to go to escape certain danger"? Is it not in some ways the land of freedom and opportunity?

IK: There's a whole tradition of immigrants, Jewish and non-Jewish, looking at America in a certain way—as a hope and a promise fulfilled. I don't look at it that way. I view it as a place where a lot of people have been ripped off. They don't have full liberties; they don't have economic opportunities. I think I would even write a harsher section right now if I were to rework that poem. The poem is fifteen years old, written just at the beginning of the Reagan era. I've never been particularly enchanted with the U.S. or "America." It is my home, though. I feel American. But I'm highly critical of this country. I know I'm part of the mainstream but I'm certainly not pleased with it.

GP: Well, the mainstream being what? The military/industrial complex? The power elite?

IK: I think that whenever I enter academia I'm part of the mainstream in the way I participate in it. Most of the time, I have white privilege. I've been upwardly mobile. Whatever my economic troubles have been, I *do* have a Ph.D. I feel like often my life is quite hard, but I also think that when I look at it comparatively, it's not so bad. At the same time, I'm aware that I'm a naturalized citizen. I don't know what these people in Congress are going to decide. I doubt that they're going to decide to throw me out, but the atmosphere these days towards non-native citizens certainly doesn't make me feel very sanguine. The hatred for foreigners is more and more overt. So, yes, I'm part of the mainstream, but I also feel quite vulnerable—as a lesbian, as a Jew, as a naturalized citizen.

GP: You still think in socialist or communist terms as a way of changing America, making it better?

IK: I am still a socialist, though I despair at how to express that these days. It's simple, so utterly simple: there ought to be fair distribution of wealth. I think the kind of economic disparity we're seeing now is obscene. I'm not saying anything radical or new. You can read it in the *New York Times;* the chasm between the rich and the poor has increased endlessly in the last two decades and that's a terrible, terrible thing. It's terrible when you consider what people's basic needs are—whether it's the vaccination of their children or affordable housing—and the obscenity of what basketball players or corporation people or HMO presidents get. Nobody needs that much money.

GP: Okay. What inspired you to write your bilingual poems, the Yiddish and English? Did you have a model for this?

IK: I didn't have any model for it. I went back to Poland in 1983. In *Dreams of an Insomniac* I included an essay called "*Oyf keyver oves:* Poland, 1983." [*Oyv keyver oves* (Yiddish) is the term for the Jewish tradition of visiting one's ancestor's graves.—GP] The trip really pushed me. My mother and I went back to Poland in 1983 on the fortieth anniversary of the Warsaw Ghetto Uprising. I had been steeped in a Holocaust consciousness. Yet it was only on that trip that I realized that I had some responsibility for Yiddish culture. I talk about this also in another essay in that collection: "Secular Jewish Identity: *Yidishkayt* in America." I was amazed that as focused as I was on words and language, it had never dawned on me that this critical part of my life—Yiddish and Yiddish culture—was totally outside of my poetry. Yet—it had everything to do with language and with my experience.

I wrote "*Bashert*" a couple of years before the trip. In looking back, I find it interesting that I picked a Yiddish word that is totally untranslatable into

English: it implies predestination, inevitability, a sense of finality, hopelessness, inexplicability. It's so rich with connotations— the perfect word for a Jewish experience—that you really can't convey in English. I knew I had to use this Yiddish word. I didn't do that with any kind of political or conscious insight. It was purely intuitive. Later, after the trip to Poland, I thought: How can I take Yiddish into myself? how can I do this? and what does it mean to reclaim a language? and what does it mean to introduce it poetically? and so on.

The first poem I wrote was "*Etlekhe Verter oyf Mame-Loshn*/A Few Words in the Mother Tongue." And that was a very interesting process because it made me realize that I couldn't just take Yiddish back uncritically. I had to take it into my poetry because of my love for it and attachment to it; at the same time I also had to critique it. I was conscious that I was a feminist, I was a woman, I was a lesbian/feminist. So I couldn't just step back into the language of my childhood. I don't think my experience is any different from anyone else who returns to a culture after having been transformed by a new perspective. You can't just go home again without questions.

So that was an interesting experiment. I was also conscious that I didn't want the Yiddish to be the Yiddish we hear on "The Late Night Show" by nightclub comics. I wanted to use the real language with its full vocabulary, not limit myself to the fourteen words that most comedians, Jewish or not, use, and which basically denigrate the language. I like to push people in my writing and to introduce them to a vocabulary that's new, but that is not artificial. I'm always sort of proselytizing in one way or another. This is an indirect way of proselytizing and teaching.

GP: The poem "*Etlekhe Verter oyf Mame-Loshn*/A Few Words in the Mother Tongue" ends with many lines of Yiddish, and you repeat the phrase "*zi kholmt*" (she dreams). Can you dream in Yiddish? Is it your visionary tongue?

IK: No, I don't dream in Yiddish; I dream in English.

GP: So there's no subtle hidden meaning to that?

IK: You mean am I trying to dream in Yiddish? I'll tell you the truth. I never thought of it. It's an interesting point.

GP: Were you one of the first to write openly about lesbian sexuality?

IK: Oh, no. There's a whole movement. I was part of a huge group of people. After Stonewall, in the early seventies, there was a huge gay and lesbian political and literary movement, especially among lesbians, which produced a remarkable number of anthologies and journals. I was very lucky because I came out in 1973–74, and this movement was already blossoming. It gave many of us the strength to create our own outlets—publishing houses, journals, bookstores, distribution companies. So in a short time, there were a lot of outlets.

And just like there are debates in the Jewish community about what makes a poem Jewish (If I write about the tree outside my house, is that a Jewish poem?), there are debates among lesbian writers about the nature of lesbian writing. What makes a lesbian or gay poem? Does it have to be about sexuality or about partners or love? Can I write about the tree outside my window and be labeled a lesbian poet?

In fact, I write very little about my private life as a lesbian, and I don't write about sexuality a lot. People certainly pay attention to me and I've gotten a lot of wonderful support and respect for my work in the lesbian community, but I'm not the poet that's going to be included in an anthology on lesbian sexuality.

GP: Let's change the focus. If you don't find a Jewish identity in the Bible or in Israel or certainly in the United States, where is it: within yourself?

IK: There was a thousand-year-old tradition in Poland that I feel far closer to than the religious traditions based on Torah and Talmud and *halakha*. Now much of that tradition is religious. But it represents *my* history, *my* Polish Jewish ancestors. Poland is the center of my Jewish cultural roots, and the destruction of that center in Eastern Europe has created the deprivation of my life. My mission is to try to figure out how to continue here. So in that sense I don't accept the Zionist premises of Diaspora and homeland—that dichotomy. I feel Jews can be Jews anywhere. They might have to work on it in different ways depending on the contexts, hostilities, support, and so on. But they have to figure it out. So, yes—neither Israel nor the Bible is the core of my Jewish identity.

GP: Can you say what it is? Is it memory?

IK: For me it is language and culture. What the Jewish Labor Bund called *national cultural autonomy*.

GP: Can you explain that a little bit?

IK: Language by itself really doesn't mean anything to me. It's because a language is the medium of a whole culture, of a literature, of a politics (socialism) that language—Yiddish—takes on meaning. Now the question for me is what happens to that combination of language and culture here in the United States.

I'm someone who is currently active in translating. I don't want that

Yiddish heritage lost to the Jews here who can't read Yiddish. So simultaneously when I translate I'm also proselytizing for people to study Yiddish so that they can read the original. What I don't know is whether we can in fact have a secular culture—meaning one not based on religious practice and ritual or on religious texts—here in the United States as they did in Europe. They had the Yiddish language to define it, we do not. Of course, I'm hoping we can and will.

So I've spent a lot of time thinking theoretically about what that means. What does it mean to translate all this material and internalize it? What does this material become after it's translated into English, when it loses its linguistic borders and boundaries? "*Etlekhe Verter oyf Mame-Loshn*/A Few Words in the Mother Tongue" is really an oral poem. It's harder to read on the page than to hear it. At the end, with the repetition of all the Yiddish words used in the early parts of the poem and the repetition of "*zi kholmt*" (she dreams), it moves into Yiddish completely. And if people don't know Yiddish they may lose some of the meaning because they've forgotten the translation of the words. But still . . . there is the dream. And there is also that dream of a Yiddish revival, which doesn't mean that we're going to abandon speaking English. Rather that maybe we'll move towards a more bilingual sense of ourselves— what our Jewish languages are if we stay here.

I understand Jews who study Hebrew because they relate to Israel or they're planning to make *aliyah*. Hebrew is obviously going to be important to them. However, in Russia today there are many of the Russian Jews who don't want to emigrate to Israel. Interestingly, there is a struggle within Israel about Israel supporting them. Israel does not want to give money to establish Yiddish schools in Russia—even when the Russian Jews want it. They're only interested in Hebrew schools with a religious base because they assume that eventually this kind of education will lead to *aliyah*. It's been documented and I'm not making it up. A lot of Russian Jews are determined to stay in Russia and want to develop their Jewish identity. Their heritage in Russia is Yiddish-based, and Israel doesn't want to acknowledge that reality by allowing them to develop their Yiddish culture.

Outside of Israel and Russia, we have our own realities, and Yiddish is "The Language That Won't Go Away." I often talk about this longing for Yiddish despite Israel, despite all the Holocaust memorials, despite all the Jewish activities that are part of American Jewish life. There's a lot of feeling about Yiddish both among an older generation and a younger generation that never even got to hear it. As I myself get older, I encounter young students whose parents don't remember Yiddish or never knew it, but perhaps whose grandparents spoke Yiddish. Yiddish for most is increasingly a vague memory. And yet this younger generation has this yearning.

It's an interesting phenomenon. What is it that's missing in Jewish American life that makes Jews think that Yiddish could fill a void? Clearly, something *is* missing. We don't know whether for them Yiddish is the answer or not; something is happening among that generation. What I would like people to think about is why at a time when there's a frenzy about the Holocaust, about memorialization, about interviewing survivors, and so on, there is a rich revival of klezmer music. Is it a desire to focus on the joy that was there before the war? I think Yiddish is something the Ashkenazi Jews really turn to to help them define themselves in terms that existed *before* the war rather than in relationship to the Holocaust or Israel. They're pointing to the issues of language and what language can express and mean and especially if it's a language that is a national language. I think writers have an important function here, and I think some of them are accepting it.

GP: Writing in Yiddish?

IK: Well, at least talking about Yiddish or using a little bit of Yiddish even to make their English less mainstream, to make their English more Jewish. People are beginning to study. I think these small steps are significant.

GP: So in some way you're memorializing that tradition.

IK: I'm hoping that I'm not so much memorializing it as taking it into the present.

GP: Through your writing?

IK: Through my writing and through encouraging other people—not just writers. I want to "activate it," so that Jews will feel that they're connected to this culture, that they can claim it as their legacy, their heritage. It's what shaped their parents—well, at this point, I'd have to say their Eastern European grandparents—and ancestors.

As I said, there's a strong sentimental attachment to anything Yiddish. I believe it represents something deeper. Today contemporary writers in Israel have an international reputation and more and more are translated into English. But the culture that they create and from which they spring is not the one my ancestors came from; though Israel and what happens in Israel touches me and all U.S. Jews in a profound way, it's not our experience. My experience is rooted in Eastern Europe. And that's why I think the force of Yiddish culture is so powerful. Most Jews who are content to live outside of Israel don't necessarily want to sit down and locate where the Galut is.

What they want is to react to their immediate environment in a direct way, they want to find their place in it. And as much as they travel to Israel, move back and forth between here and there, when they want to find their "home," they take trips to discover the towns where their ancestors came from in Eastern Europe. Every other Jew who can afford it goes to Eastern Europe. In this kind of context, the Yiddish language becomes a critical connection to "home," not to Diaspora. So this movement towards Yiddish is not just mere sentiment. I always urge people to try to find out more about their feelings and to translate that knowledge into action towards reconnecting directly with the culture.

GP: Okay, well, now I've got some questions that I've asked all the people. You just decide whether you want to take a crack at them. For example, how does one face death and can poetry help?

IK: Oh, that's interesting, because at my age you start really thinking a lot about it. It's one of those realizations that comes at this time. I'm about to be fifty-six this April and I'm thinking a lot about mortality. I'm thinking a lot about the usefulness of poetry. Does it make any difference? In a way I question it more than I ever did before. It's not that I've begun to doubt its validity, only that that's part of an inquiry that one takes up at this age. So I'm questioning everything, and poetry is not exempt. I think things are so bad in this country that it's easy to begin questioning words and the power of words.

GP: Taking what form?

IK: I had this experience in class this past Thursday. I was thinking about it in context of all this hype about the Internet and the information superhighway and how technology enables everyone to have "all knowledge and art" at our fingertips. Here at Michigan State University, I'm teaching a course in contemporary lesbian writing. One of the first works we studied was Rich's *The Dream of a Common Language*. We began with the opening poem, "Power," about Marie Curie. So, I asked the students to identify Marie Curie, and not a single one knew who she was. So I said: Didn't any of you look it up?

GP: So they didn't know the most famous woman scientist?

IK: Not only didn't they know who she was, they didn't bother to look her up. I've encountered this not only here, but in other schools. It shocks me because I know that many students own computers and have access to endless resources and even at four in the morning they can find out who Marie Curie is by accessing some encyclopedia. I felt very discouraged. The technology didn't help them. I also felt like a dinosaur. I'm still committed to books and to poetry and to literacy. I'm committed to slow reading, which poetry requires, and not zapping e-mails every three seconds. I'm not too optimistic right now, though I try to take a historical view and say: Irena, things change.

But, as you get older, you think about death, and you think about what's going to happen to your work, and whether it's even more of a losing battle than it was twenty, twenty-five years ago when I first started publishing. In that same class I once asked the students how many of them read poetry and about three hands went up. So I asked the others: How come you don't buy poetry books? And they said what I expected them to say, which is (*a*) poetry is too hard, they don't really know how to read it, or they've not been taught how to read it; (*b*) they've had horrible high school courses in poetry which made them hate poetry; (*c*) they don't understand it and so they feel that it's elitist and that they're excluded from it. In addition, they've been desensitized to language by the popular culture. Everything becomes a cliché.

GP: Well, give me an example.

IK: Like "a time for healing." When are you ever going to use the word "heal" again?

GP: Does poetry have anything to teach us about language, and can the poet with language still have something to say?

IK: Frankly, I think poets are our most important defenses against linguistic corruption. They are the reinventors of language, the defenders of language, who insist that how you express yourself, how you convey your experience, actually matters in the world.

GP: So a last defense against the deterioration of language?

IK: Yes, so that it's not clichés; it's not packaged. Poets struggle for individual, honest expression. I think they want to make their experience, not unique, but new. As I teach in my classes: it's the ordinary, the repetitious, the common that's the hardest to convey—because it's so overexposed.

GP: There's also the possibility that poetry by these young people could become in some way part of the mass culture. It already has in some sense through rock lyrics, but not the traditional poetry, of course.

IK: Also, slams are very popular, though I have mixed feelings about them and events like that. I went to one slam and wondered: why are they grading these poems? why do we have to have winners and losers and applause? why is this poem worth 8.5 and that poem 3.2? In a certain sense, I didn't even know what it was about. At the same time, I was really impressed. It was eleven o'clock on a Saturday night and the place was packed.

It reminded me how at the beginning of the women's movement in the late seventies and early eighties, women who had never been to a poetry reading . . . ever . . . who thought readings were totally elitist and academic, would pack huge halls to hear Judy Grahn or Audre Lorde or even totally unknown poets, new poets, because they felt somehow that what would be read had meaning for them, was for them. So despite all my pessimism, I have to admit that there is still a clear group of young people that is drawn to poetry.

GP: What do you wish to still accomplish as a poet, as a writer? Have you thought about that?

IK: I don't have a specific goal in mind. I'm a restless writer in a certain way. I get bored with things fairly quickly, so I'm always looking for a new way to do something. I worry about getting stuck. It's not that I don't have enough to write about.

GP: Well, so you expect your voice to actually keep changing in some way— your style?

IK: I'm interested in finding new ways of expressing myself. All of us repeat ourselves. We have obsessions or "themes" that drive us and those obsessions get manifested in different ways. Sometimes it's not even evident that they're the same obsession, but, then underneath, it often is. I think the trick is to keep doing the same thing but from a new angle so you can discover new things about your obsession and not to fall back on perspectives or techniques that have already proved successful.

I think it's been hard for me to escape some of those early Holocaust poems. Some people consider them the peak of my writing. I don't. I spoke at the beginning about the chasm between what goes on internally for me and what goes on for other people in terms of my own work. That's a difficult issue. I'm always interested in moving on and not repeating, and I think there are others who like my work and who have expectations about what I should be writing about. I'm know I'm going to continue writing poetry and hope that it's going to be new and satisfying for me, necessary. At the same time I'm also interested in Yiddish and in translating.

I don't know how old you are, Gary, and perhaps you feel this too, but I'm sort of both looking forward and looking back much more than I used to.

GP: I'm about the same age as you.

IK: I'm reevaluating the past and at the same time thinking, well, time's limited. I'm much more careful now about what I commit myself to. I recently cleared out my shelves of books I hadn't read. I said to myself: At this point you're not going to get to them. It's not like I think I'm on death's door by any means, but at fifty-six there's a greater sense of limited time.

GP: Hopefully we'll both live a lot longer. All right, we may have an answer to the next question. What place do you most identify with? I would guess that Eastern Europe might be it, but you might have another response to that question.

IK: Do you mean a geographic place?

GP: Yeah, geographic.

IK: Where I feel I should be?

GP: The place that you most want to write about.

IK: It's Eastern Europe—but at another time, certainly not now. I've been back to Poland twice and it's not my Poland. It's a totally different place. I identify historically with life in Poland and in Eastern Europe between the two wars.

GP: You're not a New York poet?

IK: I don't know that that's true. Well—you mean in a literary sense? Part of me is a Warsaw poet—always. I came to New York when I was eight years old, and I grew up in a very Jewish, and a very interesting, neighborhood in the Bronx. It was a vibrant secular Yiddish community, a shadow of the "old country." From the time I returned from graduate school in Chicago in '69, I've been living in downtown Brooklyn. I've watched the neighborhood change. And yet, I feel more rooted there than I've ever felt anywhere else. But I can't say I feel part of the "poetry scene" in New York.

GP: If you could do it again, what would you do differently?

IK: As a student, I was a purist (or so I thought). I was only focused on literature and poetry. When I was young, I resented being forced to read history. Now, I wish I had studied it more. I'm trying to catch up. In my younger years, I had a keen kind of intuitive personal sense of history, but I really didn't focus on it in a more disciplined way, and I think that that would have been a real enrichment to me, intellectually.

GP: Okay, the penultimate question: What is the most amazing thing about life?

IK: That it persists despite its fragility. Everything sort of hangs by a hair's breadth and yet somehow it manages. . . . You hear such horrible stories about people's lives . . . war, abuse, poverty—that anybody survives is remarkable. Audre Lorde once said, "None of us were meant to survive." There's truth to that, and I remain amazed that so many of us do. It's extraordinary that we can even walk around and function in a minimal way, much less in a productive way. For whatever turmoil goes on internally with people and the pain that they experience at night in their dreams, they still manage somehow to construct lives during the day which are meaningful to other people and to themselves.

GP: Okay, what's the most amazing thing about your life, same thing?

IK: Well, I think the most amazing thing about my life is that we're sitting right now and talking and that you've even heard of me.

GP: Oh my god, I've known of you for years.

IK: But when I think back of how I started and where I started, I am always surprised. There's a kind of sense that I can't believe that it really happened.

GP: That you have a literary reputation?

IK: That I got published, that people read my work. Somebody just told me there's going to be an article in *PMLA* in March '98 about my work. I'm still bowled over when someone tells me they teach my work or they use my books. I think because of my own life and my own history and partly also because I know how many writers haven't gotten any recognition—that amazement remains. After all, the chances for recognition are so slim. Think about poetry competitions; manuscripts that go to editors at commercial presses or university presses; how many get published? The percentage that get published or even known is so, so tiny. That I happen to be one of the people that anybody pays a bit of attention to seems extraordinary.

GP: Do you account for it by luck, besides what you have to say and how you say it?

IK: Yes, I think that that's true, and I do feel very lucky. I hope I'm talented and I'm getting recognition that I deserve. I just know that there are a lot of other talented people. I know I have a bigger reputation than some of my friends. And I feel bad about it because I think they're truly good poets and it seems so unfair, so impossible because I'm just not powerful enough to help them. I can help them some, but not really enough because, you know, there are levels of hierarchy in this world.

GP: Maybe we can end with this. Given all the challenges that you have described, would you still advise a person with talent and something important to say to go on with it despite the terrible odds of succeeding?

IK: I do. I teach poetry, and I encourage students and I think it always amazes me that with everything we talked about in terms of the denigration of language and pop culture and so on—how the aura of being a poet is still so captivating to young people. Many still want to be poets. In each generation, there seems to be a hard core who just never gives up on the idea. And yes, I encourage them. I'm always moved by their idealism and by their unwavering dedication. They sit in their dorm rooms, and they rework their poetry and are passionate about it. I think it's wonderful and inspiring. I never know where their desire comes from because there's nothing on TV and there's nothing in media or mainstream culture to urge them in this direction. Yet they have this sense of the importance of poetry and want to become poets and they're fierce in their determination to hold on to this ideal.

GP: Well, there's hope.

IK: I think so, and I'm always happy to meet and work with them.